MID-ATLANTIC

GETTING STARTED GARDEN GUIDE

Grow the Best Flowers, Shrubs, Trees, Vines & Groundcovers

First published in 2015 by Cool Springs Press, an imprint of Quarto Publishing Group USA Inc., 400 First Avenue North, Suite 400, Minneapolis, MN 55401 USA

Cool Springs Press titles are also available at discounts in bulk quantity for industrial or sales-promotional use. For details write to Special Sales Manager at Quarto Publishing Group USA Inc., 400 First Avenue North, Suite 400, Minneapolis, MN 55401 USA. To find out more about our books, visit us online at www.coolspringspress.com.

ISBN: 978-1-59186-435-6

Library of Congress Cataloging-in-Publication Data

Viette, André, author.
  Mid-Atlantic getting started garden guide : grow the best flowers, shrubs, trees, vines & groundcovers / André Viette, Mark Viette, Jacqueline Hériteau.
      pages cm
  Includes index.
  ISBN 978-1-59186-435-6 (sc)
  1. Gardening--Middle Atlantic States. I. Viette, Mark, author. II. Hériteau, Jacqueline, author. III. Title.

  SB453.V578 2015
  635.0974--dc23

                        2015004858

Acquisitions Editor: Billie Brownell
Design Manager: Brad Springer
Layout: Erin Fahringer

Printed in China

10 9 8 7 6 5 4 3 2 1

MID-ATLANTIC

GETTING STARTED GARDEN GUIDE

Grow the Best Flowers, Shrubs, Trees, Vines & Groundcovers

André Viette, Mark Viette, and Jacqui Hériteau

COOL
SPRINGS
PRESS
Home and Garden Experts™

MINNEAPOLIS, MINNESOTA

DEDICATION

I dedicate this book to my mother and father, Jessie and Martin Viette, who instilled in me strong family values, a good work ethic, and a deep love of plants.

—*André Viette*

ACKNOWLEDGMENTS

I want to thank the many people who have touched my life and made me a better person, especially my wife, Claire, who has been by my side throughout my career and has given me such wonderful children—Mark, Scott, Holly, and Heather. My son Mark works with me daily in the nursery, shares teaching duties with me at Blue Ridge Community College, and has been such an important part of the "In the Garden" radio programs. It has been a wonderful partnership. My father, a great plantsman, passed on to me his keen knowledge of plants and their culture. There is no substitute for the hands-on experience a parent gives to a child—digging and planting, weeding and hoeing, grafting and landscaping—that I learned at his side.

I also wish to thank the many fine professors at Cornell University who helped mold my scientific mind. Among the many who have shaped me as a nurseryman and gardener are my good friend and fellow Cornellian Dr. Marc Cathey, President Emeritus of the American Horticultural Society, who has contributed so much to the world of floriculture; Rachel Carson, who changed my approach to the way we use our planet, whom I met when I was just 24 years old; the late Harvey Barke, New York State University at Farmingdale, a great teacher from whom I learned so much about the field of biological science; my friend Robert Hebb, first director of Virginia's Lewis Ginter Botanical Garden and world-class plantsman; and my thanks to the fine plantsman Kurt Bluemel, who is responsible for the many wonderful ornamental grasses in American gardens.

And I wish to recognize all my fellow members, past and present, of the New York Hortus Club, who through the years have represented the finest in horticulture from New York City, New York, Connecticut, and New Jersey. Some members have passed on, but they leave their mark on many: Tom Everett of the New York Botanical Garden; Harold Epstein, a keen plantsman and plant collector; Dr. Alfred Graf, who wrote the impressive works *Tropica* and *Exotica*; and Don Richardson, horticulturist and world-renowned orchid specialist who was in charge of the Whitney Collection.

CONTENTS

WELCOME TO GARDENING

IN THE MID-ATLANTIC

Wonderful gardens have flourished for 400 years in the Mid-Atlantic. We are blessed with a climate that's not too hot and not too cold for almost all of the garden plants we love. Winter is mild enough to let pansies bloom, and the hellebores flower early. From February on we are graced with lavish displays of flowering bulbs, shrubs, and trees. Summer is hot and stormy, but after mid-September, many of the annual flowers revive and the flaming foliage of our maples, oaks, and burning bush light up the season of the falling leaves. A few bulbs bloom in early fall, and hollies, cotoneasters, winterberries, and barberries ripen fruits the birds love.

The plants we recommend in this book are the best of the best for the Mid-Atlantic. We chose them for their lasting beauty, ease of maintenance, and immunity or strong resistance to pests and diseases. We're not recommending specific pesticides and other deterrents; they come and go too frequently. But more important to us is that we have learned from decades of experience that the best protection you can give your garden is (1) to choose pest- and disease-resistant plants that thrive in the Mid-Atlantic, and (2) to give them the light, nutrients, and moisture they need.

Botanical Gardens

A very pleasant way to see how gardens grow in the Mid-Atlantic is to visit our magnificent public gardens. Strolling the grounds at Winterthur Museum and Gardens in Winterthur, Delaware, and Brookside Gardens in Silver Spring, Maryland, you absorb so much about garden design. Adamstown, Maryland, is home to Lilypons Water Gardens, which has wonderful annual programs for the public. And the Ladew Topiary Gardens are in Monkton, Maryland. They're the finest example of topiary training in North America. In Williamsburg, Virginia, you'll find beauty and wisdom in the sweet home gardens at Colonial Williamsburg. In Henrico, Virginia, be sure to visit Lewis Ginter Botanical Garden.

Charlottesville, Virginia is home to a personal favorite, Jefferson's home Monticello, where a sumptuous vegetable and herb terrace overlooks vineyards, orchards, and the valley below. In the District of Columbia there's so much to learn from the garden rooms at Dumbarton Oaks, the U.S. Botanic Garden on the Mall, and the many-storied collections at the U.S. National Arboretum. The American Horticultural Society, which is headquartered on a beautiful historic farm in Alexandria, offers membership to interested gardeners, and can also put you in touch with local garden groups, which are matchless sources of information about plants and gardening where you live. They're able to explain, for example, which of the Mid-Atlantic's climate zones apply to you.

Our Climate

Planting the *right* plant in the *right* place is the key to a garden that gives joy for years. Climate dictates your choices. The USDA Plant Hardiness Zone Map numbers regions according to their average lowest winter temperature. Much of Delaware, Maryland, Washington, D.C., West Virginia, and Virginia are in Zone 6 and 7. The exceptions are a few cold spots in the mountains, which are Zone 5, and hot spots in the Tidewater and Piedmont (French for "foot of the mountain") areas of southern Virginia, which are Zone 8. Nursery plant tags usually state the plant's hardiness zones. About 99 percent of the plants we recommend thrive in Zones 6, 7, and 8. Where a plant has a problem with Zone 6 cold, or Zone 8 heat, we say so.

Light

On each plant page we tell you the light in which that plant thrives. When a flowering species fails to flower, check the hours of direct sun it receives: unless we say a plant flowers in part or full shade, or part sun, it requires at least six hours of intense direct sun, which occurs from 10:00 a.m. to 6:00 p.m., to bloom well. Plants that flop forward are telling you they need more light. In warm Zone 8, some noon and late afternoon shade can help certain plants—you can supply that by placing the plant under a trellis or in dappled shade under tall trees. Plants receiving full sunlight are often the most cold hardy.

Outwitting Your Climate

Your garden is not governed entirely by the zone in which you live. There are variables that explain unexpected failures and successes. Cold air sinks, so valleys on your property are cooler than high ground. High hills are colder than their respective zones. Cities are 5 to 10 degrees warmer than the suburbs and the countryside. Bodies of water modify temperatures, as do the miles of asphalt and concrete of a town or city. In spring, the shore and ten to twenty miles inland is colder by 10 degrees or more than it is farther inland because the ocean holds winter cold. In summer, the shore is cooler because the ocean is cooler than the air.

Within every garden there are microclimates hospitable to plants normally beyond your zone. A south-facing wall can warm a corner, and shade can cool it. You can even create microclimates—a wall painted white or a reflective surface increases light and heat. The shade of a vine-covered pergola, a trellis, a tree, or a high hedge is cooling. Walls and windbreaks protect plants from sweeping winds that intensify cold. Mulch protects roots from extremes of heat and cold.

If you live in a borderline area—almost in cooler Zone 6, but not quite, for example—the safest choices are species that are well within their cold hardiness range in your garden. Borderline plants may live but not always bloom in a satisfying way. Late frosts can devastate the flower buds on a camellia though the plant itself may do well. Many plants are offered in varieties described as blooming early, midseason, or late. Where the growing season is short, plant varieties that will bloom early. If you wish to enjoy a very long season of bloom of any particular plant, plant varieties of all three types: early, midseason, and late.

Starting Seeds Indoors

You can extend the growing season by starting seeds early indoors—in winter for spring planting, in summer for early fall planting. (Starting seeds in a cold frame, or a hot bed, are projects beyond the scope of this book.) You can protect early starters from late and early cold by covering them with "hot caps," or plastic tenting. Two weeks after the date of the last annual frost is usually safe to transplant seedlings into the open garden.

For slow-growing plants, seed packets will suggest starting seeds indoors ten to twelve weeks before the planting season. For fast growers the time is four to six weeks. We recommend flats that have individual planting pockets and plastic covers. Plant in moistened commercial seed-starting mix and follow the packet instructions: some germinate best covered with soil, others need light. Label the seeds—don't forget!— and cover the flat for the germination period. Set it on a heat mat (or an old waterproof heating pad set on low and covered with plastic) to speed germination.

Plant one or two seeds per section of the seed-starting tray. Then water the soil until it is as moist as a wrung-out sponge. Depending upon the size of the sections in the seed-starting tray, you might or might not have to transplant plants into larger containers to grow before planting outside.

Check on the seeds as they're sprouting. If the top of the soil is dry, mist them with a spray bottle or very lightly water them. (Misting is better than watering because it is less likely to wash the delicate seedlings out of their spots in the trays.) Don't ever let seeds dry out while they're sprouting, or they'll die.

Seeds for most perennials are generally slow to germinate (some require cold temperature stratification), and more difficult than those for the pop-up annuals. Most annuals germinate at air temperatures of 65 to 70 degrees Fahrenheit. When they sprout, remove the cover and move the flat to a location with good light. Water from the bottom, or mist the seedlings; pouring water over their hair-thin stems flattens them. When they become crowded and have their first true leaves, transplant the seedlings to individual pots. Before moving seedlings to the open garden, wait for the soil temperature to reach 55 degrees Fahrenheit. Seedlings sulk in cold soil. Before moving seedlings to the garden, harden them off for a week in bright shade out of the wind. A fluorescent light "garden" is a worthwhile investment if you plan to start seeds indoors every year.

Soil Preparation and Improvement

Soil is your plant's support system, its drinking fountain, and its larder. In the Mid-Atlantic, two types of soil prevail. Soil is sandy in the Tidewater, along the coasts of Maryland and Delaware, and all along the Atlantic. There's a layer of hardpan under some sandy soils. Sandy soils are easy to dig and drain well, which is essential for many, many plants. But sandy soil doesn't retain water, or the nutrients dissolved in it. As the land rises on the Coastal Plain, the soil still tends to sand, but moving inland and westward, clay appears and eventually dominates. Clay soils are rich in nutrients, but the very fine particles flock together, creating a condition of poor drainage and aeration, and making it difficult for roots to develop. Whichever your soil type, the way to make it right is to mix it with the humusy organic materials—such as compost, leaf mold (rotted leaves), or peat moss—and slow-release fertilizers.

The ideal garden soil has good drainage, lots of water-holding humus, and is loose enough so you can dig in it with your fingers. We evaluate garden soil in terms of its structure or composition, its pH, and its fertility. Structure governs the soil's ability to absorb and maintain moisture. Gritty particles create air spaces, allowing tender rootlets to seek oxygen, moisture, and the nutrients dissolved in it. They also allow water to drain. Soil containing humus retains enough moisture to keep the rootlets from drying out. Roots absorb the nutrients dissolved in water. We add to new planting beds lots of humusy organic amendments to improve soil structure.

You can pick up soil test boxes from your local Cooperative Extension office. Every test result will give you recommendations for adding nitrogen, phosphorus, or potassium. Collect a soil sample to submit by digging clumps of soil from different areas of the garden, mixing them up, and submitting them for testing.

A plant's access to nutrients also depends on the soil's pH ("potential of hydrogen"), its relative acidity or alkalinity. A soil pH of 7.0 is neutral; pH 4.0 is very, very acidic; and a pH 8.0 is very alkaline. Most garden ornamentals do best in soil that has a pH between 5.5 to 6.5. Trees and shrubs are more apt to be finicky about pH than are herbaceous plants. You can use a relatively inexpensive testing kit to determine the pH of your soil. If it's above pH 6.5 to 7.0, apply water-soluble sulfur or iron sulfate. If the soil pH is below 5.5, spread finely ground limestone or hydrated lime. Ask your garden center or nursery for recommendations.

If you want plants to be all they can be, you must fertilize a new bed before planting, and all beds every year. The fertilizers we use are natural, organic, and release their nutrients slowly during the season, so we get solid stocky plants with loads of gorgeous foliage and flowers.

We plant in raised beds of improved soil. When we're digging a planting hole we add the same soil amendments and fertilizers in the same proportions. The best times to prepare a new bed are fall, and spring as soon as cold and moisture are out of the ground.

Preparing a New Bed

(1) Use a garden hose to outline the bed. A bed beside a fence, a wall, or a path can be formal or informal. For an informal look, lay out long, slow, gentle curves rather than scallops or straight lines. For a formal look, make the bed symmetrical—a half-circle, oval, square, or rectangle. Many times, formal gardens are mirror images left and right of the central axis line. An island bed can be a large oval, an elongated "S" shape, or kidney shaped. Island beds are the easiest to work since you can get at the middle from any side.

(2) Thoroughly water the turf covering the area to get the roots activated.

(3) Spray the entire area with a total weed and grass killer following the instructions on the label. Turf takes about two weeks to completely die. Alternately, you can remove the turf—the top layer of growth and its roots—but that's pretty hard work.

(4) Cover the area with enough of the most weed-free garden soil you can find to raise the soil level about 12 to 16 inches above ground level.

Outline the edges of a new garden bed by positioning a hose and then outlining its edges in powdered chalk or gypsum.

(5) Cover the bed with 3 to 4 inches of humus, enough so that one-quarter of the content of the soil is organic matter. The humus can be decomposed bark, compost, partially decomposed leaves or seaweed, sphagnum peat moss, black peat humus, decomposed animal manures, or other decomposed organic material.

(6) Next, with a rear-tine rototiller, which you can rent from a garden center, mix all this deeply and thoroughly. The bed should now be, in André's words, "as soft as chocolate pudding."

7) The next step is to determine the pH reaction of the soil, and amend it as needed to reach a pH between 5.5 to 6.5, following the steps described under Soil Preparation and Improvement.

(8) Next, for each 10 x 10 foot area (100 square feet), mix in the following and rototill or fork into the improved soil:

For a new garden in full sun	For a new garden in shade	For a new bed for bulbs
Slow-release, organic fertilizer 5-3-3: 5 to 10 pounds	Slow-release, organic, acid fertilizer 4-3-4: 4 to 7 pounds	Organic bulb fertilizer 3-5-3: 5 to 10 pounds
Rock phosphate: 5 to 10 pounds	Superphosphate: 3 to 5 pounds	
Greensand: 5 to 10 pounds	Greensand: 5 to 10 pounds	
Clay soils only: gypsum 5 to 10 pounds	Clay soils only: gypsum 5 to 10 pounds	
Slow-release fertilizer 8-month: 2 pounds	Slow-release fertilizer 8-month: 2 pounds	

(9) When you are ready to plant, rake the bed smooth and discard rocks, lumps, and bumps.

(10) Finally, tamp the edge of the bed into a long, gradual slope and cover it with mulch to keep the soil from eroding. Or, frame the bed with low retaining walls of stone or painted cement blocks, 2 × 2 red cedar or pressure-treated wood, or railroad ties.

Planting

When you are planting in a new raised bed with improved, fluffed-up soil, digging a generous planting hole is easy. Digging a big hole in a new spot, and even in an established garden, is tough. But the plant still needs a big planting hole, and soil mixed with 3 to 4 inches of humus (Step 5, above), enough so that one-quarter of the content of the soil is organic matter mixed with slow-release organic fertilizers. Each chapter has directions for planting in that chapter's introduction. Whether the plants are large or small, our basic approach is this:

(1) Make the planting hole big. For trees and shrubs, make it three times as wide and two times as deep as the rootball; for perennials and annuals, dig a hole two times as wide and two times as deep as the rootball.

(2) For perennials, annuals, and bulbs provide a base of improved soil for the rootball to rest on by half filling the planting hole with improved soil before setting the

Place the container on its side and roll it on the ground while tapping it to loosen the roots. Upend the container and gently pull it off of the plant roots. Do not pull plants by their stems.

Use your fingers to loosen any roots that may be matted, gently untangling them. Roots that are tightly coiled should be cut apart and loosened. Gently spread the roots wide so they are pointing outward as much as possible.

plant in it. For shrubs and trees, half fill the hole with improved soil, and tamp it down very firmly before setting the plant into the hole.

(3) With container plants, free the plant from matted roots. When possible, unwind roots that might be circling the rootball. If you can't untangle them, make four shallow vertical slashes in the mass. Cut off the matted roots on the bottom. Soak the rootball in a bucket containing starter solution.

(4) Set the plant in the hole. Half fill the hole with soil and tamp it down

Set the shrub into the hole so that it is at the same soil level as it was growing in the pot.

firmly; fill the hole all the way to the top with soil, then tamp it firmly. Shape the soil around the stem, crown, or trunk into a wide saucer. (The saucer is really important in collecting water for shrubs and trees, less so for perennials and annuals.)

Watering

Deep, slow, gentle watering is what keeps plants growing well. After planting, water the bed deeply, gently, and slowly. Ideal for a new bed is to put down 1½ inches of water after planting. Set an empty coffee tin—regular size—to catch the water, and record how long it takes your sprinkler to deliver 1½ inches. Water a newly planted shrub or tree by slowly pouring 10 to 15 gallons of water into the saucer around the plant. For a tree or a shrub's first season, unless there's a soaking rain, in spring and fall slowly and gently pour two to three bucketsful of water around the roots every two weeks; in summer, every week or ten days. Remember, the larger the tree or shrub, the bigger the hole and the more water needed. Flower beds thrive with 1 to 1½ inches of gentle rain every ten days to two weeks; if the sky fails you, water long enough to lay down 1½ inches of water gently over a long period of time, at least six to eight hours, every ten days to two weeks. And, of course, water any time the plants show signs of wilting.

Overhead watering is fine as long as you water deeply. There's less waste if you water before the sun reaches the garden in the early morning, or late afternoon or evening. In hot, dry periods you need to water during the day. Daytime watering lowers leaf temperatures and reduces stress in very hot, dry periods. Evening watering is fine—dew does it and plants like it. We do not recommend electrically timed mechanical watering systems that ignore the weather and water shallowly too often. However, they can do a good job if they are set up with the correct nozzles and timed to run long enough to water deeply every week or ten days. Windy, hot times, such as occur in summer, require more water, and the cool spring and fall days require less.

Staking and Stem Protection

Only a few of the tallest flowers should need staking when grown in improved soil and fertilized with slow-release organic fertilizers. Tall, weak growth can be caused by force-feeding with non-organic fertilizers. Wide spacing improves air circulation, and reduces the risk of disease and mildew. Staking is easy: Set a wood, bamboo, or metal stake close to the plant stem while it is still young. As it leafs out, it will hide the stake. Use soft green wool, raffia, or cotton string and tie the main stem loosely to the stake. Staking a tree isn't necessary unless the stem or trunk shows a tendency to lean over or to grow at an angle—and it should not need the stake for more than a year. In cold regions for their first winter, a burlap windbreak is helpful to young shrubs and trees. You may need to protect a young tree trunk from rubbing or nibbling by deer: you can surround it with stakes wrapped with mesh, or attach a rubber or plastic stem guard. Remove the wrap in spring when growth starts. To protect the tender bark of a young tree from sun scald, paint it with a wash of calcium carbonate.

Stakes are best for plants with one to seven tall main stems. Vegetables that grow single stems and bear heavy fruit, like peppers and eggplants, also benefit from being staked. Leave a little "breathing room" between the stake and the stem when you tie the stakes.

Mulches

If you love your plants, maintain a 2- to 3-inch layer of organic mulch over the roots from early spring through fall and winter. Start the mulch about 3 inches from the main stem or stems. We mulch in part to buffer soil temperatures and maintain soil moisture, to prevent erosion and control weeds. An organic mulch does more: as it decomposes on the underside it replenishes the soil's supply of humus, which is dissipated during the growing season. The mulches we use suit all plants equally well. Tests have shown that an acidic mulch, such as pine needles, has no lasting impact on the pH of the soil beneath. You can mulch with almost any healthy organic material available—seaweed or chopped leaves for example—as long as it is at least partially decomposed. The commercial mulches we recommend include cypress mulch, pine needles, fir, pine and hardwood bark, and cocoa mulch.

Maintaining Fertility

We fertilize planting beds, not individual plants. The rule of thumb is to apply a slow-release organic fertilizer to the bed before growth begins in late winter (best) or in early spring; for some plants you'll see we recommend fertilizing again in the fall. In this region, some soils have a rather high pH, that is, they are somewhat alkaline. In those situations we apply an organic, slow-release, complete fertilizer for acid-loving plants, because that tends to balance out the pH. Where soils test acidic, we apply a slow-release organic fertilizer to balance out the acidity. We use the same fertilizer or an organic fertilizer for bulbs. If plants need a boost in midseason we apply a water-soluble organic fertilizer such as fish emulsion. In high heat we don't try to force plant growth by feeding, and we avoid pruning at that time, which stimulates growth. It's natural for plants to slow their growth in extremes of weather. For more information on fertilizers, see page 222 in the Appendix.

Grooming and Weeding

To realize their potential, plants need grooming. In early spring, gardens must be cleared of the previous year's dead foliage. In summer we deadhead and shear spent blooms to encourage flowering that year or the next. We prune woody plants to keep them shapely and healthy. We weed, eliminating the competition. Weeds can even be volunteers from last year's cosmos or phlox. They start up in spring and come into their own in midsummer, along with drought and high heat. A permanent mulch discourages weeds.

But you can easily rake up the little green weeds if you do it before they're 1 inch high. When they're 6 inches high, you'll need a hoe. (After that you'll just be sorry you didn't get to it earlier!) Start clean and stay clean. Let weeds flourish in or near a newly established garden and go to seed, and they'll haunt you for years. If some get away from you, they are more difficult to dig out, especially in hard, dry soil. Water the garden first, then gently free the weeds and their roots.

Looking back on years of gardening, the moments that stand out in memory are those spent tending to the landscape. Grooming is a quiet time in the garden. Pruning boxwoods in the cool early morning, birds a-twitter, strolling the flower beds at sunset checking for spent blooms that need deadheading, weeding in summer, raking leaves in autumn—these homely chores lift us out of our everyday lives and into the life of the garden and a potential for beauty that nourishes the soul.

How to Use This Book

Each entry in this guide provides information about a plant's characteristics, habits, and basic requirements for active growth as well as our personal experience with and knowledge of the plant. This includes a plant's mature height and spread, bloom period, color, sun and soil preferences, water requirements, fertilizing needs, and general care. Because Latin names can sometimes be a challenge, there is a phonetic botanical pronunciation given for each plant selection as well as another common name (if any). Any added benefits that are unique such as drought resistance, deer and rabbit resistance, attracts beneficials, or attracts hummingbirds are represented by symbols. To help achieve positive results, we also give you our suggestions for landscape design and companion plants.

Sun Preferences

As a quick reference, we have included four symbols representing the range of sunlight suitable for each plant. Full sun means sunlight of eight hours per day to almost all of the day. Part sun is four to six hours of direct sun, preferably in the morning with protection from direct afternoon sun. Part shade is two to four hours of direct sun per day, primarily in the morning, or all day bright indirect light. Shade is shade for most of the day.

Full Sun   Part Sun   Part Shade   Shade

Additional Benefits

Plants can add a lot of special benefits to your garden. Selecting plants that enhance your landscape with special extras have a unique appeal and are indicated with the following symbols.

 Resists drought

 Deer and rabbit resistant

 Attracts beneficials like butterflies and bees

 Attracts hummingbirds

USDA Hardiness Zone Map

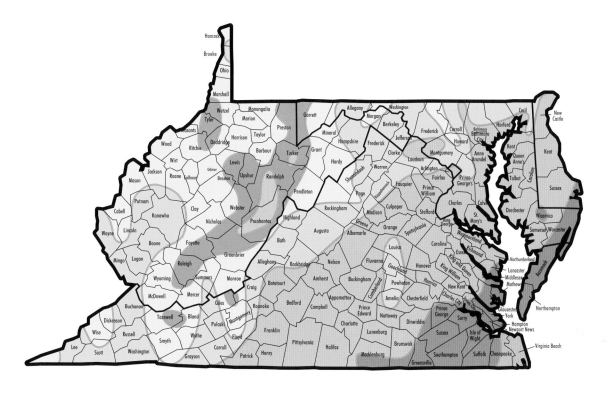

ZONE	Avg. Annual Minimum Temperature (°F)		
5a	-15	to	-20
5b	-10	to	-15
6a	-5	to	-10
6b	0	to	-5
7a	5	to	0
7b	10	to	5
8a	15	to	10

The winter of 2013–2014 was a vicious winter of cold and snow for the Mid-Atlantic states. There was tremendous winter injury. Therefore, we are using the map used in the original *Mid-Atlantic Gardener's Guide* rather than the newer map which reflects warmer temperatures.

USDA Plant Hardiness Zone Map, 2012. Agricultural Research Service, U.S. Department of Agriculture. Accessed from http://planthardiness.ars.usda.gov.

ANNUALS
FOR THE MID-ATLANTIC

Annuals and tender perennials last just one season but they're a delight to grow and dear to every gardener's heart. Just weeks after planting, annuals carpet empty spaces with lasting color and soon grow big enough to screen out the ripening of spring bulb foliage. The vivid zinnias and marigolds are so easy and so satisfying, and they're ideal for a child's garden. In dappled light impatiens, New Guinea impatiens, and coleus color well and grow more beautiful as summer advances; planted in complementary colors, they're stunning. Petunias, geraniums, and other tender (not winter-hardy) perennials keep window boxes and patio planters blooming all summer long. Some annuals self-sow and may spare you the trouble of replanting the next year. Rogue out (remove) those you don't want and transplant the others for a late show.

Many annuals have a rewarding cut-and-come-again habit: the more flowers you harvest, the more the plant produces. Many of the best cutting flowers are annuals. Knowing how to harvest—where to cut the stems—is the key to keeping them blooming. We've described the process below, and, when relevant, with each plant in this chapter. For a continuous supply of vivid zinnias, giant golden marigolds, and late-summer bouquets of pastel cosmos scented with basil, establish a cutting garden where your pleasure in harvesting won't spoil the view. Or, plant cutting flowers in a little kitchen garden with vegetables, herbs, and dwarf fruit trees.

Planting and Fertilizing

Annuals have modest root systems. To be all they can be they require sustained moisture and plenty of nutrients. The introduction to our book explains how to prepare beds for annuals to bring the soil to pH 5.5 to 6.5, the ideal range for most. Organic fertilizers release their nutrients slowly so the plants should do well the first season without further fertilization. Then every year, in late winter or early spring, fertilize beds for annuals with applications of slow-release, long-acting organic fertilizers. If your annuals seem to slow after blooming, they may benefit

Marigolds (*Tagetes* species) are among the easiest annuals you can grow.

from fertilization with one of the water-soluble organic fertilizers, such as seaweed or fish emulsion.

Nursery-grown seedlings of annuals are very tempting in mid-spring when you're looking for instant flowers. Those available at garden centers from early spring until late June are beautiful, already in bloom, healthy—and in everybody else's garden. Eventually you will want to try other alluring varieties you see in garden magazines and catalogs. Then you will have to sow seeds in the garden or—for a head start—indoors. (See "Starting Seeds Indoors" in the introduction.) The time to sow seeds outdoors for the annuals that bloom in late spring and summer is about two weeks after the last frost for your area. Please don't rush the season! Most annuals just won't take off until the ground and the air warm up in mid-spring—seeds and seedlings set out too early will sulk. Flowers whose seed packets say they are "cold hardy" can be sown outdoors a few weeks earlier than the others. Most annuals will come into bloom soonest when they are sown where they are to flower. Seeds for annuals whose show time is late summer and fall can be sown outdoors as late as June, such as cosmos.

Sow smaller seeds by "broadcasting," that is, sprinkle them thinly over the area. Larger seeds can be sown in "hills," groups of four to six, or three to five, equidistant from one another. Flowers for edging beds can be sown in "drills;" that is, dribbled at spaced intervals along a shallow furrow in the soil created by dragging the edge of a rake or hoe handle along the planting line. For planting depth, follow the instructions on the seed packet, or sow seeds at a depth that is about three times the seed's diameter, not its length. Seed packets usually suggest how much to thin seedlings in order to give the mature plants space to develop.

After sowing your seeds, give the planting bed a slow, thorough, overhead soaking. See "Watering" in the introduction for more specifics. Water often enough during the next two or three weeks to maintain soil moisture. Thin the seedlings to 3 to 5 inches apart and apply a 2-inch layer of mulch. In periods of drought, water deeply every week or ten days, or when you see signs of wilting. For window box, basket, and container plantings we recommend using a commercial potting mix. If you mix into the soil a product containing water-holding polymers, you'll find maintaining moisture much easier. These polymers hold twenty times their weight in water, and release the water (and dissolved soil nutrients) slowly.

Annuals Can Take a Lot of Pinching

To be all they can be, some annuals need pinching at several points in the season. The pinching begins right at planting time. It's a fact that once an annual starts producing flowers, the plant puts less strength into growing its root system. But the plant needs a big, healthy root system to get through hot summer days. The way to encourage a plant to grow its root system is to pinch out the flowering tips at planting time. If you are using the color of budded or opening flowers to decide where the plant goes, wait until it is in the ground to pinch out the flowers and buds. Then, at planting time, or very early in their careers, the branching tips of many, even most, annuals should be pinched out to encourage the production of side branches where flowers will develop.

Again, at midseason, when the plants are fully matured, you can encourage new branching and more flowering in some long-branching annuals, such as petunias, by shearing all the stems back by one-third or one-half. Some annuals bloom more fully and over a longer period if you deadhead them consistently and persistently. Pinch them out between your thumb and forefinger—it's fast and easy. Frequent harvesting of most annuals has the same beneficial effect. Cut the stems for bouquets just above the next set of leaves: that's where the new flowering stems will rise. Some of the newer introductions of petunias, impatiens, begonias, and vincas only need that first pinching when planting.

To Encourage Self-Sowers

Annual flowers that sow their own seeds will naturalize (come back year after year) under favorable conditions. Self-sown volunteers of petunias, snapdragons, cosmos, and little French marigolds pop up every year in our gardens. They're slow to flower, and can't be counted on for late summer and fall bloom. But we often transplant them for the fun of seeing what will happen. Other self-sowers are so productive they become weeds—morning glory comes to mind.

You can encourage self-sowing by spreading a 1- or 2-inch layer of humusy soil around the crowns of the parent plants and allowing flowers to set seed toward the end of the growing season. Keep the soil damp and gather the seeds as they ripen and scatter them over the soil. Or, wait until the seeds are dry and loose in their casings, then shake the flower heads vigorously over the soil.

Other Good Options

The annuals on the following pages are on our best-of-the-best list. Others that are "good doers" in the Mid-Atlantic are:

Bachelor's-buttons, cornflower, *Centaurea cyanus*
Browallia, bush violet, *Browallia speciosa*
Butter daisy, *Melampodium paludosum*
Corn poppy, *Papaver rhoeas*
Flowering tobacco, *Nicotiana alata* and *N. sylvestris*
Four o'clocks, *Mirabilis jalapa*
Garden heliotrope, *Heliotropium arborescens*
Globe amaranth, Globe flower, *Gomphrena globosa*
Gerbera, African daisy, *Gerbera jamesonii*
Larkspur, *Consolida ajacis (Delphinium ajacis)*
Moss rose, *Portulaca grandiflora*
Nasturtium, *Tropaeolum majus*
Ornamental kale and cabbage, *Brassica oleracea* (Acephala Group)
Wishbone flower, bluewings, *Torenia fournieri*

Angelonia

Angelonia angustifolia

Botanical Pronunciation
an-jel-OH-nee-ah an-gus-tih-FOE-lee-ah

Other Name
Summer snapdragon

Bloom Period and Seasonal Color
Late spring to October; lavender-blue, purple, pink, white

Mature Height × Spread
12 to 18 inches × 12 to 15 inches

New to many gardeners, this charming, low to mid-height annual can be counted on to keep swaths of soft pastel blooms backed by narrow green foliage in the summer border no matter how hot and muggy. Bushy natives of Mexico and the West Indies, the plants produce masses of tiny puffs of color rather like dainty snapdragons. Angelonia's success has encouraged breeders to bring to market an increasingly varied range of colors and forms. Some are upright with stiff stems, others are bushy, and some spread. The colors tend to be shades of purple, lavender-blue, pink, and there are whites and a few bicolors. The plants need little deadheading. Picked in the cool of early day, they make charming, lasting little bouquets.

When, Where, and How to Plant
Freezing temperatures kill angelonia, so wait until you are sure that all danger of frost is passed before setting out the plants. In full sun most of the day, angelonia develops stocky plants with lots of flower spikes but needs light shade late in the day. Provide well-prepared organically rich soil as described in "Soil Preparation and Improvement" in the introduction. Well before you set out the seedlings, work an organic fertilizer with equal parts nitrogen, phosphorus, and potassium into the soil. Seedlings benefit from an application of a light fertilizer when they're set out. Provide planting holes 8 to 12 inches deep. For smaller varieties, allow 6

inches between plants; for larger varieties, allow 12 inches. These are primarily bedding plants, but they also grow well in pots and containers.

Growing Tips
Apply a liquid fertilizer formulated for flowers and keep the soil nicely damp. If the plants go out of bloom, prune them back lightly and apply a liquid fertilizer.

Regional Advice and Care
Deadheading is generally not needed for angelonia, but like all bedding plants, a little grooming now and then keeps the beds looking their best. So remove browned tips and spent stems as they occur. Late in the season, tired-looking beds revive when cut back, fertilized, and watered well. After the first fall frost kills the plants, clear the beds.

Companion Planting and Design
Pink all-season roses are gorgeous when underplanted with the dark purple angelonias. But they are most often seen as rivers of pastel blues and pinks edging borders, walks, and driveways.

Try These
André likes the Serena series for very full bloom, the compact Sungelonia for early bloom, and tall, deep purple Angel Face for planters and baskets. Tall, showy purple Archangel is his choice for bedding plants.

Begonia

Begonia spp.

Botanical Pronunciation
bih-GOE-nya

Other Name
Wax begonia

Bloom Period and Seasonal Color
Mid-spring to mid-fall; white, pale pink, rose, coral, deep pink, red, bicolors

Mature Height × Spread
6 to 9 inches × 12 to 18 inches

In dappled light, the carefree *Begonia semperflorens-cultorum* hybrids produce small colorful flowers nestled in neat mounds of crisp, waxy, rounded leaves that stay handsome all season. Some strains have maroon-bronze leaves, others are bright green, and there are white-variegated forms. Bedding begonias are a maintenance-free delight, ideal edgers for partly shaded flower borders. We love them because they stay fresh in high heat, and with September rains grow even fuller and prettier. These wonderfully carefree plants need no deadheading to keep blooming. They are tender perennials that can take a lot of cold at the end of the season, but no frost. Brought indoors in October, they bloom all winter. The wax begonia's gorgeous cousin, the tuberous begonia, is a superb but challenging bedding and basket plant that does best in cool areas of the Mid-Atlantic.

When, Where, and How to Plant
You can start wax begonias indoors from seed in early January—but you will find lots of transplants available in April. They grow strong root systems and flower fully when planted right after the last frost date—April in Zone 8, early May in Zones 6 and 7. Wax begonias growing in bright dappled light bloom all season. In cool regions, they'll do better with four to six hours of direct sun. In deep shade, begonias keep their leaves but do not fill out. Wax begonias grow best in soil with a pH of 5.5 to 7.0. See "Soil Preparation and Improvement" in the introduction. Work the soil 8 to 12 inches deep. Set the seedlings high and 6 to 8 inches apart. Mulch with a 2-inch layer.

Growing Tips
To promote rapid, unchecked growth, water for two or three weeks after planting water to maintain soil moisture. After the first few weeks, water deeply when other flowers show signs of wilting. Wax begonias remain crisp even in the first stages of water deprivation. Feed monthly to keep them blooming.

Regional Advice and Care
Watch for slugs and snails during wet weather; set traps if needed. Deadhead spent flowers and remove any rotting stems if the plants are overwatered.

Companion Planting and Design
Wax begonias are perfect edgers for semi-shaded flower borders, and look just great planted in groups of three behind a ribbon of sweet alyssum.

Try These
Some of the showiest hybrid begonias are in the bigger Dragon Wing™ series. 'Picotee' is a treasure, with soft white flowers rimmed in rose. For a real show, look for the big Whopper® series. For a colorful mix of dainty plants, choose the Cocktail series. For edging, choose dwarf *B. semperflorens-cultorum* hybrids; for hanging baskets, choose hybrids with cascading branches. The attractive 24-inch hardy begonia is *B. grandis*, also known as Evans begonia (formerly *B. evansiana*). It survives winters in Zone 7, though all runners from mother plants may overwinter in Zone 6 under mulch. It thrives under tall shrubs like laurel and rhododendrons. There are white- and pink-flowered varieties.

Celosia

Celosia spp. and hybrids

Botanical Pronunciation
seh-LOE-see-uh

Other Name
Cockscomb

Bloom Period and Seasonal Color
Summer; red, pink, yellow, apricot, burgundy-red, gold, cream

Mature Height × Spread
6 to 36 inches × 6 to 12 inches

Celosia is one of the most colorful and enduring of the annuals. The "blooms" are either fanciful velvety crests (much like a cockscomb) or feathered plumes (feathered amaranth) that bloom from summer until frost touches them. The foliage is an asset and may be green or bronze, depending on the color of the blossom. There are dwarfs, and also taller types whose plumes may need staking. The feathery celosias provide strong color and graceful accents for bouquets of cut flowers. Celosia blooms are dryish to start with, so they are ideal subjects for drying. To make them into keepers, remove the lower foliage from stems 8 to 12 inches long, bundle the stems loosely, and hang them up to dry in an airy place out of bright sun. They will dry with little loss of color.

When, Where, and How to Plant

Start seeds indoors in late winter. Or, as soon as the soil has warmed, sow the seeds directly in full sun in fertile, well-drained soil worked to a depth of 8 to 12 inches. The celosias do well in almost any soil. See "Soil Preparation and Improvement" in the introduction. Transplant seedlings, or thin garden-grown seedlings, to stand 12 inches apart. The plants start well but sulk if their roots are disturbed. Provide a 2-inch mulch starting 3 inches from the plant.

Growing Tips

Water the bed well after planting and maintain the moisture the first few weeks. During the summer growing season, provide enough water so the plants do not dry out. Once established, the plants withstand some drought. Fertilize monthly with a complete organic plant food.

Regional Advice and Care

Don't overwater, as celosias are susceptible to fungus. Taller types may need staking. If they do break, they will form side shoots for more, if smaller, flowers.

Companion Planting and Design

Groups of celosias create solid splashes of vibrant color anywhere you plant them. A row of the cockscomb varieties makes a big color statement in the kitchen garden, and the feathery varieties are graceful wherever they're situated.

Try These

Our favorites are the big plume type celosias in the Fresh Look series. The dwarf 'Fairy Fountains' group has 4- to 6-inch plumes on 12-inch plants, and are charming edgers. The larger 'Century' celosias are most effective massed in beds. The handsome scarlet-plumed 'New Look' celosia has dark leaves and endures hot climates.

Coleus

Plectranthus scutellarioides

Botanical Pronunciation
pleck-TRAN-thuss skoo-tul-air-ee-oh-EYE-deez

Other Name
Painted nettle

Bloom Period and Seasonal Color
Colorful foliage all season; combinations of red, mahogany, chartreuse, yellow, white, rose, near-black

Mature Height × Spread
14 to 24 inches × 12 to 18 inches

Coleus was one of André's favorite plants as a child; he was amazed God could make a leaf so beautiful! Its gift is brightly patterned, mid-height foliage that brings eye-catching color to shaded areas. The large heart-shaped leaves emerge from lush, pale green stems that are squarish, a mint family characteristic. And coleus is as wonderfully (or terribly) "generous" as mint. If you keep the leaf tips and the untidy flower spikes pinched, the plants grow bigger and more beautiful until killed by early frosts. This is a great container plant whose color combinations get wilder every year. Coleus cuttings root quickly in water and thrive indoors in a semi-sunny window. A new group of sun- and drought-tolerant coleus, called sun or solar coleus, has revolutionized the use of coleus.

When, Where, and How to Plant
Coleus grows quickly from seed sown in flats indoors. Garden centers offer flats of seedlings of mixed foliage color combinations when the weather warms in mid-May, just in time to plant. Leaf colors are more intense when grown in part shade. In warm parts of Zones 7 and 8, grow coleus on a shaded terrace, or in the bright shade of tall shrubs or trees, or in dappled light. In cool, hilly regions, coleus can take four to six hours of morning sun; the more red there is in the foliage, the more direct sun a plant can take. Plant coleus in moderately rich, humusy soil. See "Soil Preparation and Improvement" in the introduction. Make the planting holes 6 to 8 inches deep. Allow 12 to 14 inches between plants. Apply a 2-inch layer of mulch.

Growing Tips
To promote rapid, unchecked growth, for the first two or three weeks water to maintain soil moisture. Maintain moderate soil moisture thereafter. Feed monthly.

Regional Advice and Care
When plants show signs of new growth, encourage branching by pinching out the top 3 to 4 inches of the lead stem. Encourage fuller growth by removing flower spikes as they start up, and pinch out the tips of branches that may become leggy. Coleus are sensitive to cold temperatures.

Companion Planting and Design
A container planted in mixed colors is breathtaking. In flower boxes, try combinations with impatiens in matching or contrasting colors—scarlet-variegated coleus with scarlet impatiens, and lime-green coleus with white impatiens. Sunny green and gold varieties planted with hosta lighten shaded beds. Trailing varieties are great in hanging baskets.

Try These
The Wizard series is choice for bedding and containers, and the big Colorblaze® group is hard to beat for color. Stained Glassworks™ varieties have lacy leaves and speckled and whorled foliage in sophisticated color variegations. 'Salmon Lace' is pretty, salmon-edged, green and creamy white. Yellow and green 'Highland Fling' pairs well with 'Molten Lava' whose red leaves have black-purple margins. Sun coleus 'Gay's Delight', 'Kiwi Fern', and 'Alabama Sunset' need sun to be at their colorful best.

Cosmos

Cosmos spp.

Botanical Pronunciation
KOZ-mose

Bloom Period and Seasonal Color
Late summer to frost; crimson, orange, rose, yellow, white, pink, burgundy red, bicolors

Mature Height × Spread
1 to 6 feet × 1 to 2 feet

Willowy, drought-tolerant, no-problems cosmos brings to the late summer garden airy, fresh green foliage and bright, open-faced pastel flowers that bloom until early frosts. As the plant grows, lacy foliage fills in around the other flowers in the border so it makes a great filler. As they mature, the graceful 3- to 4-feet branches are spangled with 2- to 4-inch flowers that have crested or tufted centers. Harvest the flowers, and the plants keep on producing. The flowers last well in arrangements and add lovely pastels to late summer bouquets of dahlias, blue salvia, and aromatic mint and basil. Cosmos is delicate but tough. It self-sows exuberantly. We transplant volunteers to places left empty by the passing of spring flowers.

When, Where, and How to Plant

Sow seeds or transplant seedlings outdoors after the ground has warmed. Early-flowering strains bloom from seed in eight to ten weeks. Or, sow seeds indoors in late April and plan to transplant four to six weeks later. If you are starting seeds in the garden, sow them where the plants are to bloom. Cosmos does best in full sun but makes do with four to six hours a day. It withstands drying winds but may need staking in an exposed location. Cosmos is happy in well-drained soil of only average fertility. Overfeeding and rich soil create a need for staking. See "Soil Preparation and Improvement" in the introduction. Dig the bed 6 to 8 inches deep. Space seedlings of the tall varieties at least 12 inches apart. Apply a 2-inch layer of mulch.

Growing Tips

Water for two or three weeks often enough to sustain soil moisture, but grow the plants "hard." Once established, water cosmos only if it shows signs of wilting. No fertilizer is needed.

Regional Advice and Care

If the seedlings tilt, stake the central stem. When they reach 24 inches, encourage branching by pinching out the top 3 to 4 inches of the lead stem. Repeat as the next set of branches develops. Cosmos blooms lavishly even without deadheading, but it self-sows generously so remove spent blooms to avoid too many volunteers next season. When harvesting the flowers, cut the stems to just above a branching node.

Companion Planting and Design

Cosmos is essential in a cottage garden, great in a meadow garden, and makes a good follow-on plant for spring bulbs. Use varieties as fillers for the back of the flower border. For *spectacular* color, plant orange-juice-colored *C. sulphureus* with wildly colorful Joseph's-coat, *Amaranthus tricolor* 'Molten Fire'. Cosmos combines especially well with snapdragons, blue salvia, and Shasta daisies.

Try These

For cutting, plant 'Sea Shells', which bears flowers that have creamy white, shell pink, or crimson and pink interiors; 'Sensation Mix' for large plants with single flowers; 'Psyche Mixed' for its semi-double and single flowers; and bicolored 'Candy Stripe'.

Geranium

Pelargonium × hortorum spp. and hybrids

Botanical Pronunciation
pell-are-GOE-nee-um hor-TOR-um

Bloom Period and Seasonal Color
Spring, summer, fall, some blooms in winter; shades of red, salmon, fuchsia, pink, white, bicolors

Mature Height × Spread
Zonal geranium: can be trained to tree form
Scent-leaved types: 1 to 3 feet

Geranium's special appeal is that it blooms all summer and has handsome foliage. The old-fashioned geranium with big, rounded flower heads and green horseshoe-shaped leaves banded maroon or bronze is called a zonal geranium, *Pelargonium × hortorum*. White-splashed variegated forms are perfect in containers. Ivy-leaf geranium, *P. peltatum*, covers itself and its deeply cut foliage with florets that stand out on slender stems and is perfect for urns and lofty planters. Other ivy-leaved geraniums have fewer flowers but produce cascades of thick waxy foliage on drooping stems, and make beautiful basket plants. Martha Washington geraniums, *P. × domesticum*, have exceptionally showy flowers and are used as pot plants. The several species of scented geraniums have crinkly leaves that give off a strong aroma when brushed; they are grown for their foliage and scent. The geranium is a tender perennial; bring your favorites indoors for winter.

When, Where, and How to Plant

Geraniums are safe planted after the last frost date. Although they are full sun plants, they may benefit from protection during the hottest part of the day; good morning light or a western exposure is ideal. Geraniums maintain themselves in hot, dry, windy exposures but do best where nights are cool. Plant zonal geraniums in well-drained potting or garden soil. Balcon and scented geraniums do best in a fertile humusy soil. All prefer soil with a pH of 5.5 to 6.5. See "Soil Preparation and Improvement" in the introduction. Plant the small bedding geraniums 8 inches apart. Do not mulch.

Growing Tips

Allow the soil surface to dry between deep waterings. Feed monthly with organic plant food.

Regional Advice and Care

When plants show signs of new growth, encourage branching by pinching out 3 to 4 inches of the lead stem and the side branches. Repeat once more during the growing season. Deadhead consistently to encourage flowering. Bottom water to avoid soilborne diseases. In fall, pot up geraniums and bring them indoors; in a sunny window they will bloom for weeks. Cuttings taken in January root easily in water or in a good rooting material. Geraniums can take quite a lot of cold at the end of the growing season.

Companion Planting and Design

Geraniums are great container plants. Bright red zonal geraniums combine well in a window box with silvery dusty miller, petunias, and variegated vinca. A handsome combination for a big container is pink zonal geraniums, blue ageratum, white sweet alyssum, and cascading branches of ivy-leaved geranium. For bedding, use compact varieties like the Tango series; for landscaping, use the larger Rocky Mountain group. Scented geraniums grow tall in a flowerbed, and must be brought indoors for winter.

Try These

Variegated zonal geranium 'Ben Franklin' has semi-double, rosy pink flowers and leaves splashed with beautiful, crisp white markings. Orbit series is loved for its ease of growth, compact form, and large flowers in a range of colors, including 'Apple Blossom', a favorite.

Impatiens

Impatiens spp. and *Hawkeri* hybrids

Botanical Pronunciation
im-PAY-shunz

Other Name
New Guinea impatiens

Bloom Period and Seasonal Color
Mid-spring till frost; white, red, orange, salmon, melon, pink, lavender, orchid, spotted, bicolors

Mature Height × Spread
12 to 48 inches × 18 to 24 inches

The creamy blooms of common impatiens, *Impatiens wallariana*, have been the flowers we counted on to brighten gardens and containers in partial or full shade, growing fuller and more beautiful from late spring until the first frosts. But in recent years the impatiens we know and love has been stricken by downy mildew, a disease that, we hope, is being brought under control by a new fungicide. Meanwhile, the beautiful New Guinea impatiens (*I. hawkeri*) is proving to be resistant. A superb bedding plant, it tolerates much more sun than garden impatiens especially in hybrids such as SunPatiens®. The New Guineas bloom in vibrant, showy colors, grow upright, have colorful foliage, and can withstand more cold at the end of the season. The foliage comes in a variety of colors and patterns.

When, Where, and How to Plant

Choose good-sized seedlings with lots of flower buds, and wait to set them out until night temperatures are consistently above 45 to 50 degrees Fahrenheit. New Guinea impatiens grow well with four to six hours of afternoon shade but to reach maximum size and bloom fully it needs hours of direct morning or cool late afternoon sun. Provide well-drained soil rich in humus and supplied with a slow-release fertilizer worked into the soil 8 to 10 inches deep. See "Soil Preparation and Improvement" in the introduction. Set the seedlings 10 to 12 inches apart. After planting, apply a fine mulch 2 inches deep. New Guineas thrive in big containers filled with a good quality organic potting soil that includes a slow-release fertilizer.

Growing Tips

Keep the seedlings well watered the first few weeks after planting. During the growing season, keep the soil evenly damp. For solid growth and heavy bloom, water impatiens only enough to keep it from wilting. Water early in the day or after the sun has gone by. If you can, avoid overhead watering. Once flower buds have formed, fertilize rarely, if at all, and only lightly with an organic water-soluble fertilizer such as seaweed or fish emulsion.

Regional Advice and Care

The plants are self-cleaning. Keep an eye out for slugs and snails.

Companion Planting and Design

A few New Guinea impatiens planted with coleus in similar colors makes a striking show in big window boxes and planters. Combinations we like are gray-white artemisia with light and dark pink impatiens, and white impatiens with green-and-yellow streaked coleus. The New Guinea hybrids are also great follow-on plants for bulbs growing in partly shaded locations.

Try These

The Infinity series has green foliage, and extra-large flowers in glowing shades of red, pink, rose, coral, white, and lavender. The white is luminous. They like four to five hours of shade and are good in containers. The SunPatiens series thrives in full sun as well as in part shade. It blooms on despite heat, wind, rain, and even early frosts.

Lantana

Lantana camara

Botanical Pronunciation
lan-TAY-nuh kuh-MAR-uh

Other Name
Yellow sage

Bloom Period and Seasonal Color
Summer till frost; white, cream to yellow changing to orange, lavender, yellow, red

Mature Height × Spread
2 to 6 feet × 2 to 6 feet

In color, shape, and nectar production, lantana is second only to the butterfly bush, *Buddleja*, as a butterfly magnet. A tender perennial sub-shrub, it develops quickly so we can grow it here as an annual. The cascading limbs are eventually tipped with dense, rounded or flat-topped clusters of tiny tubular florets. It's an attractive basket and container plant that provides nonstop colorful blooms summer till frost. In the species the flowers are cream to yellow and in some plants the color changes to orange, lavender, and red. There are all-white and all-red hybrids. Trained as a standard, lantana makes a handsome garden centerpiece. It thrives by the seashore. The drooping stems of *Lantana montevidensis*, purple trailing lantana, can reach 36 inches.

When, Where, and How to Plant
You'll find good-sized container-grown plants and seedlings in 4-inch pots at garden centers toward mid-spring. The time to plant lantana is as soon as all danger of frost is past. It needs full sun to bloom well, but it is not very difficult as to soil. If you are planting in containers, consider using an enriched potting soil mix, and add a water-holding polymer—grainy stuff that absorbs and holds twenty times its weight in water. If you are planting in the garden, provide generous planting holes worked 12 inches deep, and soil that is well drained and humusy. See "Soil Preparation and Improvement" in the introduction. Set the plants 2 to 3 feet apart. Water well. Surround the plants with a mulch 2 inches deep.

Growing Tips
Pinch off the branch tips of new plants to encourage lots of bushy growth. Keep the plants well watered until you see fresh new growth at all the branch tips. Mature plants tolerate drought but should be watered deeply if they show signs of wilting. Feed monthly.

Regional Advice and Care
Shear after every flush of bloom. If grown in too much shade, plants can get powdery mildew.

Companion Planting and Design
We love butterflies, so we place lantana near other plants that attract these lovely insects. *Buddleja*, butterfly bush, is one. Blue passionflower, *Passiflora caerulea*, a vigorous exotic vine that bears fragrant flowers, is another. Others are *Asclepias tuberosa* (butterfly weed), *Cosmos sulphureus* 'Bright Lights', purple coneflower, pentas, and parsley in its second year (when it flowers).

Try These
In the Tidewater area, *L. camara* 'Miss Huff' sometimes winters over. For vibrant colors, try the Luscious® and the Patriot® series. The Landmark series is ideal for large groups of plantings. *L. montevidensis* trained as a standard is lovely in bloom.

Lobelia

Lobelia erinus

Botanical Pronunciation
loe-BEEL-yuh err-EYE-nus

Bloom Period and Seasonal Color
Spring into summer; light blue, intense deep blue, wine-red spotted with white

Mature Height × Spread
4 to 6 inches × 8 to 12 inches

In semi-shade, these dainty little plants produce clouds of thin, fragile stems spangled with tiny florets in luminous, intense shades, often with a white eye. In the garden, the stems spread to carpet nearby plantings; growing in a basket or an urn, they cascade. Some varieties have fresh green foliage and some have decorative bronze foliage. In the cooler reaches of the Mid-Atlantic, in Zone 6, edging lobelia grows well throughout spring; with protection from direct sun it may continue into fall. In hot Washington, D.C., gardens, it disappears with the coming of high heat in June. If you love lobelia's intense colors, investigate the large, upright perennial blue lobelia and red cardinal flowers (*Lobelia siphilitica* and *L. cardinalis*).

When, Where, and How to Plant

Plant seedlings two weeks after the last frost date in part sun or semi-shade. In cool regions, lobelia adapts to four hours of direct sun if the soil is moist and the plants are mulched. See "Soil Preparation and Improvement" in the introduction. Prepare a well-drained humusy bed worked to a depth of 6 or 8 inches. Set the seedlings 10 to 12 inches apart, water well, and apply a 2-inch mulch between plants.

Growing Tips

To promote rapid, unchecked growth, for the first two or three weeks water often enough to sustain the moisture in the soil. Maintain soil moisture throughout the growing season, especially when the weather heats up. Feed with a complete organic food about every three weeks to keep flowers coming.

Regional Advice and Care

After every flush of bloom, shear played-out stems. The most common pests you might see are slugs and snails; set out traps if that's the case. Leaf spots are a possibility.

Companion Planting and Design

We use edging lobelia to carpet empty spaces between fading early-spring flowers. It is most beautiful dropping from a basket or an urn. For hanging baskets, choose the trailing Cascade or Fountain series, which bloom profusely.

Try These

A favorite edging lobelia is deep blue 'Crystal Palace'. The soft blue flowers of 'Cambridge Blue' are *perfect* for pots and rock gardens. The Moon series is especially heat-resistant; 'Paper Moon' is an exquisite white. The blue cardinal flower, upright *L. siphilitica*, is a perennial that naturalizes and is a long-lasting cutting flower.

Marigold

Tagetes spp. and hybrids

Botanical Pronunciation
tuh-JEE-teez

Bloom Period and Seasonal Color
Summer until frost; off white, shades of gold, orange, yellow, mahogany, bicolors

Mature Height × Spread
8 inches to 3 feet × 10 inches to 2 feet

    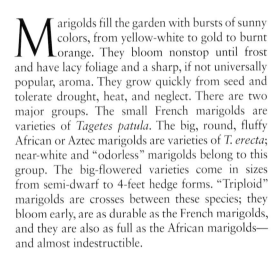 

Marigolds fill the garden with bursts of sunny colors, from yellow-white to gold to burnt orange. They bloom nonstop until frost and have lacy foliage and a sharp, if not universally popular, aroma. They grow quickly from seed and tolerate drought, heat, and neglect. There are two major groups. The small French marigolds are varieties of *Tagetes patula*. The big, round, fluffy African or Aztec marigolds are varieties of *T. erecta*; near-white and "odorless" marigolds belong to this group. The big-flowered varieties come in sizes from semi-dwarf to 4-feet hedge forms. "Triploid" marigolds are crosses between these species; they bloom early, are as durable as the French marigolds, and they are also as full as the African marigolds—and almost indestructible.

When, Where, and How to Plant

Marigolds are easy to grow from seed. Sow seeds in the garden after the soil warms, or sow seeds indoors four to six weeks earlier. Small early marigolds bloom in as little as six to seven weeks from seed sown where they are to grow. Larger types need twelve or thirteen weeks to bloom. Marigolds need full sun to develop fully, except for white varieties, which prefer a little shade. They all do best in well-drained, moderately fertile soil enriched with humus. See "Soil Preparation and Improvement" in the introduction. Space small marigolds 6 to 8 inches apart; allow 15 to 24 inches between tall marigolds. Apply a 2-inch layer of mulch.

Growing Tips

Keep plants well watered. There's no need to fertilize.

Regional Advice and Care

To encourage branching in big marigolds, pinch out the lead stem and branch tips as the plant develops. Deadhead, or shear, marigolds to keep blooms coming. Big-flowered marigolds are handsome in a vase, and last well if you strip the leaves from the part of the stem that will be immersed. The little French marigolds often self-sow, even in window boxes; gather seed for next year's garden. During dry weather, marigolds can be infested by spider mites. Keep plants watered and use an insecticidal soap if needed. Conversely, during wet weather, slugs love marigolds. Use traps if needed.

Companion Planting and Design

Use marigolds to ornament dry, neglected corners. They're great follow-on flowers for spring bulbs. When marigolds are touched by frost, replace them with ornamental cabbages, kales, or potted mums. The little French marigolds are believed to discourage soil nematodes, mosquitoes, and some insects that attack vegetables. Rototilling the big orange African marigolds into the soil seems to protect flowers planted later in the same ground from nematodes. Rows of them planted between rows of nematode-susceptible vegetables and flowers reduces infestations.

Try These

Our favorites are the Inca series that bear 4-inch double blooms on 12- to 14-inch plants; the dwarf Bonanza series, and an old favorite, 'Lemon Drop'. For hedge-sized plants, choose the Climax series, which bears huge blooms on plants 3 to 4 feet tall.

Pansy

Viola × wittrockiana

Botanical Pronunciation
VYE-oh-luh wit-rock-ee-AY-nuh

Bloom Period and Seasonal Color
Fall through early summer; shades and combinations of yellow, blue, white, orange, pink, rose, purple, black

Mature Height × Spread
6 to 10 inches × 8 to 12 inches

The pansy is a strange breed of annual. Sown and planted in fall, it can survive 15 to 20 degrees Fahrenheit; it's one of very few winter-flowering plants. A hybrid violet beloved at least since the Elizabethan era, over the centuries this lovely little flower has acquired a string of delightful common names—heartsease (Johnny-Jump-ups), ladies-delight, and stepmother's flower. Old-fashioned pansies with painted faces in combinations of white, yellow, pink, blue, purple, near-black, and mahogany red have the biggest blooms and are the showiest. Modern pansy strains are smaller-flowered and come in solid colors and tender shades. They have a faint, sweet perfume. The small-flowered Johnny-jump-ups are true violas: their little painted faces do jump everywhere, even into next year.

When, Where, and How to Plant
Pansies here are planted in early spring and again in early fall. We set seedlings out when the weather cools and replenish the plantings with new seedlings in early spring. They live longest where the light will become dappled when the trees leaf out. In cool, hilly regions, pansies can take a little more sun and often live through the summer. The ideal soil for pansies is well drained and humusy. See "Soil Preparation and Improvement" in the introduction. Make the planting holes 8 to 10 inches deep. Plant seedlings with about 3 inches between plants. Apply a 2-inch layer of mulch.

Growing Tips
Keep the soil well moistened. When the weather begins to warm in late winter, fertilize the bed with an organic liquid fertilizer.

Regional Advice and Care
As spring advances, pansies become leggy. Deadhead consistently—a killer job when done correctly since some spring-planted pansies bloom into summer. In the Washington, D.C., climate, about half are gone by June, replaced by long-lasting annuals for summer and early fall. To encourage fall-planted pansies to keep going, deadhead after the first flush of fall bloom. When the plants show vigorous growth in mid-spring, resume deadheading.

Companion Planting and Design
For a showy fall and spring display, plant a color mix of large-flowered pansies, including lots of yellows, and interplant with early tulips. For loads of blooms, plant mixed varieties of the solid-color hybrids. For a lovely spring show, carpet under daffodils with *V. cornuta* 'Sorbet Blueberries and Cream' Johnny-jump-ups. Pansies make handsome window box and container plants, and are delightful as accent plants and edgers for moist places in rock gardens, wild gardens, and woodsy places. Replace fading pansies with shade-loving edging lobelia, forget-me-not 'Victoria Blue', wax begonias, or impatiens.

Try These
'Maxim Marina', an All-America Selections winner, bears 2-inch, pansy-faced, lavender-blue blossoms on 4-inch stems. André loves the colors of the slightly smaller pansies in the 'Clear Crystal' series or the "crystal clears." They stay in bloom longer than the other pansies.

Pentas

Pentas lanceolata

Botanical Pronunciation
PENT-ahs lan-see-oh-LATE-ah

Other Name
Star flower

Bloom Period and Seasonal Color
May into October; red, rose, pink, lavender, white

Mature Height × Spread
1 × 3 feet × 12 to 24 inches

Pentas gets its common name from the shape of the little florets that cluster to form charming, rounded, mounded flowerheads with an old-fashioned look. It is beloved of children and gardeners in part because it attracts butterflies as well as hummingbirds, which linger around the red and dark pink varieties. Bees like them, too, so beware! Pentas is coming into prominence in gardens now because of the many improved varieties that flower more lavishly, come in an array of complementary colors, bloom for longer periods, and are more compact and easier to design with than the species. Even in muggy weather, pentas stays fresh and blooms all summer long. The leaves are somewhat fuzzy, lance-shaped, and dark green. The plants may be upright or low and mounding. They grow quickly in warm weather.

When, Where, and How to Plant

Set out robust seedlings after all danger of frost is past. These are native to Africa and do best when the weather is warm and the site is sunny but they will bloom in part shade as well. In the ground they need well-worked soil and thrive in slightly raised beds that are well drained. Before planting, work the soil 10 to 12 inches deep and amend it with enough humusy compost.to retain moisture. Mix in a slow-release granular fertilizer. Pentas makes a handsome show and does well set out in big window boxes and planters filled with humusy, first rate and well fertilized potting soil. In beds, space the plants 12 to 14 inches apart, and after you have set in the seedlings, add an inch or two of mulch, but keep it well away from the plant stems.

Growing Tip

You may not find plants already budded at your garden center, but pentas grows and soon buds when the weather warms and it is well watered the first six weeks. Once the plants are growing vigorously, water weekly if there is no rain. For lavish bloom, fertilize monthly with a liquid plant food formulated for flowers. In containers, fertilize weekly and water lightly every day.

Regional Advice and Care

If the plants get leggy in late summer, cut them back by one-third, and water and fertilize to encourage a new round of bloom.

Companion Planting and Design

One of the prettiest summer borders is a bed of closely planted smaller pentas set out in a variety of colors. The larger varieties are your best choice for gardens designed to attract butterflies. In planters and window boxes we like them combined with the fuzz of a low ornamental grass and trailing plants such as such as potato vine, or even wandering Jew.

Try These

For containers, André recommends the New Look® series, which grows 8 to 12 inches high. The Butterfly series are F1 hybrids and have larger, showier blooms on plants that are 18 to 24 inches.

Petunia

Petunia × hybrida

Botanical Pronunciation
peh-TOON-yuh HY-brid-ah

Bloom Period and Seasonal Color
Summer; white, yellow, orange, pink, red, blue, lavender, magenta, purple, bicolors

Mature Height × Spread
6 inches to 2 feet × 3 to 4 feet

The old-fashioned petunia with its single or double trumpet-shaped blooms comes in colors to match every dream. Cascade varieties tumble from window boxes and hanging baskets, growing fuller as summer advances. Upright forms make superb full-flowered bedding plants. Some purple and white varieties spread a sweet, cinnamon scent over the evening air; those include in their genetic makeup the night-scented *Petunia axillaris*, the large white petunia. Newer varieties don't set seed, so they last longer. The F1 hybrid single multifloras seem better able to withstand high heat. Wave™ petunias are low, dense, wide spreading, and hold their flowers up. Supertunia™ is a stronger, fuller plant. Common petunias are perennials that can't stand our winters, but the scented, full- flowering, hot magenta *P. integrifolia* can be hardy.

When, Where, and How to Plant
You can start petunias indoors from seed ten to twelve weeks before the weather warms. See "Starting Seeds Indoors" in the introduction. We prefer to choose from the many varieties of seedlings available at garden markets. Plant petunias when temperatures reach 60 to 65 degrees Fahrenheit. In midsummer we add fresh seedlings to containers to keep the displays going longer. For the fullest bloom, grow petunias where they will receive at least six hours of direct sun daily. Provide well-drained, humusy soil, with a pH of 6.0 to 7.0, worked to a depth of 8 to 10 inches. See "Soil Preparation and Improvement" in the introduction. Allow 4 to 6 inches between plants. Spread a 2-inch layer of mulch around bedding petunias.

Growing Tips
Keep the soil evenly moist. Wave™ petunias need no deadheading, pinching, or pruning, but *are* heavy feeders; add slow-release organic fertilizer at planting time.

Regional Advice and Care
Pinch out the tips of young petunias to encourage branching. Deadhead most petunias to keep them blooming. Midsummer, trim the stems back by one-third to encourage late blooming, and repeat as blooms become sparse. Surprisingly, petunias last well as cut flowers; individual blossoms fade but others on the stem open.

Companion Planting and Design
Bedding petunias make good follow-on plants for spring flowers. The sparkling whites of the Cascade varieties harmonize mixed colors in baskets and planters. The grandiflora (big-flowered) forms and doubles produce fewer flowers, but they are magnificent, worth featuring on their own. The multiflora (many-flowered) forms cover themselves with smaller, single blossoms that burst into summer's prettiest multicolor display.

Try These
For a cascade of flowers, we plant the Surfinia® and the Supertunia™ hybrids; for mixed baskets and planters, we like the tiny Million Bells® (*Calibrachoa*); for bedding we use Wave™ and Tidal Wave™ hybrids. Large-flowered Paparazzi petunias are great in containers. The Perfectunia™ series mounds and makes a beautiful filler.

Salvia

Salvia splendens spp. and hybrids

Botanical Pronunciation
SAL-vee-uh SPLEN-denz

Other Name
Scarlet sage

Bloom Period and Seasonal Color
Midsummer till frosts; many colors including lavender-blue and bright red

Mature Height × Spread
1 to 3 feet × 1 to 1½ feet

Scarlet sage (*S. splendens*) is the reddest of the summer flowers, and the parent of today's short, spiky cultivars in designer shades— aubergine to purple, gold to salmon, and, of course, red. The plant, a perennial sub-shrub we grow here as an annual, has glossy green foliage and small tubular red flowers clustered at the tops of leafy stems in thick, showy spikes. Massed in the sun, the scarlet sages make a striking display! Scarlet sage is a cousin of the lovely blue mealycup sage, *Salvia farinacea* and its varieties, which are less showy but wonderful filler plants for borders and bouquets. The blue sages bush out and produce masses of lovely, slender, lavender-blue flower spikes that are beautiful in the garden, in late summer bouquets, and in dried arrangements.

When, Where, and How to Plant
You can start salvia seeds indoors ten to twelve weeks before mid-spring; grow the seedlings at about 55 degrees Fahrenheit. Or, sow seeds in the garden in late fall or in mid-spring. Full sun is best but blue sages flower moderately well with morning sun, particularly in Zone 8. Any well-drained humusy soil is suitable. See "Soil Preparation and Improvement" in the introduction. Work the planting holes to a depth of 8 to 10 inches Space the seedlings 6 to 8 inches apart. Apply a 2-inch layer of mulch.

Growing Tips
To promote rapid, unchecked growth, for the next two or three weeks water often enough to maintain the soil moisture. The sages are drought tolerant but need watering during prolonged dry spells. Feed about every three to four weeks.

Regional Advice and Care
After every flush of bloom, remove spent stalks to promote further flowering. To encourage branching, pinch out the top 3 to 4 inches of the lead stem. Watch for spider mites, aphids, and whiteflies; use insecticidal soap if needed.

Companion Planting and Design
Aubergine scarlet sage planted with coral New Guinea impatiens makes a striking show. The blue salvias (mealycup sage) are beautiful filler plants for shrub roses and lovely with snapdragons and cosmos in complementary colors.

Try These
Heat- and drought-tolerant *S. farinacea* 'Victoria', 18 to 20 inches, and the slightly taller Wedgewood blue 'Blue Bedder' are excellent blues. *S. guaranitica* cultivars bear long spires of deep blue flowers: 'Black and Blue' is gorgeous. Choose 'Rhea', a 14-inch blue for planters and small gardens. *S. coccinea* cultivars are red; 6 to 8 inch 'Lady in Red' attracts hummingbirds.

Snapdragon

Antirrhinum majus

Botanical Pronunciation
an-tih-RYE-num MAY-jus

Other Name
Snaps

Bloom Period and Seasonal Color
Spring through early fall; clear solid shades of red, pink, rose, yellow, bicolors

Mature Height × Spread
8 to 36 inches × 6 to 12 inches

Spring through fall, snapdragons fill cutting gardens and borders with spires of colorful flowers in many colors and bicolors. There's a size and a variety for every garden purpose. Very tall snapdragons are perfect for cutting and for color at the back of a flowerbed. The Princess strain's luscious bicolors are mid-height and also good cutting flowers. Mid-height, open-faced Monarch and "butterfly" hybrids are excellent border flowers. Dwarfs like 'Tahiti' make full, fluffy edgers. In the Mid-Atlantic, we class snapdragons with the annuals, but in Washington, D.C., and Zone 8 they usually come back a year or two to provide one of spring's loveliest early displays.

When, Where, and How to Plant

Planting time for snapdragon seeds and seedlings is mid-spring, two weeks after the last frost date. For early bloom, start snapdragon seeds indoors ten to twelve weeks earlier, or buy seedlings. In Zones 7 and 8, snapdragons do best in bright, dappled light but make do with four to six hours of morning sun. In cool, hilly regions, plant snapdragons in full sun. The ideal soil pH for snapdragons is 5.5 to 7.0. See "Soil Preparation and Improvement" in the introduction. For seedlings, make the planting holes 8 to 12 inches deep, and space them 6 to 10 inches apart. Apply a 3-inch mulch layer starting 3 inches from the stems.

Growing Tips

For the first several weeks after planting, water often enough to keep the soil damp. In midsummer, water deeply every week to ten days unless you have a soaking rain. Feed monthly with an all-purpose organic plant food.

Regional Advice and Care

When seedlings are 4 inches high, pinch out the tips of the lead stems, and repeat for the next two sets of branches. When the tall varieties are 18 inches high, stake the lead stem. Where rust is a problem, plant only rust-resistant strains. When harvesting or deadheading snapdragons, cut the stem just above the next branching node to encourage continued blooming. When snapdragons that survive winter become woody, plant new seedlings beside them in the spring and discard the older plants after their first flush of bloom. Shear dwarf snapdragons after every flush of bloom.

Companion Planting and Design

The tall pastel snaps in rosy colors are beautiful with tall ageratum and silver artemisia. For windy places, choose large-flowered tetraploids like 'Ruffled Super Tetra'.

Try These

For big bouquets and a back of the border show, plant Double Supreme hybrids, which reach to 36 inches tall and bloom in clear, solid shades of red, pink, rose, and yellow. 'Floral Showers' is a good dwarf.

Spider Flower

Cleome hassleriana

Botanical Pronunciation
klee-OH-mee hass-ler-ee-AY-nah

Bloom Period and Seasonal Color
Midsummer till frosts; white, shades of pink, rose, lilac, purple

Mature Height × Spread
3 to 6 feet × 1 to 2 feet

Spider flower is an airy, wonderfully useful back-of-the-border filler flower that develops a big, rangy, multi-branched, and interesting structure. It produces masses of big, open, globe-shaped flower heads in white, pink, or purple, and elegant divided leaves. The flowers are somewhat scented and are followed by attractive seedpods. Spider flower seedlings, and even seeds planted in the open garden, fairly leap to full maturity by midsummer and they stay beautiful well into the fall. The plant handles high heat and drought and is absolutely trouble-free, but often gets to be so big it needs staking. It self-sows prolifically (unless you deadhead) and will save you the trouble of replanting next year.

When, Where, and How to Plant

You can start seeds for spider flower indoors eight to ten weeks before the last local frost date; they grow well where temperatures are about 64 degrees Fahrenheit. Cleome also flowers readily from seed sown in mid-spring in the open garden in full sun. Not all garden markets offer spider flower seedlings, but the plants self-sow so generously that once you have planted cleome it probably will maintain itself in your garden. Almost any well-worked, well-drained, light soil suits spider flower, and it does well even in sandy soil. See "Soil Preparation and Improvement" in the introduction. Space seedlings 15 to 20 inches apart and mulch 2 inches deep.

Growing Tips

Maintain soil moisture until the seedlings are growing well. Water deeply if the plants show signs of wilting in a drought. If you have sown seeds outdoors in the open garden, once the seedlings are up, water them weekly. There's no need to fertilize in fertile soil.

Regional Advice and Care

If the plants take off and begin to look like they're headed for shrub size, tie the lead stem to a sturdy stake. Since cleome self-sows abundantly, deadhead now and then to minimize the thinning you will have to do next year.

Companion Planting and Design

A mass planting of spider flowers is handsome growing against a stone wall, it is an excellent background plant for the flower border, and it's a lovely addition to a meadow garden.

Try These

'Rose Queen', with its deep pink buds and pale pink flowers, is a favorite, along with 'Purple Queen' and 'Helen Campbell', a beautiful white spider flower. New dwarf varieties such as 'Linde Armstrong' and 'Sparkler Blush' are excellent fillers for the middle of the flowering border.

Sweet Alyssum

Lobularia maritima

Botanical Pronunciation
lob-you-LAIR-ee-uh muh-RIT-ih-muh

Bloom Period and Seasonal Color
June until frosts; white, purple, pastels

Mature Height × Spread
4 to 12 inches × 6 to 18 inches

Sweet alyssum is a fragrant, frothy little edging plant that from summer through late fall just covers itself with tiny, scented florets in sparkling white, rosy violet, or purple. The plant has a dainty appearance and spreads outward, becoming a low sprawling mound by the end of the season. In extreme heat in midsummer, a slump in flower production can occur, but the blossoms return when cooler weather arrives. However you use alyssum, be sure to set at least a few plants by the porch or patio where you can enjoy its sweet scent in late summer. Alyssum is one of the plants that does exceptionally well near the sea and it can be set out around taller plants as a living mulch to keep the ground cool.

When, Where, and How to Plant

If you want to grow your own alyssum, start the seeds indoors between February 1 to 15, but be aware that alyssum is slow to germinate. Plant the seedlings outside when the soil has warmed. Sweet alyssum can do with a little less than direct sun all day, but it needs at least four to six hours of direct sun to flower at all well. The ideal for sweet alyssum is well-drained humusy soil with a pH between 6.0 and 7.0. Dig the bed, or generous planting holes, 6 inches deep. See "Soil Preparation and Improvement" in the introduction. Set the seedlings 6 to 8 inches apart. Apply a 2-inch mulch starting 3 inches from the stems.

Growing Tips

To promote rapid, unchecked growth, for the first two or three weeks water often enough to sustain the soil moisture. In midsummer, water deeply when you water the flower garden. If grown in containers, fertilize monthly. After shearing, fertilize again to stimulate blooming.

Regional Advice and Care

Shear after each flush of bloom to discourage seed-setting and to encourage flowering. Sweet alyssum self-sows and can spread like wildfire to other parts of the garden. Discard volunteers, because chances are these will turn out to be plants that have reverted to the original, less-interesting species, not the beautiful cultivar you planted originally. It has no pests or diseases to bother it.

Companion Planting and Design

Sweet alyssum makes a neat, fragrant edger for flowering borders and walks. We add sweet alyssum in hanging baskets, planters, and tubs, set so the stems will spill over the container edges as the plant fills out. It thrives tucked into moist planting pockets in a dry stone wall and is very pretty paired with purplish ornamental peppers.

Try These

For a showy white, choose the large-petaled Clear Crystal series. For compact plants 4 to 10 inches tall, André recommends the Wonderland series. For early bloom, choose the Easter Bonnet series.

Verbena

Verbena spp. and hybrids

Botanical Pronunciation
vur-BEE-nuh

Other Name
Vervain

Bloom Period and Seasonal Color
Summer till frost; white, red, pink, yellow, blue, purple, bicolors

Mature Height × Spread
6 to 18 inches × 8 to 24 inches

Common garden verbena is a spectacular basket plant and a fabulous shore-side performer. Fast growing and tolerant of drought, wind, and searing sun, it is a vigorous, free-blooming plant. It grows either as a fragrant mound or a trailer that covers itself with rounded heads of small, pale-eyed, primrose-like florets. The leaves are pretty, oval or lance-shaped, serrated, and dark green. Verbena is a great bedding plant. In Washington, D.C., it is planted as a follow-on groundcover for bulbs and remains effective through the city's hot, muggy weather. Many varieties are very fragrant. Common garden verbena is the verbena for show. To see butterflies in action, plant its taller cousin, spring-flowering South American vervain (tall verbena), *Verbena bonariensis*, which, along with the cultivar *V. canadensis* 'Homestead Purple', is perennial in Zone 7 and warmer.

When, Where, and How to Plant

Common garden verbena is a tender perennial grown here as an annual. If you want to start plants, sow seeds in January, just covering them with a little seed-starting mix, and grow the seedlings in a cool room, between 64 to 70 degrees Fahrenheit. Because the seed germinates slowly, we buy seedlings and plant them outdoors, after all danger of frost is past, where they will get full sun, or sun until the afternoon. Verbenas need light, well-drained soil and they tolerate poor, dry soil. See "Soil Preparation and Improvement" in the introduction. Work soil 8 to 12 inches deep and prepare planting holes 10 to 15 inches apart. Plant the seedlings high. Mulch 2 inches starting 3 inches from the stems.

Growing Tips

To promote rapid, unchecked growth, for the first two or three weeks water the verbenas often enough to sustain soil moisture. During the growing season, water when you water the flower beds. There's usually no need to fertilize.

Regional Advice and Care

After each flush of bloom, shear the spent flower heads. Encourage branching by pinching out the tips of each stem.

Companion Planting and Design

We most often plant baskets of common garden verbena in a single color. For bedding, we like red verbena with dianthus from the Charm series in mixed colors, dusty miller, and white sweet alyssum. A nice window box combination is verbena with petunias in a contrasting shade, variegated vinca, and indoor foliage plants (on vacation out of doors).

Try These

Many varieties of mounded verbenas are fragrant, especially the blue. Trailing verbenas, including the big Superbena® series, are excellent in big baskets and edging window boxes. The colorful Tuscany series is choice for smaller basket and pots. The showy Quartz series is compact and good for borders. One of the most popular series is the 'Showtime' hybrids, which come in many brilliant colors, some with a bold, contrasting eye. 'Sissinghurst' has bright rose-pink flowers. *V. tenuisecta* 'Imagination' has delicate leaves and produces flowers in a deep violet blue. Tappan Blue® has light blue flowers.

Vinca

Catharanthus roseus

Botancal Pronunciation
kath-uh-RAN-thuss ROE-zee-us

Other Name
Rosy Periwinkle

Bloom Period and Seasonal Color
Late spring until frosts; pink, deep rose, red, scarlet, white with a red eye, lavender-blue with a white eye, peach, apricot, orchid, raspberry, burgundy

Mature Height × Spread
6 to 18 inches × 6 to 18 inches

You can count on vinca to fill the front of your garden with pretty flowers nestled in crisp, fresh foliage from late spring until frost. It tolerates heat, drought, and pollution. The flower color never fades and the blossoms never need deadheading. The shiny leaves are dark green, and the single flowers have overlapping petals and, usually, an eye in a contrasting color. Once cut, the flowers continue to open buds for several days, and the leaves stay fresh. Both the leaves and the flowers resemble pink vinca's trailing cousins, the evergreen periwinkles or myrtles, *Vinca minor* and *V. major*. Pink vinca's standard height is 1 to 1½ feet but new strains provide plants of varying heights, some with widespreading, trailing branches suited to containers.

When, Where, and How to Plant

Seeds can be started indoors ten to twelve weeks before the average last frost. But the plants are very sensitive to cold and overwatering, so we recommend buying nursery seedlings when they come on the market in late spring. In warm Zone 8, you'll find protection from midafternoon sun beneficial; in cool regions, pink vinca does well in full sun. The ideal pH for pink vinca is 6.0 to 6.5. Any well-drained improved garden soil suits pink vinca. See "Soil Preparation and Improvement" in the introduction. Prepare planting holes 6 inches deep. Set standard vincas 8 to 12 inches apart; allow

12 to 14 inches between plants of the Mediterranean series and 'Cascade Appleblossom'. Apply a 3-inch mulch starting 3 inches from the stems.

Growing Tips

For the first two or three weeks, water lightly at ground level without wetting the foliage, just often enough to keep the seedlings from drying out.

Regional Advice and Care

Once the plants show signs of new growth, pinch out the top 3 to 4 inches of the lead stem to encourage branching. Pinch out the next two sets of branches as they develop. If the leaves curl in periods of drought and heat, don't be concerned since they'll uncurl when dew falls in the evening.

Companion Planting and Design

Pink vinca's clear colors, bright contrasting eyes, and crisp green foliage have a cooling effect that enhances flowers with hot colors. It's attractive with blue or scarlet salvia, and makes a pretty low hedge for the front of the garden.

Try These

Cora series vincas are disease-resistant and stand a lot of heat: The Cora® Cascade series is a glorious trailing variety ideal for containers. 'Bright Eye' is a white dwarf.

Zinnia

Zinnia elegans and hybrids

Botanical Pronunciation
ZINN-ee-uh ELL-ih-ganz

Bloom Period and Seasonal Color
Summer through early fall (if kept deadheaded);
shades of red, pink, orange, magenta, yellow,
white, bicolors

Mature Height × Spread
6 inches to 3 feet × 12 to 42 inches

We love the zinnia's sparkling colors, wild and wonderful flower forms, and cut-and-come-again attitude. One of the very best annuals for vibrant color and lasting vase life, it's a staple in our gardens. Zinnias are fun because there are so many varieties to experiment with. These are upright plants that branch when the tips are pinched, and they come in colors and sizes suited to every design purpose. The petals of some varieties are quilled like a cactus, others curl, and some are ruffled. There are flat-petaled forms, doubles, and singles. The large-flowered zinnias bloom less freely than the small-flowered forms, and need more time to come into bloom.

When, Where, and How to Plant
You can sow seeds indoors about four weeks before planting time, which is when the soil has warmed. The smaller varieties bloom in four to five weeks from sowing. Zinnias do best with full sun, but bloom with four to six hours of sun. Dig the soil 8 to 12 inches deep. See "Soil Preparation and Improvement" in the introduction. Set seedlings of miniatures 6 inches apart, and the larger zinnias 18 inches apart. We can't do without zinnias, but they are subject to leaf spot and mildew so avoid mulch and crowding, which encourages mildew.

Growing Tips
In a drought, water every ten days to two weeks; overwatering encourages mildew. Fertilize monthly with organic plant food.

Regional Advice and Care
When seedlings are 6 inches high, pinch out the tips of the lead stems to encourage branching. Deadhead consistently and harvest flowers at will. Cut the stem just above the next branching node and new flowering stems will develop, rising from between each pair of leaves and the main stem. Where mildew is a problem, choose mildew-resistant cultivars. Cornell University research suggests that spraying with a solution of 1 tablespoon ultrafine or horticultural oil plus 1 tablespoon baking soda (sodium bicarbonate) per gallon of water protects against mildew.

Companion Planting and Design
Zinnias are ideal follow-on plants for spaces left empty by the passing of spring flowers. Dwarfs like 'Dasher' and 'Liliput' make colorful edgers. Ribbons of award-winning 'Peter Pan' zinnias, small plants with big flowers, brighten a garden path. Little *Zinnia angustifolia* is a spreading form to use in hanging baskets and as an edger. An annual that makes a delightful edger for zinnias is the pretty little "creeping zinnia," *Sanvitalia procumbens*.

Try These
Two AAS winners André likes are 2- to 3-feet bold, colorful, lasting 'Zowie!' and a unique bicolor, 'Starlight Rose'. For double blooms in a colorful pink, look for Senora™. For cutting choose the very popular Cut & Come Again series. Magellan series is an outstanding double-flowered dwarf.

BULBS, CORMS, RHIZOMES & TUBERS
FOR THE MID-ATLANTIC

The earliest flowers come from bulbs, tubers, and corms planted in September and October the fall before. The little bulbs open first, about February when the witch-hazels bloom at the U.S. National Arboretum. We plant these early risers under shrubs and trees tall enough to allow them dappled light. We edge flowerbeds with them, and woodland paths, and set them adrift in rock gardens. We keep a few near entrances so they can report on the progress spring is making. Each small bulb adds just a scrap of color to the winter landscape, so we plant them in drifts of twenty to a hundred. Small bulbs thrive and perennialize even in lawns. They may be grown in large containers outdoors in Zones 7 and 8 and some can be forced into flower indoors.

The next wave of color from fall-planted bulbs peaks in April and May. The earliest of the big bulbs are the perfumed hyacinths, which we plant near entrances. Then come the daffodils and the tulips. The large spring bulbs are most effective planted in groups of ten in flower borders and naturalized in drifts of twenty or more. We plant dozens in flower borders accompanied by perennials (and annuals) that will grow up and hide the fading bulb foliage, which must be allowed to ripen before it is removed. That's their major drawback: for the larger bulb flowers to bloom well the following year, the foliage must be allowed to ripen—yellow—before it is removed. It takes weeks and the process is unsightly.

Summer-flowering bulbs provide great screening for the fading foliage of spring-flowering bulbs. They come into bloom when the nights turn warm—mid- to late June, and some last until mid-September. Those that are winter hardy can be planted the fall before; tender bulbs should be set out in the spring. To be effective, these big bulbs need to be in sets of five or ten. We like to add a few real tropicals, including canna and the ornamental banana, for their exotic foliage: they're available pot-grown in late spring. They often winter over successfully stored in their containers in a cool basement.

Bulbs that bloom when all other flowers have faded have a special place in the gardener's heart. The silky petals and tender colors look so fragile, but they endure fall rains and windstorms. Fall-flowering bulbs can be planted in spring and anytime up until July—as soon as they're available. These small bulbs are most effective planted in groups of twenty, fifty, and one hundred.

Tulips bordered by violas in a spring landscape are a cheerful sight.

When, Where, and How to Plant

Bulbs-in-waiting can be stored in the crisper, or a cool garage or cellar. (Do not store them with apples, which put out a gas that will cause the bulbs to rot.) If you can, plant them as soon as you get them. Planted late, they have shorter stems and late blooms. Most bulbs bloom earliest when growing in full sun; in part shade, they open later. Their first year, spring-flowering bulbs will bloom planted in shade. But to perennialize and bloom fully, they need at least bright or dappled light under deciduous trees, or bright shade under a tall evergreen. The ideal site is a sunny, sheltered location where the soil is dryish in summer and in winter.

The ideal soil for bulbs is light, very well drained, and improved by additions of organic matter such as peat moss, compost, or aged pine bark, along with an organic, blended bulb fertilizer at the rate of 5 to 10 pounds per 100 square feet. The ideal pH range for most is 6.0 to 7.0. See "Soil Preparation and Improvement" in the introduction. Set bulbs so the pointed tips are upright; set corms and tubers with the roots facing down. For bulbs under 2 inches tall, provide holes at least 5 inches deep and 1 inch wide. Or, prepare a planting bed 5 to 6 inches deep. Set the small bulbs 2 inches apart. Plant bulbs that are 2 inches or larger in holes 8 inches deep and 3 inches wide. Or prepare a planting bed 8 to 10 inches deep. Set the bulbs 4 to 6 inches apart. To create naturalized drifts, dig an irregularly shaped planting bed, throw the bulbs out by the handful, and plant where they fall.

Caladiums provide striking color in a garden.

But before planting bulbs, inventory the vole population. For voles, your bulbs are the local gourmet counter. Squirrels shop there, too, and store their catch for later use. When they forget where they stored your bulbs, they come up in totally unexpected, sometimes delightful, places. To foil the sweet dears, plant your bulbs in pockets of VoleBloc™ or PermaTill®. Either one improves drainage, by the way. Daffodils don't need protection from voles: they're toxic to wildlife. Place 2 inches of VoleBloc™ or PermaTill® in the bottom of the hole. Set the bulb on top of it, and fill in all around with VoleBloc™ or PermaTill® leaving just the tip exposed. Fill the hole with a mix of 50 percent VoleBloc™ or PermaTill® and improved soil from the hole. Mulch with 2 inches of pine needles, oak leaves, composted wood chips, or shredded bark.

Care

Most of the bulbs we recommend come back, at least for a season or two. Allow the stems and foliage of the large bulbs to ripen six to seven weeks before removing them. Daffodils and some of the small bulbs are likely to rebloom and to multiply indefinitely without deadheading. Large bulbs benefit from deadheading. Remove only the flower itself. Allowing the flower stem as well as the foliage to ripen nourishes the bulb and that enhances next year's flowering. Small bulbs do not need deadheading. Tulip foliage may be cut when it yellows halfway down. If well fertilized, some tulips perennialize, but the following year many just put up puny foliage and fail to bloom. We dig and discard those. Most bulbs require ample moisture during the season of active growth from the moment the first pip breaks ground. Once the foliage disappears, the bulbs are dormant, and excess watering can be detrimental. After flowering, but before the foliage disappears, spread an organic, slow-release fertilizer over the bulb plantings, 4 to 6 pounds per 100 square feet.

A Seasonal Approach

There are so many wonderful bulbs to choose from, it can be overwhelming. One way to simplify the selection is to categorize them by seasons.

Late Winter and Early Spring Bulbs

Early crocus, *Crocus vernus*
Glory-of-the-snow, *Chionodoxa luciliae*
Grape hyacinth, *Muscari* spp.
Miniature cyclamen, *Cyclamen coum*
Miniature daffodils, *Narcissus* 'Tête à Tête' and other early daffodils
Netted iris, Reticulated iris, *Iris reticulata*
Snowdrop, *Galanthus nivalis*
Species tulips, *Tulipa saxatilis, T. tarda, T. turkistanica*, and others
Squill, *Scilla tubergeniana*
Striped squill, *Puchkinia scilloides*
Windflower, *Anemone blanda*
Winter aconite, *Eranthis hyemalis*

Early and Mid-Spring Bulbs

Bearded iris, *Iris* hybrids
Daffodil, *Narcissus* spp.
Fritillaria, *Fritillaria imperialis* 'Rubra Maxima'
Hyacinth, *Hyacinthus orientalis*
Late crocus, *Crocus vernus* hybrids
Lily-of-the-valley, *Convallaria majalis*
Silver bells, *Ornithogalum nutans*
Starflower, *Ipheion uniflorum* 'Wisley Blue'
Tulip, *Tulipa* spp.
Wood hyacinth, Spanish bluebell *Hyacinthoides hispanica* (syn. *Scilla campanulata*)
Wood sorrel, *Oxalis adenophylla*

Summer Bulbs

Crocosmia, *Crocosmia* spp. and hybrids
Dahlia, *Dahlia* hybrids
Dwarf canna, *Canna* hybrids
Flowering onion, *Allium giganteum*
Gladiolus, *Gladiolus* spp.
Lily, *Lilium* spp.
Peacock orchid, *Acidanthera bicolor*
Peruvian daffodil, *Hymenocallis narcissiflora*
Poppy anemone, *Anemone coronaria*
Rain lily, Zephyr lily, *Zephyranthes* spp.
Spider lily, Naked lady, *Lycoris* spp.
Summer hyacinth, *O. candicans*, formerly *Galtonia candicans*
Tuberose, *Polianthes tuberosa*

Fall and Winter Bulbs

Colchicum, Autumn crocus, *Colchicum autumnale*
Fall crocus, *Crocus kotschyanus* syn. *C. zonatus, C. speciosus*
Hardy cyclamen, *Cyclamen hederifolium*
Lily-of-the-field, Autumn daffodil, *Sternbergia lutea*
Winter daffodil, Saffron crocus, *C. sativus, Narcissus asturiensis* and *N.* 'Grand Soleil d'Or'

Other Options

This chapter presents the best bulbs, corms, and tubers for the Mid-Atlantic, but there are others we like also:
Canna, *Canna* × *generalis*
Ornamental banana, *Musa velutina* (though technically not a bulb)

Crocosmia

Crocosmia spp. and hybrids

Botanical Pronunciation
kroe-KOZ-mee-uh

Other Name
Montbretia

Bloom Period and Seasonal Color
July and August; orange-red, red, yellow

Mature Height × Spread
1 ½ to 3 feet × ½ to 1 ½ feet

Crocosmia is a tall, exceptionally beautiful and showy summer-flowering bulb that will remind you of a gladiola. Like the gladiola, it grows from a corm and sends up fresh, handsome, sword-shaped leaves followed by slender, branching spikes of deep orange-scarlet flowers. The blossoms must be loaded with nectar because they are dearly loved by butterflies and hummingbirds. The most famous of the cultivated varieties is 'Lucifer' whose large, silky flowers are a vivid flame red. Crocosmia is a long-lasting garden perennial that lives through winters without cover even in Zone 6. In Zone 7 and southward it perennializes, multiplies, and provides many weeks of vivid color for the garden in the dull summer months. Crocosmia is also an excellent cutting flower.

When, Where, and How to Plant

Crocosmia may suffer in cold winters in Zone 6, so plant it in a protected spot and provide a winter mulch. If your winters are colder than Zone 6, plant corms and plan to lift and store them for the winter. Garden centers offer container-grown crocosmia in spring, the planting season. In cool regions, crocosmia needs full sun to be all it can be, but where summer gets very hot it needs some protection from noon sun. Crocosmia is tolerant as to pH, but needs a well-drained site and humusy, fertile soil. See "Soil Preparation and Improvement" in the introduction. Set corms 3 inches deep and 5 inches apart. Plant container-grown crocosmia according to the planting instructions at the beginning of the Perennials chapter. Water well. Mulch 2 inches deep starting 3 inches from the edge of the planting.

Growing Tips

Water deeply every week to ten days for the first four to six weeks unless you have a soaking rain. Crocosmia does best given sustained moisture, but the plant is adaptable. Fertilize the bed between late winter and early spring with slow-release, organic, acid fertilizer.

Regional Advice and Care

Crocosmia is self-cleaning, so it doesn't need deadheading. The flowers are followed by attractive seed capsules that can be left until fall; then the foliage should be cut down to a few inches above the crown. For winter protection in Zone 6, mulch with evergreen boughs or hay; in cooler regions lift the corms and store them for the winter.

Companion Planting and Design

Use crocosmia to screen the last of the foliage of the late spring bulbs: it will grow up and make a wonderful splash of color in the hot dry months. Plant crocosmia in a flowering border in groups of five or ten and toward the center of the bed. It needs lots of space all around.

Try These

'Lucifer' is our favorite, so this could be headed "Try This One."

Crocus

Crocus spp. and hybrids

Botanical Pronunciation
KROE-kuss

Bloom Period and Seasonal Color
Late winter, early spring, and fall; white, pink, lavender, purple, yellow, orange; many striped or streaked with contrasting colors

Mature Height × Spread
½ to 6 inches × 1 to 6 inches

There are both fall-blooming and spring-blooming crocus. The late winter, early spring crocuses are planted the fall before, and begin to bloom about the same time as the snowdrops raise their tiny white bells. Often enough these early birds face up to and bloom through the last snowfall. The brightly colored, little cup- or chalice-shaped flowers have vivid yellow anthers and come in many colors. Some have beautiful contrasting stripes or streaks. The grassy green leaves come up after the flowers and in some varieties have white or silver midribs. The fall crocuses produce their elegant cup-shaped blooms in early and mid-fall. They are planted in August or September. The following year the grassy leaves come up in the spring, and then die down in summer.

When, Where, and How to Plant
Plant the bulbs in September or October, and set them out in full sun; in part shade they open later. The ideal location is a sunny, sheltered place where the soil is dryish in summer and in winter. The ideal soil is light, well drained, and improved by additions of organic matter and an organic, blended fertilizer. The ideal pH range is 6.0 to 7.0. See "Soil Preparation and Improvement" in the introduction and the planting instructions at the beginning of this chapter, including instructions on discouraging voles and squirrels. Provide holes 5 inches deep and 1 inch wide, or a planting bed 5 to 6 inches deep. Set the bulbs 2 inches apart. Avoid leaving bits of bulb casing around the planting: squirrels notice these. Mulch the bed area.

Growing Tips
After flowering, and before the foliage disappears, spread an organic, blended fertilizer over the area where the bulbs have been planted, at the rate of 4 to 6 pounds for every 100 square feet.

Regional Advice and Care
Crocus naturalize easily, and will perennialize in lawns. If you plant crocus in the lawn, you must be prepared to allow the foliage a little time to ripen before the grass can be mowed. Voles, mice, and chipmunks may eat the bulbs.

Companion Planting and Design
To really show, they need to be planted in drifts of twenty to one hundred. We like lots of spring-blooming crocuses near house entrances, early reminders that spring is coming, and for edging flowerbeds and borders, fronting shrub borders, and planted along woodland paths. With fall-blooming crocus, André plants *Colchicum autumnale* under tall trees.

Try These
André's choices are varieties of *C. vernus*, with 3-inch flowers, some striped or feathered, which has been in cultivation since 1765, and the Dutch hybrid cultivars. For fall flowering *C. speciosus*, which blooms early, is the showiest, the easiest, and can stay in bloom until hard frosts. Also try these fall bloomers: *C. kotschyanus* (syn. *C. zonatus*), which bears 4- to 6-inch-tall rose-lilac flowers, and the later blooming saffron crocus, *C. sativus*.

Daffodil

Narcissus spp. and hybrids

Botanical Pronunciation
nar-SISS-us

Other Name
Jonquil

Bloom Period and Seasonal Color
Spring; white, yellow, gold, orange, pink, bicolors

Mature Height × Spread
4 to 24 inches × 2 to 8 inches

D affodils are flowers that announce the coming of spring with a splashy show of gold, cream, or bicolored "ta-da-ta-da" trumpets on straight 4- to 24-inch stems. In the hills of Virginia and Maryland, Zone 6, early daffodils often bloom with the thawing of the snow. But in southern Virginia and along the shore, early daffodils and miniatures such as 'Tête-à-Tête' often flower in December and January, or even earlier. Daffodils perennialize readily and are safe from rodents because they are toxic to them. The names "daffodil," "*Narcissus*," and "jonquil" cause confusion: *Narcissus* is the botanical name, though "daffodil" may be used in its place. Jonquils are a specific type related to the species N. *jonquilla*, late bloomers that bear a cluster of flowers on each stem and are exquisitely scented. The paperwhites we force for winter bloom are jonquils too tender to survive winter.

When, Where, and How to Plant
Plant bulbs in September or October in full or part sun. The ideal soil is well drained and slightly acidic. Provide well-worked fertile loam with excellent drainage. See "Soil Preparation and Improvement" of the introduction. Some bigger daffodil bulbs are really two or three bulbs attached—don't separate them. Set the bulbs 8 inches deep, about 3 to 6 inches apart. Mulch.

Growing Tips
To perennialize, after flowering and before the foliage disappears, spread organic, blended fertilizer over the area, 4 to 6 pounds for every 100 square feet.

Regional Advice and Care
Deadheading isn't essential. Allow the foliage to yellow about six weeks before cutting it back. Don't bind the leaves during that period—that cuts off light and oxygen. When daffodils get smaller and crowded, divide them just before the foliage has died. Replant them at once, or store them in well-ventilated trays at 50 to 80 degrees Fahrenheit. Cut daffodils last well. A note of caution: before combining just-cut daffodils (which contain toxic substances) with other flowers, soak the daffodils in water overnight and discard the water.

Companion Planting and Design
Plant daffodils in irregular drifts of ten, twenty, or more. Large daffodils are breathtaking in woods, fronting evergreens, edging meadows, and along the banks of ponds and streams. The miniatures are exquisite in rock gardens, containers, or tucked into rocky nooks. By choosing bulbs that come up early, midseason, and late there can be daffodils from late winter until early summer. In warm climates, a few will flower (whether you want them to or not) before Christmas.

Try These
For over fifty years nurseryman Martin Viette, André's father, tested daffodils to find those that perennialize best. Here are a few: 'February Gold', 'Avalanche', 'Geranium', 'Hawera', 'Sir Winston Churchill', and 'Tête-à-Tête'. A few are fragrant such as 'Cheerfulness,' and 'Pheasant's Eye', 'Ice Follies', 'Thalia', 'Peeping Tom', 'Carlton', and 'Silver Chimes'.

Dahlia

Dahlia spp. and hybrids

Botanical Pronunciation
DAL-yuh

Bloom Period and Seasonal Color
Late summer, early fall; pastels and jewel tones of pink, salmon, white, cream, lemon, heliotrope, mauve, red, bicolors

Mature Height × Spread
1 to 6 feet × ½ to 2½ feet

The dahlia is one of the great flowers of late summer and early fall, an easy-to-grow, bushy perennial with lush foliage and many-petaled flowers in extraordinary forms. The American Dahlia Society recognizes fourteen distinct types of this New World flower, discovered in the sixteenth century in the mountains of Mexico by members of the Cortez expedition. But for gardeners, there are two main groups: the seed-grown bedding plants sold in flats of mixed colors; and the big show dahlias grown as staked specimens in containers or at the middle or back of the border. The flowers range from 6- and 7-inch "dinner plates" to 1½- and 2-inch pom-pom charmers. Cut dahlias last well. Their crisp, almost translucent petals catch the light and in paler shades can be luminous.

When, Where, and How to Plant

Plant tubers, or container-grown dahlias, when lilacs bloom. Provide an open sunny site and soil improved as described in the introduction—light, fertile, well drained, humusy, pH 6.0 to 7.5. Set tubers or container-grown plants 18 to 24 inches apart. For 5-footers, provide sturdy, equally tall stakes. For tubers, dig planting holes 6 to 8 inches deep with the eye portion nearest the stake, if there is to be one. Cover the tuber with 2 to 3 inches of soil. Water when a shoot appears about four weeks later. Then add a few more inches of soil, water, and repeat at intervals as the plant grows until the hole is filled. When the stem is 12 inches tall, tie the stem to its stake. Tie on other branches as the plant matures.

Growing Tips

Dahlias require watering every week to ten days unless there's a good soaking rain. Feed monthly with an organic plant food.

Regional Advice and Care

Harvest the blooms or deadhead. To harvest, place cut dahlia stems in water at 150 to 160 degrees Fahrenheit to harden overnight before re-cutting the stems and arranging them. Given a deep winter mulch, dahlias may perennialize. But growers recommend digging and storing the tubers when the yellowing tops die back after the first killing frost. Lift the crown with a spading fork, remove the foliage, and wash off the dirt. Dry them out of direct sunlight for a day or so. Label and store them in cedar chips, vermiculite, sand, or peat moss in a cool, dry place at 40 to 45 degrees Fahrenheit. In spring when the eyes begin to sprout, divide the tubers, providing each with at least one eye, and replant. If slugs and snails are a problem, set traps.

Companion Planting and Design

We plant dahlias in the cutting and vegetable gardens—5-footers get a row of their own. We use bedding dahlias to edge perennials and with blue salvia, mint, asters, lavender, purple basil, and statice. In the flowerbeds, we front tall dahlias with baby's breath and grassy liriope.

Try These

For cutting, we favor the long-stemmed cactus-flowered dahlias and the large pom-poms.

Fancy-Leaved Caladium

Caladium bicolor

Botanical Pronunciation
kuh-LAY-dee-um BI-ko-lor

Other Name Dancing ladies

Bloom Period and Seasonal Color
All-season foliage; green overlaid with patterns
in white, pink, rose, salmon, crimson

Mature Height × Spread
8 to 30 inches × 12 to 30 inches

Caladiums, which grow from tubers, are not winter hardy in our area, but we can't imagine summer without these beautiful foliage plants brightening semi-shaded areas with their incredible colors. Unlike the time-bound show that flowers provide, the caladium's rich glow is with you all season long, growing more beautiful as the plants fill out. The leaves are large and shield-shaped, held on slender stems 8 to 30 inches tall. The old-fashioned name for them is "dancing ladies" because they flutter in the wind. The fanciful leaf patterns are pink, red, and/or white on green, and in some varieties are almost translucent. The leaves are used in flower arrangements, but the flowers are insignificant and should be removed so the strength of the plant can go to the leaves.

When, Where, and How to Plant
We start caladium tubers indoors in a warm room about eight weeks before the weather turns warm enough to put out tropicals—55 degrees Fahrenheit. We lay them on 2 to 3 inches of peat moss or sterile soilless mix on shallow trays. Place them about 8 inches apart with the knobble side up and the little straggle of dry roots facing the bottom; even if you plant them upside down, they'll grow but may have smaller leaves. They're rather slow to start up but then they grow quickly. They develop well on a grow-light stand and in a sunny glassed-in porch. Once the tubers sprout, transplant them to pots filled with soil fertilized with a slow-release fertilizer. You can also plant caladiums outdoors when nights are above 60 and day temperatures are at or above

70 degrees Fahrenheit. Set them out in groups of four to six, about 2 inches under well-drained, rich soil mixed with humus or peat moss. They do best in a semi-sunny or a lightly shaded location.

Growing Tip
Keep the soil evenly moist. Fertilize all summer during the growing season.

Regional Advice and Care
In autumn as the temperature drops, gradually dry out caladium tubers and store them in dry peat moss, vermiculite, or perlite at 70 to 75 degrees Fahrenheit. Note: Deer love caladiums.

Companion Planting and Design
Caladiums are superb bedding and pot plants, glorious growing with impatiens whose colors complement the leaves such as red impatiens with red-centered caladiums, or white impatiens with white-green caladiums. We also use caladiums to keep color in late spring, summer, and early fall borders.

Try These
The *Caladium bicolor* cultivars of great beauty include 18- to 24-inch tall, cool, white and green 'White Christmas'; the lovely, light-as-air, 10- to 20-inch white and green-lined-red 'White Queen'; 8- to 16-inch dark green, white frosted rose and red 'Rosebud'; solid red-bordered green 'Frieda Hemple'; rosy 12- to 18-inch 'Florida Sweetheart'; luminous 12- to 18-inch shell pink touched with green 'Pink Symphony'.

Grape Hyacinth

Muscari spp. and hybrids

Botanical Pronunciation
muss-KAIR-ee

Bloom Period and Seasonal Color
Early to mid-spring; many shades of blue, white, yellow

Mature Height × Spread
6 to 12 inches × 3 to indefinite spread

The most familiar grape hyacinths are blue as blue can be, a tribe of little bulb flowers that bloom toward mid-spring almost anywhere there is sun or dappled light. *Muscari* perennializes and naturalizes readily, and growing in good soil in open sunny woodlands, will eventually carpet the earth with an extraordinary "river" of blue. The flowers of the grape hyacinth are thickly clustered on stems to 6 to 12 inches high. In some forms the flowers are open and fertile, so they look a little like miniature hyacinths. Other types are sterile and the unopened buds look like tiny grapes enveloping the stems. Some varieties combine both fertile and infertile flowers. The leaves are grassy. Some have a faint spice-and-grape fragrance, especially *M. macrocarpum*, a rather rare yellow species.

When, Where, and How to Plant

Plant in September or October, in full or part sun. The ideal soil is light, well drained, and improved by additions of organic matter and an organic, slow-release 4-10-6 fertilizer. The ideal pH range is 6.0 to 7.0. See "Soil Preparation and Improvement" in the introduction and the planting instructions at the beginning of this chapter, including instructions on discouraging voles and squirrels. Provide holes 5 inches deep and 1 inch wide, or a planting bed 5 to 6 inches deep. Set the bulbs 2 inches apart. Mulch the area.

Growing Tips

Grape hyacinths multiply if they are well fertilized after blooming every year. To encourage grape hyacinth to multiply, after flowering and before the foliage disappears, spread a blended, organic fertilizer over the area, 4 to 6 pounds for every 100 square feet. Keep them watered.

Regional Advice and Care

There's no deadheading. Sometimes newly planted bulbs fall victim to squirrels and chipmunks; try sprinkling them with cayenne pepper at planting. Mark the bulbs' location to avoid digging them up.

Companion Planting and Design

Plant blue grape hyacinths in large groups, drifts of twenty to one hundred. White grape hyacinths stand out more, so fewer are effective. Grape hyacinths add solid blue to the front of flowerbeds. We like them naturalized in drifts, along paths, and at the foot of stone walls and white picket fences. They're pretty at lawn edges, as a carpet between larger bulbs, in bulb baskets or shallow pots, and as underplanting for large white daffodils. 'Blue Spike' is lovely planted with daffodils like white 'Thalia' and early, pale yellow 'Hawera'.

Try These

André favors the 6- to 8-inch *M. botryoides* 'Caeruleum'. *M. azureum* has both infertile (buds) flowers and fertile, open flowers and these have a darker stripe of blue on the lobes. *M. armeniacum* 'Blue Spike' is a popular cultivar whose flowers are light blue and double. It is the *Muscari* usually chosen for planting in "rivers." The feather hyacinth *M. comosum* 'Plumosum' has fluffy, double, mauve-lilac flowers on 6-inch stems, blooming a little later than other species.

Hyacinth

Hyacinthus orientalis spp. and hybrids

Botanical Pronunciation
hye-uh-SIN-thuss or-ee-un-TAY-liss

Other Name Oriental hyacinth

Bloom Period and Seasonal Color
Early to mid-spring; pure white, yellow, coral, pink, rose, shades of blue and purple, midnight purple

Mature Height × Spread
8 to 12 inches × 3 to 6 inches

The Oriental hyacinths open with the daffodils and the early tulips and they bring us spring's most extraordinary perfume. The plant is composed of wide, grasslike leaves and a thick, fleshy flower stem that rises right up out of the middle, completely covered with starry, outfacing bells. Hyacinths are rather rigid, which makes them somewhat difficult to fit into a casual garden design. But their perfume is worth the effort. Hyacinths grow from bulbs that are quite large, a fair handful. Some varieties bloom early, others at midseason, and some quite far along in spring, so you can, if you plan carefully, keep hyacinth perfume in your garden all spring. Hyacinths can be forced to bloom indoors long before they come into flower out in the garden.

When, Where, and How to Plant
Plant hyacinth bulbs in September or October in full sun or partial shade. Some shade can prolong the hyacinth's flowering but in our cooler regions full sun is recommended. Provide well-worked fertile loam with excellent drainage. Look up the information about soil for bulbs in the "Soil Preparation and Improvement" section in the introduction. Plant following the instructions at the beginning of this chapter. Set the bulbs 8 inches deep, about 3 to 4 inches apart. Mulch the area.

Growing Tips
To encourage hyacinths to come back, after flowering and before the foliage disappears, spread a blended, organic fertilizer over the area, 4 to 6 pounds for every 100 square feet.

Maintain moisture in spring, but avoid it in summer and winter.

Regional Advice and Care
In the cooler reaches of their hardiness range, hyacinths come back for at least two or three years if the flower is removed after flowering and the foliage is allowed to mature fully before it is removed. In the South, the sudden onset of summer heat often prevents this. Heads up: chipmunks, voles, and mice love hyacinths.

Companion Planting and Design
Plant early, midseason, and late types in groups along paths, in pockets near patios and entrances. In flower beds, plant hyacinths in groups of five to fifteen; in containers, plant the bulbs in sets of three to five. For bedding, choose slightly smaller bulbs; they'll have outstanding blooms the first year and a looser cluster the second. For forcing indoors, choose the largest bulbs of white 'Carnegie', 'Pink Pearl', deep blue 'Ostara', and clear pink 'Anna Marie'.

Try These
Generally, white hyacinths are the most fragrant, then the pastels, but some deeply colored hyacinths have a powerful scent. The luscious pink 'Chestnut Flower', an 1880 heirloom, has large, double scented blooms. Old Standards are 'Delft Blue' and 'Pink Pearl'. Some related species André recommends are endymion, *Hyacinthoides*, a frost-hardy European bluebell that naturalizes easily; the Spanish bluebell, *H. hispanica*; and the English bluebell, *H. non-scripta* (syn. *Scilla non-scripta*).

Lily

Lilium spp. and hybrids

Botanical Pronunciation
LIL-ee-um

Bloom Period and Seasonal Color
June to August; white, every color but the blue range, bicolors, spotted, brush-marked

Mature Height × Spread
1 ½ to 7 feet × 1 ½ to 2 feet

The lilies are among the tallest of all garden flowers. They're also the most stately, probably the most beautiful, and, in the case of the Oriental lilies, the most exquisitely perfumed. A 6- or 7-foot lily is a commanding plant, not at home everywhere. But there's a place in every garden for medium and small lilies which, planted in groups, provide welcome color just when you need it most in summer. They bloom in a wide range of colors for three to four weeks beginning in most areas in June. The three major groups—Asiatic, Trumpet, Oriental—bloom in that order. Their periods of bloom overlap since there are late Asiatics and early Trumpets and Orientals. By thoughtful selection you can have lilies flowering from late spring until frost.

When, Where, and How to Plant
A container-grown lily in bloom adapts to transplanting almost anytime during the growing season, but to plant a bulb with a shoot over 2 inches long is death—believe us! Growers ship big dormant bulbs in damp peat; keep them there until planted, or in a crisper. Six hours of full sun, plus partial sun the rest of the day, is the rule of thumb; where temperatures soar over 90 degrees Fahrenheit, lilies benefit from protection from noon and afternoon sun. Pastel shades are more successful in bright shade. A lily requires perfect drainage and very fertile soil, with enough humus to keep moisture around the roots. Most need rather acidic soil and will fail where lime or wood ashes have been applied. The exceptions are the Martagons and the species *L. candidum*, which thrive in alkaline soils. See "Soil Preparation and Improvement" in

the introduction. Provide planting holes worked to a depth of 24 inches to guarantee good drainage, and space the big lilies 12 to 18 inches apart. Stake taller varieties. Water well. Mulch 3 inches deep.

Growing Tips
Lilies tolerate a dry period after flowering. In fall and late winter fertilize the bed with a slow-release, organic fertilizer for acid-loving plants. Mulch the area.

Regional Advice and Care
As they fade, pinch blooms off the stalk. For bouquets, cut the stalks less than one-third of the overall height of the plant, or the lily will be smaller next year. When flowering is over, cut the stalks to just above the leaves; when the leaves yellow, cut the stalks to the ground—or leave them to mark the locations. Move or divide lilies every four years in the fall. Mice, voles, and chipmunks will feed on bulbs; take precautions.

Companion Planting and Design
All lilies enjoy cool feet. A mulch of groundcover such as alyssum or petunias or short marigolds does that job beautifully. For tubs or flowerbeds, group mid-sized lilies in threes to fives. For big borders, mass taller lilies in sets of ten to fifteen.

Try These
An extraordinarily fragrant, beautiful lily is pure white, 2- to 4-foot 'Casa Blanca', which has wide petals, and colorful stamens (that stain!). It blooms in midseason.

Ornamental Onion

Allium spp. and hybrids

Botanical Pronunciation
AL-ee-um

Other Name Flowering onion

Bloom Period and Seasonal Color
Late spring and late summer; blue, purple, pink, white, yellow

Mature Height × Spread
6 to 60 inches × 4 to 15 inches

The strap-shaped leaves of flowering onions do smell like onions but several species have appealing flowers, and all are excellent pest-proof plants. There are two types of flowers. The most interesting are perfect spheres composed of many blue-purple or white-pink florets, on leafless stalks above tufts of dark green, strap-shaped foliage. Think huge chives. The tallest is *Allium giganteum*, giant onion, whose round 6-inch reddish purple flower heads top stems 36 to 60 inches tall. The ornamental onions create striking accents in a mixed border. They're also lasting, eye-catching cut flowers and excellent for drying.

When, Where, and How to Plant

Plant the bulbs for flowering onions in late fall in full sun or light shade. The ideal soil is well-drained, humusy, and fertile, pH 6.0 to 7.5. You'll find instructions on improving soil for bulbs in "Soil Preparation and Improvement" in the introduction. Plant the bulbs, large or small, following the instructions at the beginning of this chapter. Set the bulbs, depending on their size, 3 to 5 or 8 inches deep, 3 to 6 or 8 inches apart. Mulch the area.

Growing Tips

Maintain moisture during the flowering onion's growth period; after that it can be according to the weather, average to dry. To encourage the plants to come back, after flowering, and before the foliage disappears, spread an organic, blended fertilizer, 4 to 6 pounds for every 100 square feet.

Regional Advice and Care

In the cooler reaches of the flowering onion's hardiness range, plants come back at least two or three years if the flower is removed after flowering and the foliage is allowed to mature fully before it is removed. Deadheading helps.

Companion Planting and Design

Plant flowering onions where the foliage of other flowers serves as a filler and screens the onion foliage while it is fading. The giant onion is striking in arrangements of flowers fresh or dried.

Try These

There are dozens of interesting ornamental onion species. *A. aflatunense* is a smaller version, 12 to 24 inches, of the giant allium that blooms earlier. *A. cristophii* (syn. *A. albopilosum*), star-of-Persia, has a much larger flower, 8 to 10 inches around. *A. sphaerocephalum*, called drumsticks or round-headed leek, bears small, egg-shaped, reddish lavender flower heads on stalks 24 to 36 inches tall. *A. karataviense*, a superior bedding plant recommended for rock gardens, bears fragrant, round, lilac-pink flowers and has decorative gray-purple leaves spotted violet. *A. schubertii* is an early summer bloomer with large flower heads composed of forty or more little pink or purple florets on stems of very unequal length. The flower of the lily leek, or golden garlic, *A. moly*, is made up of clusters of bright yellow, star-shaped florets. 'Globe Master' has 8- to 11-inch lavender globes on 20- to 30-inch stems.

Tulip

Tulipa spp. and hybrids

Botanical Pronunciation
TEW-lih-puh

Bloom Period and Seasonal Color
Late winter to late spring; every color but true blue

Mature Height × Spread
4 to 28 inches × 5 to 12 inches

Tulips are with us from very early spring, or late winter, right through late spring. There's every size and shape, almost every color—including midnight purple—and almost every combination of colors imaginable. Tulips can bloom in your garden for months on end. We group them for design purposes according to their season of bloom. The earliest are the low-growing little species (botanical) tulips—bright, perky, and informal. The big cup-shaped tulips on round, jade-green stems are showstoppers from late March through May. Some bloom as singles, others are bunch-flowering. There are early, midseason, and late bloomers in a range of colors and forms that are a delight to explore; plant a series of all types for a long bloom season. Put your nose right into a tulip cup, and you'll discover a faint, hauntingly sweet scent, more pronounced in a few varieties. Many Single Early tulips are scented, and the vivid orange, lily-flowered 'Ballerina' has fragrance.

When, Where, and How to Plant
Plant tulips in September or October, well before the ground freezes. Planting results past mid-December are poor. Tulips need only six hours of sun daily to perform well, preferably morning or afternoon sun. Ideal soil is slightly acidic, well drained, deeply dug, enriched with compost and humus. Find information about soils for bulbs in the "Soil Preparation and Improvement" section in the introduction. Plant following the instructions at the beginning of this chapter and follow the instructions on discouraging voles and squirrels. Squirrels really love tulips! Set large tulips 4 to 6 inches apart, 8 inches deep; set small bulbs 3 to 4 inches apart, 4 to 5 inches deep. Deeper planting can be successful but is not recommend below 10 inches. Mulch.

Growing Tips
To encourage tulips to perennialize, after flowering and before the foliage disappears, spread a slow-release organic bulb fertilizer over the area, 4 to 6 pounds for every 100 square feet. Keep soil moist but not overwatered.

Regional Advice and Care
In ideal conditions, some tulips perennialize. Some come back under most conditions for at least four years. Deadheading helps; take just the bloom, leaving the stem intact. Allow foliage to yellow about seven weeks before cutting it back. *Don't* bind the leaves during that period—that cuts off light and oxygen. If the following year all you get is foliage, dig and discard the little bulbs that produce it. They may never bloom well. Deer love tulips.

Companion Planting and Design
Plant the little early botanical tulips with small bulbs. Big annual flowers make fine screening for ripening tulip foliage: tall snapdragons and big marigolds and zinnias, for example. André likes pastel tulips growing with creeping phlox, (*Phlox subulata*), white candytuft (*Iberis*), big multicolored pansies, scilla, crocuses, and snowdrops.

Try These
Good tulips include 'Apricot Beauty', 'Ollioules', 'Beau Monde', 'Marilyn', 'Angelique', 'Red Riding Hood', and 'Gudoshnik'.

CONIFERS

FOR THE MID-ATLANTIC

E vergreens are key foundation plants. In this chapter we've grouped the needled and scale-leaved conifers, large and small. The shrub sizes of familiar tree species—pines, yews, cedars, junipers, spruce, and hemlock—are discussed on the same pages as the tree sizes.

We find the small, shrubby conifers extremely useful for anchoring color and as background in flowerbeds and shrubbery borders. The shrubby evergreens also make the best dense hedges and windbreaks, and sturdy edgers for paths and driveways. For tall privacy screening and windbreaks we use big, naturally columnar evergreens, such as American arborvitae. To furnish neglected corners, and for mid-height or low screening, we like the bold branching of the sprawling dwarf junipers, and upright little yews like 'Pygmaea', which stays under 18 inches. Elegant columnar junipers— like 'Gray Gleam' and 'Skyrocket'—are ideal where a stylish accent is wanted and they make great verticals for small spaces.

A big, needled evergreen that has a considerable presence is the Canadian hemlock, a pyramidal conifer with short needles. Hemlock grows into a handsome shade tree, and a hemlock hedge can be pruned for decades. A hemlock and a holly make a lovely background for white-barked birch, and for azaleas and ornamental grasses. For a hurry-up tree and for really tall screening, nothing beats the Leyland cypress, which grows at least 3 feet a year. It can be pruned for many years without losing its beauty. Mature, it becomes a big stately tree with graceful, feathery, bluish green, scalelike foliage and red-brown bark. Weeping evergreens, such as the blue Atlas cedar, *Cedrus atlantica* 'Glauca Pendula', add grace notes to the landscape.

Fossil records indicate dawn redwood (*Metasequoia glyptostroboides*) is an ancient species dating nearly 50,000,000 years ago.

Other lovely conifers that do very well here are varieties of blue spruce, silver fir, lacebark pine, and the beautiful dwarf hinoki cypress. The tall, longleaf pine that is native to our sandy coastal plain is too tall and coarse to be considered a garden ornamental.

Delayed leaf drop is one of the advantages you gain by planting conifers: practically no leaves to gather and grind in the fall. It's reassuring to know that yellowing needles most often are a normal part of a needled evergreen's cycle and not symptomatic of a problem. The term "evergreen" is misleading. Every plant must renew its foliage. White pines shed aging needles every year. And most other conifers shed some aging needles every year, but they don't, like the deciduous trees, lose all their older needles at once.

Planting and Pruning Evergreens

Conifers need well-drained soil and are moderate drinkers. You will find general information on planting and care for shrubs in the Shrubs chapter, and for

In winter, conifers can provide great structural interest.

trees in the Trees chapter. Specific soil needs and planting information for each conifer appears with the plant.

Most often we prune an evergreen only to shape the plant or to make it bushier. To encourage dense branching to the ground, begin pruning when the evergreen is three to five years old. In summer after its main spurt of growth is the time to prune an evergreen to slow, dwarf, or maintain its shape. The rule is to prune strong growth lightly, and weak growth hard. Never trim more than one-third of the branches from a conifer. You should not remove more of the top growth (the leader) than the growth of the last year or two. You can cut the main stem back to the first side shoots. This doesn't apply for trimmed hedges.

Light pruning of the branch ends of many evergreens, including hemlocks, junipers, and yews, is acceptable throughout the growing season, but not when they are dormant. Yews and junipers can take heavy pruning and fill out again very quickly. Firs, pines, spruces, and other conifers whose growth is initiated by "candles" should be pruned in spring when the candles appear at the branch tips. Cutting back the new candles by one-half to two-thirds will make the tips branch. Heavy pruning in fall isn't a good idea, because the pruning stimulates a new flush of growth which could be damaged by winter weather, and wounds heal more slowly in seasons of reduced activity. But you can save some pruning of your coniferous evergreens, and the hollies, too, to make swags and roping for the holiday season.

Other Good Conifers

Dawn redwood, *Metasequoia glyptostroboides* (a deciduous conifer)
Lawson's false cypress, *Chamaecyparis lawsoniana*, and its cultivars

Arborvitae

Thuja occidentalis spp. and hybrids

Botanical Pronunciation
THOO-yuh ock-sih-den-TAY-liss

Other Name
American arborvitae

Bloom Period and Seasonal Color
Insignificant blooms; small erect cones

Mature Height × Spread
20 to 30 feet × 10 to 15 feet

Arborvitae is perhaps the most beautiful of all the formal conifers. A tall shrub, it is used as a specimen, windbreak, hedge, and foundation plant. Densely clothed with scalelike, lacy leaves in flat sprays that are an attractive deep green and aromatic when crushed, the tree is symmetrical, slow growing, long lived, and can be sheared repeatedly. It also is easy to grow. In cultivation, the height of American arborvitae is between 20 to 30 feet. Its fruits are small, erect cones. Cultivars in many shapes and shades are available. There are narrow forms, round forms, and broadly pyramidal forms, and cultivars in shades of blue-green and yellow. 'Emerald' ('Smaragd') maintains brilliant green color in winter and has considerable heat tolerance. 'Holmstrup' is a slow-growing arborvitae and stays under 10 feet.

When, Where, and How to Plant
Container-grown and balled-and-burlapped arborvitae transplant easily in early spring and fall. It adapts to light shade but unless it's growing in full sun it loses the furry texture that is one of its major assets. It flourishes in slightly acidic soil, pH of 6.0 to 7.0, neither very wet nor very dry. It tolerates clay and limestone as long as the site is fertile, well drained, and sustains moisture. See "Soil Preparation and Improvement" in the introduction, and planting instructions in the Trees chapter, because it is a *big* plant. Provide a planting hole three times the rootball's width and twice as deep. Position so the crown is an inch or two above ground level. Shape the soil around the crown into a wide saucer. Water slowly and deeply. Mulch 3 inches deep starting 3 inches from the trunk.

Growing Tips
The first year, unless there's a soaking rain, in spring and fall slowly and gently water two to three buckets around the roots every two weeks; in summer, water every seven or ten days. Water deeply during drought. Using a slow-release organic fertilizer, fertilize lightly in fall and again in spring. Maintain mulch.

Regional Advice and Care
Arborvitae generally does not need pruning. A heavy snowfall can open up the tight branching at the top; the solution is to tie the top of the plant in fall. Any pruning should be done before spring growth begins. Deer love them all.

Companion Planting and Design
It's excellent as a formal specimen, as a backdrop for deciduous trees and flowering shrubs, and in windbreaks and hedges. Deer will crop arborvitae to the core at grazing height; the radical solution is to surround the plants with 8-foot wire fencing.

Try These
For the warmest reaches of our area 18- to 25-foot Oriental arborvitae, *Thuja orientalis*, might be a better choice. It's a small tree with grass-green foliage when it's young that changes to a darker green as it matures. A 30- to 50-foot tree that does well in wet places is fast-growing, cinnamon-barked Western red cedar, *T. plicata*. It does *not* tolerate salt spray.

Blue Atlas Cedar

Cedrus atlantica 'Glauca'

Botanical Pronunciation
SEE-druss at-LAN-tih-kuh GLAW-kuh

Bloom Period and Seasonal Color
Insignificant blooms; upright cones

Mature Height × Spread
40 to 60 feet × 30 to 40 feet

The blue Atlas cedar is a needled evergreen; when it's mature, it is perhaps the most beautiful of the large evergreens, especially when featured as a specimen in a large landscape and surrounded by green lawn. It is narrowly pyramidal in youth, and with maturity becomes a picturesque, flat-topped tree, 40 to 60 feet tall, with slightly drooping horizontal branches, steel blue needles, and handsome upright cones. It grows quickly when young. For a smaller landscape, consider the weeping form, 'Glauca Pendula', which has pendulous branches 15 to 20 inches wide that drip icy blue foliage. This cedar will be fine in warm Zones 7 and 8, but it is borderline hardy near the West Virginia border, in Zone 6.

When, Where, and How to Plant
True cedars are difficult to transplant, so set out young container-grown plants in early spring, and handle rootballs carefully. Cedars require lots of space as they develop, but they do not do well when exposed to icy blasts of wind—avoid the crests of hills with northern exposures, and areas where there's pollution. Atlas cedar tolerates partial shade but the other species named need full sun. Cedars do best in soil that is somewhat acidic, pH 5.0 to 6.5, but Atlas cedar withstands some alkalinity. It tolerates clay and sandy soils as long as they are well drained. See "Soil Preparation and Improvement" in the introduction, and planting instructions in the Trees chapter. Provide a planting hole three times the width of the rootball and twice as deep. Position so the crown is 1 or 2 inches above ground level.

Shape the soil around the crown into a wide saucer. Water slowly, deeply, thoroughly. Mulch 3 inches deep starting 3 inches from the main stem.

Growing Tips
The first year, unless there's soaking rain, slowly and gently water two to three bucketsful around the roots every two weeks in spring and fall; in summer, water every week or ten days. Using a slow-release organic fertilizer for acid-loving plants, fertilize lightly in fall and again in spring. Maintain mulch.

Regional Advice and Care
Allow plenty of room so you won't have to prune, except any dead or dying branches. It's generally free of pests or disease problems.

Companion Planting and Design
Blue Atlas cedar is superb in a group with 'October Glory' red maple and low-growing evergreen azaleas. Use blue-foliaged trees with discretion; more than one in a small landscape can be too much.

Try These
Also consider the picturesque deodar cedar, *Cedrus deodara*, which has needles that are light blue or grayish green. Zone 7 is the northern end of its range. 'Kashmir' is hardy to minus 25 degrees Fahrenheit. *C. libani*, the legendary cedar of Lebanon celebrated since biblical times, is like blue Atlas cedar in form, but has dark green needles; *C. libani* var. *stenocoma* can stand severe winters.

Canadian Hemlock

Tsuga canadensis

Botanical Pronunciation
SOO-guh kan-uh-DEN-siss

Other Name
Eastern hemlock

Bloom Period and Seasonal Color
Insignificant blooms; coppery brown cones

Mature Height × Spread
40 to 70 feet × 25 to 35 feet

Long-lived, tolerant of years of shearing, and easy to transplant, the Canadian hemlock is a superb evergreen for screening, shade, and display as a specimen. The shape is pyramidal and the branches are graceful, feathery, slightly drooping, and covered with short, aromatic, deep green needles that have two white bands beneath. It's a favorite nesting place for birds. The fruits are pretty little coppery brown cones ½ to 1 inch long. The cinnamon-brown bark in time becomes attractively ridged and deeply furrowed. The Canadian hemlock grows to between 40 and 70 feet in cultivation, but in its native lands—the Midwest, Northeast, and the Appalachian regions—it can reach 100 feet and more. The boughs are harvested for Christmas decorations and roping.

When, Where, and How to Plant
Plant a young balled-and-burlapped or container-grown hemlock in fall before Indian summer, or in early spring, while the tree is still dormant. Canadian hemlock does well in full sun or in partial shade. It does best in cool, moist, acidic soil, pH 5.0 to 6.5. It also succeeds on rocky bluffs providing there is shelter from icy winds, and in sandy soil, providing there's enough humus in it to keep moisture around the roots. See "Soil Preparation and Improvement" in the introduction, and planting instructions in the Trees chapter. Provide a planting hole three times the width of the rootball and twice as deep. Set the tree so the crown will be an inch or two above ground level. Shape the soil around the crown into a wide saucer. Water slowly and deeply. Apply mulch 3 inches deep starting 3 inches from the trunk.

Growing Tips
The first year, unless there's a soaking rain, slowly and gently pour two to three bucketsful of water around the roots every two weeks in spring and fall; in summer, water every week or ten days. Maintain the mulch throughout the summer. Using a slow-release, organic, acid fertilizer, fertilize lightly in early spring. Replenish the mulch as needed.

Regional Advice and Care
Prune away dead wood anytime of year. Light pruning or shearing of new growth on the branch ends is acceptable after the main spurt of growth and throughout the growing season, but not after the plant becomes dormant.

Companion Planting and Design
Canadian hemlock is an excellent tall foundation plant. Limbed up, it becomes a graceful evergreen shade tree. Trimmed, it makes a superb 6-foot hedge that can be maintained for decades.

Try These
We recommend the eye-catching variety 'Sargentii', a spreading, weeping tree. 'Pendula', weeping Canadian hemlock, is a dark green, prostrate form that takes decades to reach 5 feet by 8 to 10 feet and thrives in shade. The Carolina hemlock, *T. caroliniana*, is somewhat less graceful than the Canadian hemlock, but is the best hemlock for city conditions.

Colorado Blue Spruce

Picea pungens 'Glauca' and spp.

Botanical Pronunciation
PYE-see-uh PUN-jenz

Bloom Period and Seasonal Color
Insignificant blooms; green cones mature to light brown

Mature Height × Spread
40 to 60 feet × 10 to 20 feet

The spruces are the aromatic, symmetrical, conical evergreens we buy for Christmas trees, both cut and live. The needles are thin, rigid, ½ to 1¼ inches long with four sides and sharp points. The 2- to 4-inch cones start out green and turn light brown. A hardy native of the high Rocky Mountains, it lives for 600 to 800 years. Majestic 'Glauca' has soft, blue-gray foliage that turns silver-gray to blue-green as the tree grows slowly to 40 to 60 feet. There's a gorgeous weeping form, 'Glauca Pendula', and several other cultivars with special characteristics: 'Hoopsii' has the bluest needles; 'Moerheim' is a narrow, conical, blue tree; 'Thompsonii' has whitish silver-blue foliage and is considered one of the best of the blue spruces.

When, Where, and How to Plant

Plant balled-and-burlapped or container-grown spruces in early fall or early spring. They have spreading root systems (rather than deep ones), so large specimens can be transplanted successfully. The Colorado blue spruce needs full sun to color well and does best in well-drained, moderately moist soil in the acid range, pH 5.0 to 6.0. See "Soil Preparation and Improvement" in the introduction, and planting instructions in the Trees chapter. Provide a planting hole three times the width of the rootball and twice as deep. Set the tree so the crown will be about 1 or 2 inches above ground level. Shape the soil around the crown into a wide saucer. Water slowly and deeply. Apply mulch 3 inches deep starting 3 inches from the main stem.

Growing Tips

The first year, unless there's a soaking rain, in spring and fall slowly and gently pour two to three buckets of water around the roots every two weeks. In summer, water every seven or ten days. Maintain mulch throughout the summer. In early spring before growth begins, broadcast the recommended dose of a slow-release organic fertilizer for acid-loving plants; water it in. Replenish the mulch.

Regional Advice and Care

To encourage density, or to change the shape of the plant, periodically prune the tips.

Companion Planting and Design

The Colorado blue spruce is best featured as a specimen out in the open in a large landscape; parked in a small lawn it soon grows out of scale with the dwelling. Grouped with smaller evergreens and planted at a distance from a dwelling, it becomes the anchor for a beautiful screen.

Try These

Our favorite compact varieties of *P. pungens* are bluish white 3- to 5-foot 'Glauca Globosa', and silver-blue 'Montgomery'. For screening we suggest fast-growing green Norway spruce, *P. abies* and *P. abies forma pendula*, and the compact 4- to 6-foot bird's-nest spruce, 'Nidiformis'. For high style there's the narrow 60-foot Serbian spruce, *P. omorika*, whose cascading branches droop, then curve upward. The graceful Oriental spruce, *P. orientalis*, is beautiful and has exfoliating bark.

Douglas Fir

Pseudotsuga menziesii

Botanical Pronunciation
soo-doe-TSOO-guh MEN-zeez-ee-eye

Other Name Green Douglas fir

Bloom Period and Seasonal Color
Insignificant blooms; cones

Mature Height × Spread
50 to 80 feet × 12 to 20 feet

The Douglas fir is a stately pyramidal evergreen that is straight as a spear at maturity, and one of North America's most important timber trees. It's also used as a cut or live Christmas tree. A dramatic landscape ornamental 50 to 80 feet tall, in the wild it towers to heights of 250 and 300 feet and lives 800 to 1,000 years! When young, the upper branches of the Douglas fir are ascending while the lower branches are somewhat drooping, a characteristic that becomes accentuated as the tree matures. The needles are flattish and blue-green. The pendulous cones are 3 to 4 inches long and bear seeds; when they mature in late summer they become an important source of food for small mammals and birds.

When, Where, and How to Plant

Balled-and-burlapped, or container-grown, the Douglas fir transplants well in early spring. The ideal site is open, airy, and sunny with space all around and moist air. It does not succeed in dry, windy areas. Plant a Douglas fir where the soil is well drained, with enough humus to maintain moisture around the roots, and slightly acid, pH 6.0 to 7.0. See "Soil Preparation and Improvement" in the introduction, and planting instructions in the Trees chapter. Provide a planting hole three times the width of the rootball and twice as deep. Set the tree so the crown will be about 1 or 2 inches above

ground level. Shape the soil around the crown into a wide saucer. Water slowly and deeply. Mulch 3 inches deep starting 3 inches from the main stem.

Growing Tips

The first year, unless there's a soaking rain, in spring and fall slowly and gently pour two to three buckets of water around the roots every two weeks; water again in summer every week or ten days. Maintain the mulch throughout the summer. Using a slow-release, organic, acid fertilizer, fertilize lightly in fall and again in early spring. Replenish mulch as needed.

Regional Advice and Care

Prune as needed.

Companion Planting and Design

Douglas fir is a dramatic ornamental tree for large landscapes, such as parks, golf courses, and estates.

Try These

The beautiful Douglas fir variety *glauca*, or Rocky Mountain Douglas fir, grows more slowly and makes a long-lasting live Christmas tree. The needles are a beautiful soft blue. Unfortunately, after Christmas it often gets lovingly planted on a small front lawn where it soon grows out of scale in relation to the grounds and the dwelling.

Dwarf Hinoki Cypress

Chamaecyparis obtusa
'Nana Gracilis' and spp.

Botanical Pronunciation kam-ee-SIPP-ur-iss ub-TOO-zuh

Other Name Dwarf false cypress

Bloom Period and Seasonal Color
Insignificant blooms; bluish cones changing to red-brown

Mature Height × Spread 3 to 6 feet × 2 to 4 feet

Shrubby forms of the false cypress are first-rate landscape plants. The dwarf hinoki cypress, 'Nana Gracilis', is an exceptionally graceful shrub 4 to 6 feet tall with deep green, lustrous foliage that is white on the underside, flat, and scalelike. The branch tips turn down in an interesting half-twist that gives the plant an appealing texture and the appearance of greater softness than is usual in a conifer. An excellent yellow form is the golden cypress, *Chamaecyparis obtusa* 'Crippsii', a dense, pyramidal evergreen, whose branchlets are tipped a rich yellow-gold. It's a slow-growing shrub that needs a decade or two to reach 8 to 10 feet but may eventually reach 30 feet.

When, Where, and How to Plant
Plant a young container-grown false cypress in fall before Indian summer, or in early spring, while the tree is still dormant. The hinoki cypress requires full sun and does best with some protection from wind. It prefers soils that are well drained, with enough humus to maintain moisture around the roots, and neutral to slightly acidic, pH 6.0 to 7.0. See "Soil Preparation and Improvement" in the introduction, and planting instructions in the Shrubs chapter. Provide a planting hole three times the width of the rootball and twice as deep. Set the shrub so the crown will be an inch or two above ground level. Shape the soil around the crown into a wide saucer. Water slowly and deeply. Apply mulch 3 inches deep starting 3 inches from the crown.

Growing Tips
The first year in spring and fall, unless there's a soaking rain, slowly and gently pour two to three buckets of water around the roots every two weeks; water in summer every week or ten days. Maintain the mulch throughout the summer. Using a slow-release organic fertilizer for acid-loving plants, fertilize lightly in fall and again in early spring. Replenish the mulch as needed.

Regional Advice and Care
Pruning is rarely needed. Hinoki false cypress resists most pests and diseases, but juniper tip blight during moist, cool weather may lead to tip dieback.

Companion Planting and Design
This is a first-rate, shrub-size evergreen for use in hedges, as background to a shrub border of azaleas, and as a foundation plant. The golden foliage of 'Crippsii' is striking against darker evergreens.

Try These
A fascinating relative is the blue- or gray-green weeping Nootka, or Alaska, false cypress, *C. nootkatensis* 'Pendula', a variety with pendulous branches that droop. It can live to be over 1,000 years old. In cultivation it reaches 30 to 45 feet. A yellow species that is hardier than 'Crippsii' and holds its striking yellow hue in summer is the 8- to 12-foot golden threadleaf Sawara cypress, *C. pisifera* 'Filifera Aurea'.

Juniper

Juniperus spp. and hybrids

Botanical Pronunciation
joo-NIP-ur-us

Bloom Period and Seasonal Color
Insignificant blooms; berrylike cones

Mature Height × Spread
Varies according to species and variety

Junipers are really tough conifers that come in amazingly variable shapes, from 60-foot trees to 1- to 2-foot groundhugging plants like creeping juniper, *Juniperus horizontalis*, covered in Groundcovers. Juvenile growth has awl-shaped needles and the adult growth is scalelike; when that transition occurs depends on the variety. The male cones are yellow, and resemble catkins; the female fruits are berrylike cones. Many superb shrubs have been developed from the Chinese juniper, *J. chinensis*, whose foliage may be bright blue- or gray-green. 'Hetzii' is a beautiful gray-green shrub about 10 feet by 10 feet at maturity. Mint Julep® is a compact, bright green, fountaining shrub, 4 feet by 6 feet. 'Pfitzeriana', the most hybridized, has drooping branches, bright green foliage, and averages 5 feet by 8 feet.

When, Where, and How to Plant

Junipers have a spreading root system that transplants easily. Set out container-grown plants in spring or fall. Plant in full sun; they accept some shade when young, but will get open and ratty unless growing in full sun. Eastern red cedar, *J. virginiana*, does well in acidic and in alkaline soils, but most junipers prefer soil in the pH 5.0 to 6.5 range that is light, even sandy, and moderately moist. But they are tolerant of dry, clay soils and pollution. See "Soil Preparation and Improvement" in the introduction, and planting instructions in Shrubs. Provide a planting hole three times the width of the rootball and twice as deep. Set the shrub so the crown will be an inch or two above ground level. Shape the soil around the crown into a wide saucer. Water slowly and deeply. Mulch 3 inches deep starting 3 inches from the trunk or main stem.

Growing Tips

In spring and fall the first year, unless there's a soaking rain, slowly and gently pour two to three buckets of water around the roots every two weeks; in summer, every week or ten days. Maintain mulch through summer. Using a slow-release organic fertilizer for acid-loving plants, fertilize lightly in fall and again in late winter or early spring. Replenish mulch as needed.

Regional Advice and Care

Minimize shearing and pruning by choosing junipers whose growth habits fit your purpose. The best time to prune to minimize growth or enhance their shape is just after new growth. Junipers can experience a variety of problems, including cedar apply rust galls and twig blight; prune off and destroy affected branches.

Companion Planting and Design

For groundcover we use 24-inch, slow-spreading *J. sabina* 'Tamariscifolia', which spreads 8 to 10 feet. For edging, try 1- to 2-foot creeping juniper, *J. horizontalis* 'Plumosa' and 'Plumosa Compacta', whose foliage turns purplish in winter. For columnar accents we like *J. scopulorum* 'Skyrocket' and 'Pathfinder', narrow, 20-foot, blue or blue-gray trees.

Try These

A 40- to 50-foot tree we recommend for landscaping and seashore planting is eastern red cedar, *J. virginiana*, available in pyramidal and columnar forms. Another is the rare temple juniper, *J. rigida* 'Pendula', a columnar weeping small tree.

Lacebark Pine

Pinus bungeana and spp.

Botanical Pronunciation
PYE-nus bun-gee-AY-nuh

Bloom Period and Seasonal Color
Insignificant blooms; cones are scalelike

Mature Height × Spread
30 to 50 feet × 20 to 35 feet

You can tell a pine from similar conifers by its needles, which are soft, thin, 2 to 5 inches long, and grow in bundles of two to five. The pine group includes dwarf, compact forms that are useful in landscaping, as well as tall, pyramidal trees. Lacebark pine is one of the most appealing species—a multiple-stemmed tree that grows very slowly to 30 to 50 feet. Its major and unique asset is bark that exfoliates and becomes mottled. When the tree is young, the several stems are a mixture of green with white and brown. As the trunks mature, they show a great deal of chalky white. Where winters are severe, try the Korean pine, *Pinus koraiensis*, a similar, faster-growing tree.

When, Where, and How to Plant

Pines have taproots and are best moved as young, container-grown or balled-and-burlapped plants in early spring. They require full sun and well-drained, somewhat acidic soil, pH 5.0 to 6.0. The lacebark pine tolerates some alkalinity. See "Soil Preparation and Improvement" in the introduction, and the planting instructions in the Trees chapter. Provide a planting hole three times the width of the rootball and twice as deep. Set the shrub so the crown will be an inch or two above ground level. Shape the soil around the crown into a wide saucer. Water slowly and deeply. Apply mulch 3 inches deep starting 3 inches from the trunk.

Growing Tips

Unless there's a soaking rain, the first year, in spring and fall slowly and gently pour two to three buckets of water around the roots every two weeks; in summer, every week or ten days. Maintain the mulch throughout the summer. Using a slow-release organic fertilizer for acid-loving plants, fertilize lightly in fall and again in late winter or early spring. Replenish the mulch.

Regional Advice and Care

To encourage density or to change the shape of a pine, in June, when new candles are fully grown, cut them back by half. This pine is generally resistant to pests and diseases.

Companion Planting and Design

Several species of pine are used in landscaping. For edging urban gardens and anchoring perennial beds we like dwarfs of the mugo pine, *P. mugo*, which have small, attractive, dark green bundles of needles. They also do well by the shore. Plant lacebark pine where you can appreciate the mottled bark.

Try These

One of the hardiest and most attractive of the big trees is *P. strobus*, the eastern white pine, straight as a ship's mast with long, bluish green needles, 6- to 8-inch cones, and rapid growth to 50 to 80 feet. The drooping branches of 'Pendula' sweep the ground; 'Nana' is slow-growing and can take seventy-five years to reach 10 feet. Coastal gardeners love the Japanese black pine, *J. thunbergii*, a salt-tolerant tree sometimes used as a sand binder. It will grow from 20 to 60 feet depending on the environment.

Leyland Cypress

Cupressocyparis × leylandii

Botanical Pronunciation
kew-press-oh-SIP-uh-ris LAY-lund-ee-eye

Bloom Period and Seasonal Color
Insignificant blooms; dark brown cones

Mature Height × Spread
60 to 70 feet × 10 to 20 feet

The Leyland cypress is a stately columnar hybrid of the cypress family, a group of narrow shrubs and trees with flat, scalelike leaves. It has graceful branches and bluish green, feathery foliage. The red-brown bark is a nice warm color, interestingly scaly, and it bears small roundish cones that are dark brown. In addition to its grace, what makes the Leyland cypress unusual is that it grows up to be a big tree 60 or 70 feet tall very quickly—3 feet a year. That makes it an exceptionally good evergreen for screening. It tolerates heavy shearing, and makes a fine tall hedge. It also tolerates salt, and is used along the coast as a screen to protect the garden from salt spray.

When, Where, and How to Plant
Plant a container-grown or balled-and-burlapped tree in fall before Indian summer, or in early spring. In shade, the branching is more open and informal; in full sun the foliage grows more densely. Leyland cypress adapts to a variety of soils, acidic or alkaline, but grows most rapidly in moist, fertile soil containing enough humus to maintain moisture around the roots. If you are planting a hedge, make the bed at least 5 feet wide. See "Soil Preparation and Improvement" in the introduction, and planting instructions in the Trees chapter. Provide a planting hole at least three times the width of the rootball and twice as deep. Set the tree so the crown will be about 1 or 2 inches above ground level. Shape the soil around the crown into a wide saucer. Water slowly and deeply. Apply mulch 3 inches deep starting 3 inches from the main stem.

Growing Tips
The first year, unless there's a soaking rain, in spring and fall slowly and gently pour two to three buckets of water around the roots every two weeks; in summer every seven or ten days. Maintain soil moisture during droughts. Maintain mulch through summer. Using a slow-release, organic, acid fertilizer, fertilize in fall and again in late winter or early spring. Replenish the mulch.

Regional Advice and Care
Periodically prune or shear a Leyland cypress during July. For a formal hedge, allow the tops to grow 6 to 12 inches beyond the intended height, then cut the leaders off to just above a lateral branch 6 inches below the intended height.

Companion Planting and Design
Provide Leyland cypress plenty of room as it is too vigorous for narrow spaces that restrict growth. In a new landscape, Leyland cypress is sometimes planted with a slow-growing evergreen that is more desirable for the long term, then, when the star specimen attains a desired height, the Leyland cypress is cut down to allow space for the other.

Try These
A very graceful Leyland is 30- to 40-foot 'Naylor's Blue', whose bright, gray-blue foliage is intensely colored in winter. The new growth of narrow 20-foot 'Castlewellan Gold' is tipped yellow-gold, bronze in winter.

Umbrella Pine

Sciadopitys verticillata and spp.

Botanical Pronunciation
sigh-uh-DOP-ih-tiss ver-tiss-ill-LAY-tuh

Other Name
Japanese umbrella pine

Bloom Period and Seasonal Color
Insignificant blooms; green cones turn to brown

Mature Height × Spread
25 to 30 feet × 15 to 20 feet

Consider an umbrella pine if you'd like something different in an evergreen. It's a rather small tree with a strongly textured look that to some seems primitive, as though it belonged to an earlier time. Considered unique and artistic in appearance, it has two types of needles: one type is small and scalelike, arranged at the tips of the twigs; and the other is 2- to 5-inch-long, dark green needles bunched at the ends of the branches. When the tree begins to mature, the bark turns orange to red-brown and begins to peel in plates and strips. A young umbrella pine has a compact pyramidal shape and the branches are stiff, twiggy, and spread in whorls. As it matures, the branches droop and loosen. It grows very slowly.

When, Where, and How to Plant
The best time to plant an umbrella pine is in early spring. Buy a young, container-grown or balled-and-burlapped plant and handle the rootball with great care. The site can be in partial shade or in full sun as long as there is protection from the hot late afternoon sun and from sweeping winds. The umbrella pine does not tolerate pollution or drought. The ideal site is well drained and has rich, moist, and somewhat acidic soil. See "Soil Preparation and Improvement" in the introduction, and planting instructions in the Trees chapter. Provide a planting hole three times the width of the rootball and twice as deep. Set the tree so the crown will be about 1 or 2 inches above ground level. Shape the soil around the crown into a wide saucer. Water slowly and deeply. Apply mulch 3 inches deep starting 3 inches from the main stem.

Growing Tips
The first year, unless there's a soaking rain, in spring and fall slowly and gently pour two to three buckets of water around the roots every two weeks; every week or ten days in summer, water. Maintain the mulch throughout the summer. Using a slow-release organic fertilizer for acid-loving plants, fertilize lightly in fall and again in early spring. Replenish the mulch.

Regional Advice and Care
The umbrella pine should not be sheared and should not need pruning. It's free of any serious pests or diseases.

Companion Planting and Design
The umbrella pine is best used as an accent tree in a group of trees and shrubs, or as a specimen out in the open.

Try These
Plant the species.

White Fir

Abies concolor and spp.

Botanical Pronunciation
AY-beez KON-kull-ur

Other Name
Concolor fir

Bloom Period and Seasonal Color
Insignificant blooms; green shading to purple cones

Mature Height × Spread
30 to 50 feet × 15 by 30 feet

The firs are long-lived, stately trees native to the Rockies. Pyramidal conifers like the spruces, they also are used as live Christmas trees, and the boughs are sold to make Christmas decorations. In silhouette, the white fir looks like a blue spruce, but it's more refined. The silvery, blue-green needles are flatter than those of the spruces, soft, 2 to 3 inches long, and have two pale bluish bands underneath. The cones are 3 to 5 inches long and greenish when new, shading to purple. Most other fir species are big forest trees that live at high altitudes and do poorly in hot, dry cities. The white, or silver, fir has some tolerance for long, hot summers like those in Washington, D.C., and it endures city conditions, heat, cold, and drought. But it may not do well in the Tidewater area.

When, Where, and How to Plant

Plant a young, container-grown or balled-and-burlapped tree in early spring. The white fir prefers full sun, but tolerates all-day, bright filtered light. Firs do best in acidic soil, pH 5.0 to 6.0. The white fir can live on almost bare rock, but it does poorly in heavy clay soil. Ideal soil is rich, moist, sandy loam. Prepare the soil well! See "Soil Preparation and Improvement" in the introduction, and planting instructions in the Trees chapter. Provide a planting hole three times the width of the rootball and twice as deep. Handle the rootball with great care. Set the tree so the crown will be about 1 or 2 inches above ground level. Shape the soil around the crown into a wide saucer. Water slowly and deeply. Mulch 3 inches deep starting 3 inches from the main stem.

Growing Tips

The first year, unless there's a soaking rain, in spring and fall slowly and gently pour two to three buckets of water around the roots every two weeks; in summer, water every week or ten days. Maintain mulch throughout the summer. Using a slow-release organic fertilizer for acid-loving plants, fertilize lightly in fall and again in early spring. Replenish mulch.

Regional Advice and Care

White fir generally doesn't need pruning, except to shape, especially if you're growing it as a holiday tree. Protect young trees from deer.

Companion Planting and Design

The dark green needles make a handsome backdrop for ornamental plants and in fall and winter they lend life to the sleeping garden. It is generally used as a specimen in lawns and parks.

Try These

In addition to the white fir, we recommend the graceful Caucasian, or Nordmann fir, *Abies nordmanniana*, whose tiered branches sweep downward and then curve up. It's a big tree, 35 to 50 feet, whose needles are a lustrous black-green. The ideal pH for the Caucasian fir is soil in the 5.8 to 7.0 range; it needs full sun, a very well-drained site, and does best in a somewhat sheltered situation.

Yew

Taxus spp. and hybrids

Botanical Pronunciation
TACKS-us

Bloom Period and Seasonal Color
Insignificant blooms; fleshy red berries in winter

Mature Height × Spread
Cultivars vary in size; many are as wide as they are tall, or wider

Yews are the most adaptable, durable, and useful evergreens. Dark-needled shrubs and trees with reddish brown, scaly bark, the female plants bear pea-sized fleshy red berries. Native to the Northern Hemisphere, yews are disease resistant. They grow slowly and tolerate extensive pruning, so they're often used for clipped hedges, green screens, walls, archways, topiary, and foundation plants, small and tall. Yews come in almost all sizes, shapes, and colors. Among the very best for hedges, screening, and foundation plantings are cultivars of the medium to deep green intermediate yews (*Taxus* x *media*), including pyramidal 'Hatfieldii'; columnar 'Hicksii'; low, spreading, 3- to 4-foot 'Densiformis'; and rounded, 8- to 10-foot 'Brownii'. Seeds and foliage of yews contain toxic compounds.

When, Where, and How to Plant
Plant a balled-and-burlapped or container-grown yew in fall before Indian summer, or in early spring while the shrub still is dormant. A yew will do well growing in full sun or bright shade, but the needles will brown in winter if the plant is exposed to strong, cold winds. Yews generally prefer somewhat alkaline soil; they are not good companion plants for azaleas, rhododendrons, or other acid-loving evergreens. The ideal site has excellent drainage—yews do not tolerate wet feet. See "Soil Preparation and Improvement" in the introduction, and planting instructions in the Trees chapter. Provide a planting hole three times the width of the rootball and twice as deep. Set the tree so the crown will be about 1 or 2 inches above ground level. Shape the soil around the crown into a wide saucer. Water slowly and deeply. Apply mulch 3 inches deep starting 3 inches from the main stem.

Growing Tips
The first year, unless there's a soaking rain, in spring and fall slowly and gently pour two to three buckets of water around the roots every two weeks; in summer, water every week or ten days. Maintain the mulch throughout summer. Using a slow-release organic fertilizer, fertilize lightly in fall and again in spring.

Regional Advice and Care
Prune away dead wood anytime, but do not cut beyond the area where green needles are growing. Yews accept shearing of the branch ends throughout the growing season. To keep a yew compact, follow an early spring pruning by the removal of the soft new summer growth. To create a natural looking hedge, remove the longest growth every other year.

Companion Planting and Design
Yews tolerate extensive pruning, so they're also often used for clipped hedges, green screens, and walls, archways, and even topiary.

Try These
The tree form we favor is 'Capitata', a pyramidal 25- to 30-foot cultivar of the very hardy light green Japanese yew, *T. cuspidata*. A single plant that can make a hedge almost by itself is 'Repandens', a cultivar of the big English yew, *T. baccata*, which grows 2 to 4 feet tall and 10 to 15 feet wide. It has beautiful dark or black-green foliage.

GROUNDCOVERS
FOR THE MID-ATLANTIC

Groundcovers create a unified field that harmonizes and pulls together the various elements of the landscape—shrub borders, flowerbeds, and specimen trees. Groundcovers can be any height. Even daylilies can be a groundcover. Those we recommend here are low-growing, need almost no maintenance once established, can do what lawn grasses do where mowers can't go, and can replace lawns you are weary of mowing. The most attractive and enduring groundcovers for Mid-Atlantic gardens are the plants on the pages that follow, but not every one of these is perfect for every site. They are designated as groundcovers because, like weeds, most of them spread rapidly, so think twice about planting any of these where they might later invade stands of native plants or woodlands we are trying to preserve.

The toughest low evergreen groundcovers are ajuga, periwinkle, ivy, and creeping juniper. Ajuga and periwinkle bear sweet little flowers in early spring and can be walked on—with discretion. Ivy can take months to expand, but once started spreads irrepressibly. Creeping juniper withstands sun, heat, drought, and salt, and it's a good bank holder.

A beautiful groundcover for shade is silvery lamium, which produces masses of small hooded flowers in spring. Leadwort has handsome glossy foliage and in late summer bears long-lasting, gentian blue flowers. For cooler regions, dappled light, and a formal look, pachysandra is the perfect choice. The ferns we recommend also do well in dappled light and are lovely in transitional areas edging woodlands.

Combining several compatible groundcovers adds texture to an area and it's a safeguard should one of the plants run into difficulties. For a richly varied lawn substitute we like drifts of small winter-flowering bulbs, overplanted with aromatic Greek oregano and thyme, ajuga in the sunny places, periwinkle in part sun, and lamium under the trees.

Planting Groundcovers

We recommend starting groundcovers with flats or pots of rooted cuttings. If you will be replacing turf, in early spring or fall when the soil is dry, spray the area with a product containing glyphosate according to the directions on the label, or remove the top layer. Top the area with 2 or 3 inches of compost or decomposed leaves and broadcast over it slow-release fertilizers, along with greensand (with its thirty-two micronutrients) and rock phosphate. Follow the rates recommended on the packages. Rototill all this 8 inches deep three times over a two-week period. If you are installing an invasive groundcover such as ivy or ajuga, bury a 6-inch metal barrier around the perimeter to keep it from overrunning neighboring plantings.

Another fern worthy of consideration is *Osmunda regalis*, royal fern. It is a lovely addition to a garden.

The genus *Sedum* is quite diverse and includes creeping forms, such as this *Sedum spurium* 'Red Carpet'.

At planting time, cover the area with 3 inches of mulch and plant through it. Working in even rows and starting at the widest end, dig a row of evenly spaced planting pockets 8 to 14 inches apart. Set the plants into the pockets and firm them into place. On a slope, set the plants so their backs are a little lower than their fronts. Position the second row plants zig-zag style between those of the row above. Row three repeats row one, and row four repeats row two. Maintain the mulch until the groundcover shades out weeds. Plan on at least two years for the plants to grow enough to cover well.

If weeding won't be possible, plant your groundcover through a porous landscape fabric. Push the edges of the fabric sheet into the ground and weight them with rocks, or heel them in. Make rows of X-shaped slits in the fabric, and insert the plants through the slits with a trowel. Landscape fabric slows the rooting of the aboveground branches, so plant densely. In fall clear your groundcover of fallen leaves with a blow-vac. Certain groundcovers, when fully mature, benefit from shearing every year or two in early spring before growth begins.

Companion Planting and Design

We use groundcovers in one-of-a-kind plantings to carpet, protect, and enhance untended slopes and the areas at the feet of tall trees where shade is too intense for grass to flourish. We also combine groundcovers with trees, shrubs, ornamental grasses tall and small, flowers, and bulbs to naturalize rocky fields and transitional areas between gardens and woodlands, bodies of water, the road, or the next property. No-maintenance shrubs that work well in this type of planting include several roses, such as the rugosa rose and the Virginia rose. *Rosa virginiana* and the ground-hugging memorial rose, *R. wichuraiana*, are good choices for erosion control of slopes. You can combine low-growing groundcovers with *Forsythia × intermedia* 'Arnold Dwarf' in full sun almost anywhere. Summer-flowering shrubs and trees that go well with groundcovers are crape myrtle, butterfly bush, and blue spirea, which all bloom on new wood so they can be cut back every spring. Some of the flowers we like to include in these naturalized areas are columbine, butterfly weed, coreopsis, purple coneflower, rudbeckia, and goldenrod.

The plants on the following pages are the best of the best, but we do have other favorites:

Other Groundcovers Worthy of Consideration

Barren strawberry, *Waldsteinia fragarioides*
Bloody cranesbill, *Geranium sanguineum*
Creeping phlox, *Phlox subulata*
European wild ginger, *Asarum europaeum*
Goldenstar, Green-and-gold, *Chrysogonum virginianum*
Soapwort, *Saponaria officinalis* 'Rosea Plena'
Sedum, *Sedum spurium* 'John Creech' and other cultivars
Snow-in-summer, *Cerastium tomentosum*
Sweet woodruff, *Galium odoratum*
Wintergreen, checkerberry, *Gaultheria procumbens*

Other Ferns Worthy of Consideration

Beech fern, *Phegopteris (formerly Thelypteris) hexagonoptera*
Cinnamon fern, *Osmundastrum cinnamomea*
Deer fern, *Blechnum spicant*
Japanese shield fern, Autumn Fern, *Dryopteris erythrosora*
Maidenhair fern, *Adiantum pedatum*
Marsh fern, *Thelypteris palustris*
Massachusetts fern, Bog fern, *Thelypteris simulata*
New York fern, *Thelypteris noveboracensis*
Ostrich fern, *Matteuccia struthiopteris*
Rock Polypody, American wall fern, *Polypodium virginianum*
Royal fern, *O. regalis*

Barrenwort

Epimedium spp. and hybrids

Botanical Pronunciation
ep-ih-MEE-dee-um

Other Name
Bishop's hat

Bloom Period and Seasonal Color
Spring foliage and flowers, fall foliage; flowers in yellow, pink, orange, rose, lavender, white, bicolors

Mature Height × Spread
6 to 24 inches × 9 to 24 inches

The barrenworts are spring-flowering plants that, given time, carpet the earth under trees, shrubs, and in woodlands with clumps of beautiful, long, heart-shaped semi- or evergreen (Zones 7 and 8) leaves. The foliage colors reddish or gold in cold weather, bringing new vitality to the fading fall scene. In spring, exotic little flowers rather like columbines, some long-spurred, are borne in clusters on slim, gracefully arching stems. Among many wonderful barrenworts for our area are red barrenwort, *Epimedium* × *rubrum*, whose graceful sprays of flowers are red with yellow; bicolor barrenwort, *E.* × *versicolor* 'Sulphureum', which bears delicate yellow flowers with long rosy spurs; and *E. pinnatum* (syn. *E. colchicum*), which has handsome brownish foliage and bears up to twenty-four short red-spurred yellow flowers.

When, Where, and How to Plant

You can set out container-grown barrenworts anytime during the growing season. The plants do best in bright shade. But in the cooler regions of the Mid-Atlantic, especially in Zone 6, barrenworts can tolerate full sun. Once established, they grow well in dry shade. They thrive in well-drained, rich soil with an acid pH of 4.5 to 5.5. It's an ideal groundcover for land that was forest and for wooded areas. Follow the planting instructions at the beginning of this chapter, and provide planting holes 8 to 12 inches deep. Space the plants, which are slow to establish, about 12 inches apart. Spread a permanent 1-inch mulch of pine needles, or rotted leaf mold.

Growing Tips

Keep the plants well watered the first two months, and weekly thereafter unless you have a good soaking rain. Established barrenworts can handle some drought, but they need sustained moisture to get off to a good start. Light feeding twice yearly is enough.

Regional Advice and Care

In late winter fertilize and replenish the mulch in new beds; once established, barrenworts make a dense mat so they will need no mulch in subsequent years. In early spring just before new foliage emerges, shear old foliage. You can multiply your holdings by dividing mature clumps of barrenworts in very early spring or toward the end of summer. There are no pests to speak of.

Companion Planting and Design

The barrenworts make beautiful groundcovers for the earth under trees, shrubs, and in woodlands. We love seeing them bordering a woodland path planted with fall flowering anemones, ferns, and hostas. They're handsome growing with hellebores in the shade of a tall shrub border.

Try These

We especially like *E.* × *versicolor* because it is beautiful and grows vigorously. We use *E. grandiflorum* 'Rose Queen', a long-spurred barrenwort, for planting nooks and crannies of stone walls.

Bugleweed

Ajuga reptans and hybrids

Botanical Pronunciation
uh-JOO-guh REP-tanz

Other Name
Carpet bugleweed

Bloom Period and Seasonal Color
Foliage in green, multicolored, rose, burgundy; in early spring, flowers are white, reddish blue, deep blue, pink, rose

Mature Height × Spread
2 to 10 inches × 12 to 36 inches

Bugleweed covers the earth with flat rosettes of colorful leaves 3 to 4 inches long, an excellent groundcover for small, partially shaded areas, and poor soil. It's a tough plant that can be walked on, in moderation. Fast-growing *Ajuga reptans* is our choice for quick cover. Some forms are green-leaved; others are splashed with cream or pink or have a metallic sheen. In mid- to late spring *Ajuga* is misted with blue florets on short, squarish flower spikes. Bugleweed is evergreen here and the leaves take on an attractive bronze-plum tint when the weather turns cold. In severe winters the leaves flatten and some turn brown. Cold that persists without snow cover damages the leaf tips but in spring the plants soon fill out.

When, Where, and How to Plant
Plant clumps of rooted plantlets in early spring or early fall. Where summers are muggy, bugleweed does best in high, bright shade; in dense shade, the leaves will be smaller and it will spread toward the sunlight. In cool upland areas, bugleweed can handle full sun. The colored varieties are showiest growing in some direct sun. Rooted plants are fairly expensive, but you can minimize the cost by choosing the rapidly spreading species *A. reptans* and setting the plants 6 to 12 inches apart. You can also divide the clumps into individual plantlets and make more. Bugleweed does best in well-drained ordinary garden soil whose pH range is between 6.0 to 7.0. Follow the soil preparation and planting instructions at the beginning of this chapter, but omit the fertilizer. Prepare a planting bed 6 to 8 inches deep. Space slower-spreading *Ajuga* species 3 inches apart and be prepared to divide the plants—or prune them back—the following summer. Mulch the area.

Growing Tips
Water a new bed every week to ten days the first season, unless rain is plentiful. Bugleweed growing in full sunlight in Zones 7 and 8 may need watering during droughts. In early spring, scratch a little slow-release fertilizer in beside young plants. In the following years, when you fertilize your lawn, water in a long-lasting organic fertilizer.

Regional Advice and Care
If too well fed, bugleweed will "melt out" with diseases. Clear autumn leaves to avoid crown rot; if a fungal problem develops, ask your garden center to recommend a fungicide. Rooted plantlets of *A. reptans* can be cut from the parent and replanted during the growing season; divide other species in early spring.

Companion Planting and Design
We use bugleweed to cover a small area with a low dense mat. Its growth is expansive, so avoid growing it close to flower beds and other areas that are easily invaded.

Try These
For something different, plant *A. reptans* 'Alba', whose flowers are off-white. Or try 'Burgundy Glow', whose leaves are cream, pink, rose, and green. 'Rosea' has green leaves and showy rose-pink flower spikes. Where crown rot is a problem, choose blue bugle, *A. genevensis*.

Christmas Fern

Polystichum acrostichoides

Botanical Pronunciation
puh-LISS-tih-kum uh-kross-tih-koe-EYE-deez

Other Name
Dagger fern

Bloom Period and Seasonal Color
Evergreen crown of dark green foliage

Mature Height × Spread
1 to 1½ feet × 1 to 1½ feet

Ferns have a cool graceful presence that no other type of plant quite duplicates. The lush greens evoke woodlands and romantic glades and no cottage garden is complete without them. The Christmas fern is a forever plant, a lifetime fern with beautiful, lance-shaped leathery fronds up to 24 inches long by 5 inches wide, growing in arching, circular clusters from the crown. And it is evergreen here! A woodland native, it offers practical solutions to the challenges presented by the north side of a house, the north slope of a wooded stretch, and sun-dappled stream edges with poor drainage. It can tolerate more sun than many ferns if given adequate moisture. Please insist on purchasing *only* plants propagated by nurseries, not those gathered from the wild.

When, Where, and How to Plant

Set out container-grown plants of Christmas fern after the last frost. They do best in partial shade. Some direct morning sun is acceptable if the soil has been well prepared. Like most ferns, the Christmas fern thrives in moist, humusy soil in the pH range 5.0 to 6.0. Follow the planting and soil preparation instructions at the beginning of this chapter, and enhance the soil mix by mixing in 50 to 75 percent of humusy forest soil or decayed shredded leaves, and a natural or slow-release organic fertilizer for acid-loving plants. Since the fern lives long and multiplies all around, dig wide planting holes 18 to 20 inches apart. Set the rootball just a little higher than the level at which it was growing before. Mulch all around with pine needles, shredded leaves, or leaf compost.

Growing Tips

Maintain soil moisture for the first season. A little overhead watering in high heat and drought is helpful. Fern glades are often misted. In following seasons, in late winter scatter a light application of organic fertilizer for acid-loving plants under the foliage. Allow the duff (layer of decaying vegetation covering the soil) to remain undisturbed.

Regional Advice and Care

Avoid cultivating next to the crown; pull weeds by hand.

Companion Planting and Design

This evergreen fern is a beautiful groundcover and it is especially lovely in a ferny glade planted with hostas and astilbes. Christmas fern fills its space throughout the year so it makes a charming background for garden plants such as wildflowers, begonias, columbines, lilies-of-the-valley, primroses, Solomon's seals, trilliums, and lady's slippers. Shallow-rooted, Christmas fern competes successfully with tree roots and in rock gardens for moisture and space.

Try These

Evergreen and long-lived, Christmas fern is André's favorite. But in alkaline soils, you will do better with Braun's holly fern, *Polystichum braunii*. It is semi-evergreen with graceful, arching fronds to 36 inches tall, and has twice divided leaves covered with hairlike scales at the edges. It needs cool, deep shade and tolerates somewhat alkaline soil.

Creeping Juniper

Juniperus horizontalis spp.

Botanical Pronunciation
joo-NIP-ur-us hore-ih-zun-TAY-liss

Other Name Groundcover juniper

Bloom Period and Seasonal Color
Foliage turns plum in winter, or deeper green or deeper blue, depending on variety

Mature Height × Spread
4 to 12 inches × 6 to 10 feet

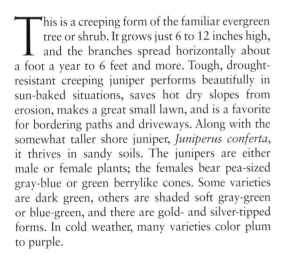

This is a creeping form of the familiar evergreen tree or shrub. It grows just 6 to 12 inches high, and the branches spread horizontally about a foot a year to 6 feet and more. Tough, drought-resistant creeping juniper performs beautifully in sun-baked situations, saves hot dry slopes from erosion, makes a great small lawn, and is a favorite for bordering paths and driveways. Along with the somewhat taller shore juniper, *Juniperus conferta*, it thrives in sandy soils. The junipers are either male or female plants; the females bear pea-sized gray-blue or green berrylike cones. Some varieties are dark green, others are shaded soft gray-green or blue-green, and there are gold- and silver-tipped forms. In cold weather, many varieties color plum to purple.

When, Where, and How to Plant
Container-grown junipers can be planted at any season. If the plants are rootbound, make shallow vertical cuts through the binding roots, and slice 1 inch off the bottom. Junipers need six hours or more of direct sun; in shade they get thin and ratty. The creeping junipers do best in soil with a pH of 5.0 to 6.0, but can handle slightly alkaline soils. The shore juniper, *J. conferta*, can be planted in areas reached by salt spray. Juniper colors most intensely in infertile sandy loam that is somewhat moist. Follow the soil preparation and planting instructions at the beginning of this chapter but omit the fertilizer. Set the plants about 3 feet apart in generous planting holes and spread out the roots. Water thoroughly. Spread a 3-inch mulch of pine needles, bark chips, or rotted leaf mold.

Growing Tips
Water a new planting every week or two the first season. Local rainfall should be enough for established plants. They grow without extra watering among the rocks at Bar Harbor, Maine. Do not fertilize unless the soil is extremely poor. Replenish the mulch in late winter.

Regional Advice and Care
If the branches are rusty, chances are spider mites are at work; spray with a miticide. Where branches are beginning to overlap, prune in midsummer. Where branches touch the soil they will eventually root; in early spring you can sever rooted branches and replant them.

Companion Planting and Design
We plant creeping juniper as a bank holder, and as a groundcover for neglected areas among rocks and edging masonry walls. These low-growing junipers can be interplanted with early daffodils and other medium-height spring-flowering bulbs.

Try These
Among the finest junipers are 6-inch-high, silver-blue 'Blue Rug' ('Wiltonii'); gray-green, 12-inch-high 'Bar Harbor'; 9- to 18-inch-high shore juniper, *J. conferta*, which thrives by the sea; and little 6- to 12-inch-high, dense blue-green, mosslike *J. procumbens* 'Nana', dwarf Japanese garden juniper. For a taller groundcover we use Chinese juniper, including 24-inch, blue-green *J. chinensis* var. *sargentii*, and 4- to 6-inch-high, dark green *J. communis* 'Green Carpet'.

Dead Nettle

Lamium maculatum

Botanical Pronunciation
LAY-mee-um mack-you-LAY-tum

Other Name
Spotted dead nettle

Bloom Period and Seasonal Color
Green and silver foliage; flowers in pink, lavender-pink, white

Mature Height × Spread
6 to 12 inches × 12 to 30 inches

Beautiful but tender-leaved, nettle (André hates the term "dead" nettle) produces a year-round froth of silvered leaves in the shade where even hostas and impatiens do poorly. A low, fast-growing creeper of the mint family, its dark green, oval leaves are splashed or striped silver or white along the midrib. Between late spring and midsummer, it sends up small hooded flowers. In summer, it throws 1- to 2-foot horizontal stems toward sunnier reaches of the garden. The stems root at the nodes and the plantlets can revert to other foliage and flower colors. Nettle is evergreen most years in Washington, D.C., but in sizzling heat and in very cold winters without snow cover, the new stems may die back; the rooted parent plants remain and re-grow in the spring.

When, Where, and How to Plant

Plant root divisions in early spring in partial shade. *Lamium* can take full shade and tolerates more sun in the cool upland areas. Nettles do well in almost any soil, but spread rapidly in light, well-drained loam. Follow the soil preparation and planting instructions at the beginning of this chapter. Prepare planting holes 6 to 8 inches deep and set the plants 12 to 18 inches apart. Water well. Mulch between the plants to keep weeds at bay until the plants completely shade the ground.

Growing Tips

For the first month or two, water weekly or biweekly, unless there is a good supply of rain.

Thereafter, water *Lamium* when you water the flowers. If it dries repeatedly, it will die back to scattered plantlets that take months to re-establish vigorous growth. In spring, remove winter-damaged stems and scatter a little slow-release fertilizer and compost through the bed. Replenish the mulch if weeds begin to take hold.

Regional Advice and Care

If the plants become straggly toward midsummer, cut them back to 6 to 8 inches to keep the growth full and within bounds. In late fall, remove dead stems and clear away fallen leaves. To multiply your holdings, dig rooted plantlets that have not reverted to an unwanted color and replant at once. Terminal cuttings taken from parent plants during the growing season will root easily in water and can be planted once the heat of summer has gone by.

Companion Planting and Design

Dead nettle lightens the shade under trees, and is quite lovely edging shaded flowerbeds and as a filler in a bed in a formal parterre.

Try These

André recommends 'Album', which bears white flowers and has a silver stripe down the middle of the leaves. The most beautiful for foliage is 'Beacon Silver', whose silver leaves are edged with a narrow band of green. The leaves of 'White Nancy' are silvery with a green edge, and the blossoms are white.

Foamflower

Tiarella cordifolia

Botanical Pronunciation
tee-uh-RELL-uh kore-dih-FOE-lee-uh

Other Name
Allegheny foamflower

Bloom Period and Seasonal Color
May; species flowers are white; some cultivars
are pink

Mature Height × Spread
6 to 12 inches × 12 to 24 inches

The foamflower is a charming wildflower native to the rich, moist woodlands of the eastern U.S. and Canada. Evergreen in the warmer areas of the Mid-Atlantic, it forms small clumps of overlapping crinkled leaves that spread by runners. In mid-spring, the foliage is covered with a foam of fluffy little white flowers on tall stems. The blooms fade in a couple of weeks revealing fresh new foliage. Foamflower is easy to grow and spreads so energetically that it makes an excellent woodland groundcover. Breeding by our friend Sinclair Adams has extended the beauty of the foliage color and markings so that now many interesting new hybrids are coming onto the market, some with flowers that are white, cream, pink, or deep rose.

When, Where, and How to Plant
Plant rooted divisions or runners of foamflower in early spring in partial or full shade. Good-sized plants of the newer varieties are being offered by growers, with many more anticipated in the years ahead. Foamflower thrives in soil with pH between 5.0 to 6.0 and is an excellent low groundcover for damp, shady places where the soil is rich in humus. Follow the soil preparation and planting instructions at the beginning of this chapter, and mix in 50 to 75 percent of humusy forest soil or decayed shredded leaves; fertilize with a slow-release organic fertilizer for acid-loving plants. Provide planting holes 6 to 8 inches deep, and 8 to 12 inches apart. Water well after planting and mulch 2 inches deep between the plants with shredded leaves, leaf compost, or peat moss.

Growing Tips
Maintain soil moisture for the first season. Mature plants tolerate brief periods of drought. In late winter scatter a light application of acidic fertilizer under the foliage.

Regional Advice and Care
Pull weeds by hand, selectively. *T. cordifolia* sends out runners that creep over or just under the soil surface, between fallen logs, and over or between rocks. You can control its growth by chopping off the runners. You can multiply your holdings by clipping off rooted plantlets and transplanting those with good root systems.

Companion Planting and Design
With ferns, *Tiarella* makes a lovely living mulch for clematis. We use it as underplanting for drifts of bleeding heart along woodland paths and in sun-dappled glades. In shaded corners, it's pretty with hellebore, creeping phlox, and ferns. The new varieties make attractive container plants.

Try These
'Pink Brushes' is a newer, very cold-hardy *Tiarella* cultivar whose pink blooms gradually change to white. 'Pink Pearls' blooms over a long period. The foliage of both these cultivars acquires bronze-red tones in fall. The leaves of 'Rambling Tapestry' are marked attractively with maroon veins; the leaves of 'Eco Running Tapestry' have wine-red centers. *T. wherryi*, is a clump-forming foamflower—no runners.

Golden Moneywort

Lysimachia nummularia 'Aurea'

Botanical Pronunciation
liss-ih-MAK-kee-uh numm-you-LAIR-ee-uh

Other Name Golden creeping Jenny

Bloom Period and Seasonal Color
Early summer; blooms in yellow

Mature Height × Spread
3 to 6 inches × indefinite spread

reat in shaded areas with moist soil, *Lysimachia* is a rapidly spreading perennial with round, dark green leaves that are evergreen in all but the coldest areas of the Mid-Atlantic. It bears masses of small, bright yellow, cup-shaped flowers and is an excellent groundcover for stream borders, wet banks, and the edges of damp woodlands. A European plant that has naturalized here, it rambles along the ground, rooting as it goes and forming a ruffled carpet. This golden-leaved variety produces rounded, penny-shaped, 1-inch leaves that start out yellowish in spring then turn lime-green in summer. In the shade, the foliage fairly glows. The flowers are yellow and faintly fragrant. It can grow in water up to 2 inches deep.

When, Where, and How to Plant

Set out container-grown plants anytime after the last spring frost and before the first frost in autumn. In Zone 8, *Lysimachia* does best in bright shade and it can multiply even in deep shade. In Zone 6, it can stand sun. Golden moneywort prefers somewhat neutral soil. If the planting bed is in or near woodlands and somewhat acidic, apply lime to raise the pH to between 6.5 to 7.0. Follow the soil preparation and planting instructions at the beginning of this chapter. If the bed is not naturally moist, increase the humus content by digging in a 2-inch layer of peat moss or chopped leaves along with a 1-inch layer of compost, or an application of a slow-release organic fertilizer. Set the plants 12 to 18 inches apart. Water thoroughly. Provide a permanent mulch of well-rotted leaf mold to keep weeds at bay until the plants cover the ground completely.

Growing Tips

Water a new planting every week to ten days unless the ground is naturally moist. Fertilize a new planting early in the spring after you set out the plants by scratching a slow-release fertilizer into the soil beside young plants. Once established, these plants do well on their own without fertilization (or spraying).

Regional Advice and Care

Golden creeping Jenny spreads aggressively in moist conditions and can become invasive, so keep an eye on its development. You can multiply your holdings in early spring or in early fall by digging up and replanting rooted sections of the stems or small divisions of the crown. Prune the plants back in late winter if they are becoming matted. Neither pests nor diseases seem to come their way—but they will suffer if the soil surface is dry for days at a time. Maintain mulch until the plants spread enough to shade out weeds.

Companion Planting and Design

'Aurea' is an excellent groundcover for wet, difficult places. It's lovely in rock gardens, between paving stones, and as an edger in patio containers. It's attractive planted with golden-leaved coleus.

Try These

For golden cover, we plant 'Aurea'. For green cover, we plant the species.

Japanese Painted Fern

Athyrium niponicum 'Pictum'

Botanical Pronunciation
uh-THEER-ee-um nih-PON-ih-kum

Other Name Painted fern

Bloom Period and Seasonal Color
Seasonal; blended silver-green foliage, maroon fronds

Mature Height × Spread
12 to 18 inches × 18 to 24 inches

Japanese painted fern is a strikingly beautiful specimen plant for the wild garden. An exotic looking variegated fern, it has gray-silver, lance-shaped fronds with wine-red stems and a graceful weeping habit. It grows vigorously and easily in partial shade almost anywhere. Unlike the Christmas fern, which is evergreen here, the Japanese painted fern dies down in winter but it stands up to a lot of cold, greening wooded lots long after the trees have dropped their leaves. In a suitable habitat—partially shaded, moist soil—it grows more lush every year, doubling and tripling its size and competing successfully with tree roots. In the 1940s, Alex Summers, founder of the American Hosta Society, introduced the plant to André's father, nurseryman Martin Viette, who introduced it to the trade.

When, Where, and How to Plant

Root divisions of Japanese painted fern are available from nurseries and through garden catalogs. Set them out after the last frost in partial to deep shade. Some direct morning sun is acceptable if the soil has been well prepared. This fern thrives in moist, humusy soil in the pH range 5.0 to 6.5. It lives long and multiplies all around, so dig wide planting holes 25 to 30 inches apart. Follow the soil preparation and planting instructions at the beginning of this chapter and improve the soil by mixing in 50 to 75 percent of humusy forest soil or decayed shredded leaves fertilized with a slow-release organic fertilizer for acid-loving plants. Set the rootball a little higher than it was growing before and mulch with shredded leaves, leaf compost, or peat moss.

Growing Tips

Maintain soil moisture for the first season. A little overhead watering in high heat and drought is helpful. In following seasons, in late winter scatter a light application of acid fertilizer under the foliage. Allow the duff (a layer of decaying vegetation that covers the soil) to remain undisturbed.

Regional Advice and Care

Pull weeds by hand to avoid disturbing the plants. Protect from frosts; in spring it is as sensitive to frost as impatiens. Japanese painted fern can be divided in early spring or fall by digging and separating the crown into smaller divisions.

Companion Planting and Design

We love Japanese painted fern paired with white impatiens and with wild ginger and creeping thyme. We have edged a water garden set in a rocky outcropping with Japanese painted fern, astilbes, white bleeding heart, and Japanese irises, and they are very pretty together.

Try These

The silvery Japanese painted fern is our first choice, and we also recommend 'Pictum Red', which has a reddish tinge in the fronds. We love Japanese painted fern's green cousin, the lady fern, *Athyrium filix-femina*, which forms thick clumps of graceful, lacy fronds 24 inches long that appear throughout the growing season. It spreads at a moderate rate in moist conditions but is tolerant of fairly dry soils.

Japanese Spurge

Pachysandra terminalis

Botanical Pronunciation
pack-ih-SAN-druh tur-mih-NAY-liss

Other Name
Japanese pachysandra

Bloom Period and Seasonal Color
Spring; flowers are insignificant

Mature Height × Spread
6 to 12 inches × indefinite spread

Japanese spurge is a beautiful, rather formal, low-growing evergreen groundcover that does best in light shade and in the cooler areas of the Mid-Atlantic. It makes a handsome "lawn" though it cannot be walked on, and succeeds under tall shrubs and even under maples, beeches, and sycamores where roots are shallow and competitive. The plant consists of upright rosettes of rich green, scalloped or saw-toothed leaves on fleshy stems 8 to 10 inches tall. In early spring, there is a flush of light green new growth and small green-white flower spikes appear. The flowers can reappear in fall when Indian summer warmth follows a cold snap. We can't do without *Pachysandra*, but it can have problems in our region, especially when growing in the sun.

When, Where, and How to Plant
Plant rooted cuttings in the early spring and fall in the bright shade of tall trees, in daylong dappled light, or shade. In direct sun, especially where summers are hot and muggy, pachysandra has problems. Humusy, well-drained acidic soil, pH 4.5 to 6.0, is best. Follow the soil preparation and planting instructions at the beginning of this chapter and mix in a 2-inch layer of peat moss or chopped leaves along with a 1-inch layer of acidic compost. Provide planting holes 6 inches deep and set the cuttings 4 to 6 inches apart. Water thoroughly. Spread a 3-inch mulch of shredded pine bark, pine needles, or rotted oak leaves.

Growing Tips
For the first season, water your planting well every week, especially where pachysandra is competing with the roots of trees and shrubs. In late fall or winter, apply a slow-release organic fertilizer for acid-loving plants. Maintain the mulch.

Regional Advice and Care
Remove autumn leaves. Especially growing in sun, pachysandra is susceptible to volutella stem blight and to scale and mites. For the stem blight, use a copper fungicide, and use ultrafine or horticultural oil to control scale and mites. Keep the bed airy and cool by thinning and cutting. If leaves wilt where soil is reasonably moist, treat the area with a fungicide. Cuttings of new growth taken in summer will root in damp sand tented with plastic; mist often for six weeks. Clumps of pachysandra dug with lots of soil attached transplant well in early spring; keep the transplants well watered.

Companion Planting and Design
Pachysandra is perfect as a groundcover for formal plantings anywhere, beautiful under rhododendrons, azaleas, tall trees, and in open woodlands.

Try These
The most attractive variety is deep green 'Green Carpet', which has wide, compact, rather smooth leaves. Glossy 'Green Sheen' has a more formal look. 'Variegata' and 'Silver Edge' are beautiful but tolerate less direct sun and are less vigorous. Our native Allegheny pachysandra, *P. procumbens*, is not as good an evergreen groundcover but it withstands heat and sun and has showier flowers.

Leadwort

Ceratostigma plumbaginoides

Botanical Pronunciation
sur-at-oh-STIG-muh plum-bay-jih-no-EYE-deez

Other Name
Plumbago

Bloom Period and Seasonal Color
Late summer and early fall; bright blue blooms

Mature Height × Spread
6 to 12 inches × 12 to 18 inches

This is a beautiful groundcover for small sunny or partly shaded areas and it bears one of the bluest of all blue flowers in late summer and fall. The plants form sprawling 6- to 12-inch-high mats of glossy leaves. The peacock blue flowers tip new growth from midsummer to frosts, perfectly set off by rusty red calyxes and bracts. With frost, leadwort dies, leaving behind a tangle of not very attractive brown stems. Leadwort takes a year or two to get under way, but once established, it throws new growth in every direction, overwhelming lower-growing groundcovers such as pachysandra and periwinkle. It handles more than the usual Mid-Atlantic cold and tolerates our high heat. Butterflies—large and small—love it.

When, Where, and How to Plant
In early spring, plant rooted divisions or container plants in sun or moderate shade. Leadwort needs a well-drained site. It does best in rich, acidic loam but tolerates other soils. Follow the soil preparation and planting instructions at the beginning of this chapter, but omit the fertilizer. Make the planting holes 6 to 8 inches deep. Set the divisions 9 to 15 inches apart: leadwort spreads rapidly. Water well. Mulch with salt hay, straw, or compost to keep weeds at bay until the plants shade the ground so completely that weeds cannot get started. That will take two or three seasons. Once established, it gives the garden a weed-free groundcover.

Growing Tips
The first three or four weeks after planting, maintain soil moisture. Overhead watering is suitable. Half an inch or so of compost applied in late fall or winter every two or three years keeps leadwort a good green.

Regional Advice and Care
Cut leadwort back after frost wilts the leaves to keep the bed tidy and healthy, and to promote the new growth on which flowers will appear the next season. Leadwort blooms on new growth. If you do not cut it back, you will get lots of foliage but you will miss out on its really beautiful flowers. We shear the tops of leadwort growing in an all-leadwort bed in winter and then mow with a sharp rotary mower. Leadwort spreads by underground stems, rooting as it rambles. It gets matted in time, and every three or four years benefits from dividing. To multiply your holdings, in early spring cut all around rooted clumps to free them from the parent plants, then dig them and replant.

Companion Planting and Design
We like leadwort combined with other flowering groundcovers, such as myrtle and lamium. It's lovely with flowering perennials. Confine it to 3-gallon pots to keep it from spreading so much that it overwhelms its neighbors.

Try These
If you live in Zone 8, try *Ceratostigma willmottianum*, Chinese plumbago, a shrubby form 2 to 24 inches tall; the flowers are violet-blue and quite beautiful.

Lenten Rose

Helleborus orientalis

Botanical Pronunciation
hell-EBB-ur-us orient-TAY-lus

Other Name
Hellebore

Bloom Period and Seasonal Color
Late winter through mid-spring; green-white, rose to maroon, pink, black-maroon

Mature Height × Spread
1 to 1½ feet × 1 to 1½ feet

Imagine a flower blooming in the cold of February and March! That's the Lenten rose, the best of the hellebores, and one of the toughest and hardiest groundcovers we have. Growing in lightly shaded areas, under rhododendrons and other tall shrubs for example, the plants develop dense stands of shining, leathery, deeply divided foliage as beautiful in winter as it is in summer. Unique nodding flowers appear in late winter. In clear colors, or speckled, mottled, or streaked with color, these are the finest, most long-lasting of any winter flower. Rather like small nodding roses, they are composed of five petal-like sepals and persist for two to three months. Undisturbed, beautiful colonies form and self-sow.

When, Where, and How to Plant
Set out large container-grown plants in early spring or early fall. In Washington, D.C., and other warm areas, the hellebores do best in light shade; in Zone 6 they tolerate morning sun. The hellebores thrive in well-drained, humusy, nearly neutral woodland soil. Follow the soil preparation and planting instructions at the beginning of this chapter and, unless you are planting in woodland soil, mix in 50 to 75 percent of humusy forest soil or decayed shredded leaves mixed with slow-release, organic, acid fertilizer. Make the planting holes twice as wide and as deep as the container. Set the rootball a little higher than the level at which it was growing in the pot. Water well. Mulch with shredded leaves or leaf compost.

Growing Tips
During the first six weeks after planting, water often enough to keep the soil damp to the touch.

Established clumps are relatively drought tolerant. Fertilize in early winter and remove old foliage.

Regional Advice and Care
Lenten rose self-sows; eventually you'll find seedlings growing. Lift them with as much soil as possible, and transplant to a similar environment. Baby the seedlings with sustained moisture and yearly feeding of an organic acidic fertilizer until they are growing lustily. August to mid-September is the best time to divide the plants.

Companion Planting and Design
The hellebores are especially handsome under tall evergreen shrubs. To make sure you get to fully enjoy this rare winter flower, plant hellebores along well-used paths and where they can been seen from a window. They're especially attractive growing with narcissus, skimmia, hostas, and *Pulmonaria saccharata* 'Mrs. Moon'.

Try These
There are hellebores in many strains and colors now, but the Lenten rose and its cultivars are the best of the best. Other species we plant with the Lenten rose are musty-smelling stinking hellebore, *Helleborus foetidus*, which bears panicles of drooping, bell-like, pale apple-green flowers edged with red in Zone 7 as early as January, and in Zone 6 in April; and *H. atrorubens*, which has deep green foliage and deep purple flowers that fade to green.

Lily-of-the-Valley

Convallaria majalis

Botanical Pronunciation
kon-vuh-LAIR-ee-uh muh-JAY-liss

Bloom Period and Seasonal Color
Spring; white, pink

Mature Height × Spread
6 to 12 inches × indefinite spread

One of the world's great perfumes, Joy, is derived from lily-of-the-valley, a slim stem of pure white bells topping foliage that starts out looking like a tiny furled umbrella. The leaves pop up in early spring, and the flowers rise up through them a few weeks later. Lily-of-the-valley is loved for its fragrance; it's also a great groundcover. In light woodlands and shaded wild gardens it naturalizes, and rapidly colonizes surrounding territory with deep—and hard to eradicate—underground roots. You can get lily-of-the-valley to put up flower stems tall enough to cut easily by interplanting it with pachysandra. Pre-cooled pips (pointed tips) of lily-of-the-valley can be forced into bloom early indoors. Note: lily-of-the-valley is listed among toxic plants.

When, Where, and How to Plant

You can plant container-grown lily-of-the-valley anytime. Bare-root divisions or rhizome segments are best planted in early spring or early fall. Lily-of-the-valley is most successful in part sun, shade, or in dappled light. The cooler the region, the more sun it can handle. It thrives in somewhat acidic soil that is well-drained, humusy, and moist. Follow the soil preparation and planting instructions at the beginning of this chapter. Set planting holes for bare root divisions 6 to 8 inches apart and place the pips just below the surface with the roots bunched up underneath. Space plants from 4- or 5-inch containers 8 to 10 inches apart. Water well. Provide a 2-inch mulch for the area.

Growing Tips

During the first six weeks after planting, water often enough to keep the soil damp to the touch. Thereafter, water when you water your lawn. Fertilize in fall with a light topdressing of slow-release organic fertilizer for acid-loving plants.

Regional Advice and Care

If the foliage browns in late summer, spider mites are at work, so apply a miticide according to label directions. If the flowers become smaller and less fragrant, it means the roots are crowded; dig out clumps in the fall, and replant them elsewhere with space all around. Lily-of-the-valley roots go deep, so push your spading fork way down and make sure you get all the roots; fill the empty space with improved soil and the plants all around will move into the new ground.

Companion Planting and Design

When well tended, lily-of-the-valley stays a fresh green all during the growing season and is charming as a groundcover for garden plants as well as wildflowers. It's delightful in a woodland garden with columbines, primroses, Solomon's seals, trilliums, and lady's slippers.

Try These

We recommend the cultivar called 'Fortin's Giant', a tall, full-flowered white that has larger flowers than the species. If you are planting for the beauty of the flowers, plant 'Plena', a double-flowered variety, and little 'Rosea', a less fragrant variety whose flowers are lavender-pink.

Lily-Turf

Liriope muscari

Botanical Pronunciation
lih-RYE-uh-pee mus-KAIR-ee

Other Name
Blue lily-turf

Bloom Period and Seasonal Color
August and September; blue, lavender, purple, white

Mature Height × Spread
1 to 1½ feet × 1 to 1½ feet

Lily-turf looks like a graceful clump of grass, but is in the lily family, and it produces lovely flower spikes, is as tough as any groundcover, evergreen here, and spreads rapidly. The grasslike leaves are tall, coarse, and broad, about ½ to ¾ inches wide. The flowers appear in late summer and early fall. They look a little like slim stems of grape hyacinth but much taller. They bloom in shades of blue, purple, lilac, or white, and are followed by attractive shiny black fruits that persist through early winter. A tough and resistant plant, it takes several seasons of growth to fill out, but once established it's almost indestructible. It's ideal for edging and can handle the Mid-Atlantic climate in cities as well as in the suburbs.

When, Where, and How to Plant

In early spring or early fall, set out container-grown root divisions. Lily-turf thrives in bright shade under tall trees, but spreads even in dense shade. It is not particular as to soil pH, tolerates high-alkaline soils, and succeeds in hot, dry locations. Following the planting instructions at the beginning of this chapter, prepare a planting bed, or planting holes twice the width of the container, with well-drained, moderately fertile soil. Set the plants 12 inches apart. Water thoroughly, and provide a permanent mulch.

Growing Tips

Keep the planting watered during droughts the first summer. Lily-turf withstands muggy weather and high humidity, and spreads as long as the soil doesn't dry out completely. Feed annually in spring.

Regional Advice and Care

In late winter, cut the foliage down to the crown to allow for fresh growth, and replenish the mulch. In continuing wet weather, slugs and snails may chew the edges of the leaves; the control is to wait until the soil dries then sprinkle diatomaceous earth around each plant. Repeat the treatment as necessary. Well-established clumps can be divided in early spring before growth begins.

Companion Planting and Design

We plant clumps of several together as filler for flowering borders. The white-flowered cultivar 'Monroe's White' is lovely with variegated liriope and lavender-flowered 'Gold Band', whose leaves have gold edges and form a mound. 'John Burch', whose foliage is variegated, bears attractive crested lavender flowers. Dwarf mondo grass, *Ophiopogon japonicus* 'Nana', and 'Silver Mist', the variegated form, are fast-spreading dwarf lily-turf relatives.

Try These

For edging flowerbeds and garden paths, we like the effect of 'Christmas Tree', which produces a large, full flower spike in lavender-lilac. Another beauty is 'Royal Purple' whose flowers are deep purple. For groundcover foliage, one of the best is silver and green 'Variagata'. Creeping lily-turf, *L. spicata*, spreads rapidly by underground stolons and is excellent as a bank holder and to cover very large areas. It is a slightly smaller species with ¼-inch leaves and pale violet or white flowers.

Periwinkle

Vinca minor

Botanical Pronunciation
VINK-uh MY-nur

Other Name
Myrtle

Bloom Period and Seasonal Color
March to May; periwinkle blue, white

Mature Height × Spread
3 to 6 inches × 2 to 3 feet long trailing stems

Small-leaved *Vinca minor* is a low-to-the-ground flowering evergreen plant with trailing branches and dainty, shiny, dark green leaves. It creates a beautiful green carpet for open woodlands, rocky slopes, and shrub borders. Though it tolerates only a little foot traffic, it's a handsome lawn substitute. *Vinca* stems root every few feet, but unlike ivy, periwinkle does not cling to masonry so it's ideal for edging walls and terraces. The little flowers that appear in very early spring are a real asset, almost flat, wide open, a beautiful periwinkle blue; they're lovely against the dark green foliage. Like other rapidly spreading groundcovers, periwinkle can crowd out desirable natives and exotics, so plant it only where you are sure it will remain under your control.

When, Where, and How to Plant

Set out flats of rooted cuttings of *V. minor* in early spring or fall. Periwinkle does best in bright shade under tall shrubs or trees and in the partial shade created by a building. It prefers well-drained soil with a pH between 5.5 to 7.2 that is well-worked, fertile, and loamy. Follow the soil preparation and planting instructions at the beginning of this chapter. Provide planting holes 6 to 8 inches deep and space the plants 8 inches apart. Water thoroughly. Mulch with pine needles, or composted leaf mold.

Growing Tips

Do not allow the soil to dry out the first season. Water periwinkle during extended droughts. Scratch in a slow-release organic fertilizer in the spring.

Regional Advice and Care

In early spring before growth starts, use a mower or shear periwinkle to keep the bed thick. To multiply your holdings, divide and replant rooted stems as growth resumes in early spring, or during wet weather in late summer and fall. You can also bunch up root divisions or offsets and plant them.

Companion Planting and Design

For small areas, we like the look of groundcovers grouped in richly varied combinations rather than in single-species displays. A combination that has everything—flowers, fresh foliage, fall color—is *Viola odorata*, *Vinca minor*, pachysandra, plumbago, and ferns. It includes plants for shade, semi-shade under tall trees, and sun. In planters we sometimes combine variegated forms of *Vinca major* and *V. minor*. *V. major* has larger leaves, is a paler green, and produces 3- to 4-foot-long branches that are lovely trailing over the edges of containers. *V. major* 'Variegata' has jade green leaves edged with creamy white. It isn't reliably winter hardy in the Mid-Atlantic, but often survives mild winters.

Try These

Some of the most beautiful cultivars are 'Alba', which has creamy white flowers and is somewhat less vigorous; 'Bowles', which has large blue flowers; 'Miss Jekyll', which bears small white flowers; and 'Sterling Silver', which has midnight blue flowers and beautiful white margins around the leaves.

HERBS
FOR THE MID-ATLANTIC

In the long ago and far away, our forebears grew aromatic kitchen herbs alongside the roses, cinnamon-scented pinks, spicy nasturtiums, and other perfumed flowers with which they flavored food—so the old-time herb garden was a place of beauty and fragrance. But enhancing food was just one of the ways in which herbal plants improved life. You can get a sense of the past—and present—importance of herbs by visiting the U.S. National Arboretum in Washington, D.C. There, The Herb Society of America has established a beautiful 2-acre herb garden planted with medicinal and dye herbs, early pioneer and Native American herbs, industrial and fragrance herbs, Oriental herbs, and beverage herbs. Herbal trees and shrubs occupy the center of this grouping.

Growing together, the herbs become an aromatic sprawl of greens. The knot garden at the National Arboretum illustrates the classical solution to herb sprawl, which is to group herbs within ribbons of low boxwood hedges. "Knot garden" originally referred to any garden with an intricate design but has become almost synonymous with the growing of herbs.

The most indispensable kitchen herbs are those on the following pages. We grow our cooking herbs in beds of ornamentals handy to the kitchen door. The lush greens of parsley and cilantro enhance the flower borders. Low-growing thyme makes an aromatic edger for the path to the kitchen steps. Basil hides the yellowing foliage of small spring bulbs. Dill adds grace to the flower-filled tub by the door.

Herbs are easily grown in containers.

How to Plant and Grow

Seeds of most herbs are slow to germinate and growing the seedlings on can be a challenge. So, unless we need many plants of one kind—basil for bouquets, creeping thyme for tucking between steppingstones—we buy potted plants, rooted cuttings, or seedlings and set them out usually about mid-spring. Most herbs thrive in full sun and well-drained soil with a pH between 5.5 to 7.0. A few kitchen herbs do well in part shade, among them dill and basil. To prepare soil for herbs, see "Soil Preparation and Improvement" in the introduction.

To encourage an herb to bush out and be more productive, early on pinch out the tip of the main stem. Remove herb flowers as they develop—they're edible and make charming garnishes. When the plants have filled out, you can harvest the tender tip sprigs of the youngest branches at will without harming the plant. Never strip a plant of more than one-third of its foliage or it will have trouble maintaining itself. In summer's high heat—especially in a very warm summer—herbs may go into semi-dormancy. During this season, you should pick herbs sparingly, as the plants are unable to replace the missing foliage and will look awful and be slow to recover.

How to Harvest and Dry

Herbs are most flavorful harvested in the early morning before the sun dissipates the essential oils that give them flavor. Rinse herbs only if they're muddy. You won't have to rinse the foliage if you surround your herbs with a clean mulch. We find herb foliage stays fresh for a week or so when we seal it in a vegetable bag lined with damp paper towels and store it in the crisper.

Fennel, like this *Foeniculum vulgare* 'Purpureum', can be both ornamental and an edible.

To dry herbs, harvest clean, healthy stems 12 to 14 inches long, and strip off the lower leaves. Tie them loosely in small bunches and hang them upside down in an airy, dry, preferably dark place. Direct sunlight fades the foliage. When they're crackling dry, strip off the leaves and discard the stems. Rub the leaves between your palms to break them up. Pour the leaves into jars, label, and seal them. We try to find time to renew our supply every season; old herbs lose much of their flavor.

Ornamental Herbs

Some of the many other herbs we include in ornamental gardens, mainly for their beauty and fragrance, include these:

Catmint, *Nepeta mussinii*
Fennel, *Foeniculum vulgare*
Feverfew, *Tanacetum parthenium*
Italian oregano, *Origanum majoricum*
Lemongrass, *Cymbopogon citratus*
Rue, *Ruta graveolens* 'Jackman's Blue'
Summer and winter savory, *Satureja* spp.
Sweet woodruff, *Galium odoratum*

Basil

Ocimum basilicum

Botanical Pronunciation
OH-sih-mum bah-SIL-ih-kum

Bloom Period and Seasonal Color
Summer; lavender flower spikes

Mature Height × Spread
1 to 2½ feet × 10 to 15 inches

The basils are vigorous, upright annuals or short-lived perennials with light green, often slightly puckered leaves that have the cool strong bite of mint (a close relative), with hints of anise, or sweet licorice, clove, and thyme. The leaves are used to flavor Mediterranean dishes, raw tomatoes, salads, pasta sauces, and pesto, and in sauces for lamb, fish, and beef. We wouldn't be without basil for cooking, but we also plant basil for the aroma, color, and texture its colorful varieties add to garden plantings. To have fragrant fillers for bouquets we plant opal basil, which has purplish leaves with green markings, and 'Dark Opal' basil, which has little green markings, red stems, and a sweet, anise-like flavor. 'Red Rubin', purple leaf basil, is a European selection that holds its color well.

When, Where, and How to Plant

Pots of seedlings can be set out after the weather has warmed. You can start seeds indoors four to six weeks before that, or sow basil seeds in the garden once night temperatures stay above 50 degrees Fahrenheit. Basil prefers full sun but will tolerate some afternoon shade. It does well in well-drained humusy soils whose pH is between 6.0 and 7.0. See "Soil Preparation and Improvement" in the introduction. Provide planting holes 8 to 12 inches deep, and allow 6 to 8 inches between plants. Water well with diluted fertilizer. Basil wilts quickly and easily in summer heat, so apply a 3-inch layer of mulch starting 3 inches from the stem to help keep in moisture.

Growing Tips

To promote rapid growth, water often enough to sustain the soil moisture for two or three weeks. After that, water weekly unless you have a soaking rain. Fertilize every three to five weeks through August with a liquid fertilizer such as seaweed.

Regional Advice and Care

Pinch out the central leader and harvest branch tips and flowers early and often to encourage leaf production. If you have planted seeds, keep weeds away. At mid-season, cut the plants back by about half. Pick tip sprigs at will when the leaves still are young. Big harvests for making pesto can begin when flower spikes start to form. Basil will go on through Indian summer if you protect it from early frosts.

Companion Planting and Design

The purple varieties especially are beautiful tucked into flower borders and growing in containers planted with flowers in pastel colors. They're lovely with cosmos. In window boxes and for edging containers use tiny bush basils like 'Spicy Globe', which grows into a perfect 6 to 12 inch ball; the flavor is quite good.

Try These

Our favorite basils for flavoring are common sweet basil and holy basil, *Ocimum sanctum*. We plant purple-leaved basils, which aren't very flavorful, for the fragrance and rich color they bring to flower beds and bouquets. The opal basils and 'Purple Ruffles', an All-America Selections winner, are our current favorites.

Chives

Allium schoenoprasum

Botanical Pronunciation
AL-ee-um skee-no-PRAY-zum

Bloom Period and Seasonal Color
Spring and summer; mauve to lavender-pink

Mature Height × Spread
12 to 18 inches × 12 to 18 inches

Chives are perennials. They develop attractive mounds of perfectly round, hollow, dark green leaves that look like grass at first glance. Beginning in June, pretty, dryish, lavender-pink globes appear and these are edible too. It's a charming display that continues all summer if you pick the blooms. Chive leaves impart a mild onion flavor. They're used chopped as a garnish and flavoring agent for salads, dips, stews, casseroles, and laid full size over fish or meat that will be roasted. Chopped chives put a flavorful finishing touch to one of the world's great cold soups, vichyssoise, and the flowers, pulled apart, make an elegant garnish for eggs Benedict. Chives keep well frozen, or dried on a screen and sealed into airtight containers.

When, Where, and How to Plant
Chives can be started from seed indoors six to eight weeks before the last frost date; they grow best at a temperature of 75 degrees Fahrenheit. The clumps enlarge over the years so unless you are planting lots for the garden display, we suggest you buy a few potted seedlings. Potted chives can be planted spring, summer, or early fall. They thrive in full sun and in soils between pH 6.0 to 7.0. Choose a well-drained site—chives hate puddles—and work the soil to a depth of 8 to 12 inches. See "Soil Preparation and Improvement" in the introduction. For each plant, mix in a handful of either compost or composted manure. Set the plants 12 to 18 inches apart and water with diluted fertilizer. Mulch all around 2 inches deep.

Growing Tips
To promote rapid, unchecked growth, for the first two or three weeks water often enough to sustain soil moisture. After that, water deeply only during prolonged droughts. In early spring, fertilize the bed with a slow-release organic fertilizer.

Regional Advice and Care
Keep weeds away: they're hard to get out of a clump once the chives are well established. To encourage more foliage, pinch out the flower heads. Use sharp, clean scissors to harvest chives and cut no lower than 2 inches from the crown. Never take more than one-third of the plant at one time and harvest sparingly in summer's high heat. Divide chives every three to four years in early spring or early fall. In late summer, you can pot chives in a clay container and bring a clump indoors for modest winter harvests.

Companion Planting and Design
Chives are pretty little plants, lovely in bloom and attractive tucked into a flowering border or edging an herb or a vegetable garden. They do well in large containers.

Try These
For cooking, we recommend the variety called 'Fine Chives'. There are interesting other species. One we plant for cooking and for its flowers is *Allium tuberosum*, the tall garlic, or Chinese, chives. The leaves are flat, not round, and the flowers are white.

Dill

Anethum graveolens

Botanical Pronunciation
uh-NEE-thum gruh-VEE-uh-lenz

Bloom Period and Seasonal Color
Late summer; yellow-green flower heads

Mature Height × Spread
1½ to 6 feet × 2 to 3 inches

Dill is a willowy annual with foliage as fine as asparagus fern. It looks a lot like fennel, *Foeniculum*, and tastes of parsley-carrot-lemon-anise. The foliage is called "dill weed." Flower heads resembling yellowish green Queen Anne's lace develop as the season warms. They are edible and eventually produce seeds that can be dried and bottled for winter seasoning of casseroles and stews—and for pickling. Dill foliage dries quickly on screens and also can be bottled for later use. Snipped fresh dill weed is excellent in salads and with salmon, potatoes, green beans, salads, and in chicken soup. It's also a really pretty garnish. We use whole stems of aromatic dill weed as a garnish for platters of cold cuts, salmon, tomatoes, and cheese.

When, Where, and How to Plant

You can start dill from seed indoors six to eight weeks before the last frost. Dill's taproot doesn't transplant easily, so sow the seeds in peat pots and transplant the seedlings in their pots. Or, sprinkle the seed over the soil surface after the ground has warmed; sow where the plants are to grow. Dill needs sun but deteriorates in prolonged, intense heat. In our area, shade at noon helps keep dill going longer. Avoid growing dill where walls or white-painted surfaces intensify the heat. Dill prefers soil in the acidic range, pH 5.5 to 6.5. See "Soil Preparation and Improvement" in the introduction. Work the soil 8 to 12 inches deep and set seedlings about 12 inches apart. Water with diluted fertilizer. Apply a 2-inch mulch starting 3 inches from the stem.

Growing Tips

To promote rapid, unchecked growth, for the first two to three weeks, water often enough to keep the soil moist. Then, water deeply every week unless you have a soaking rain. If you have fertile soil, you don't need to fertilize.

Regional Advice and Care

Pinch out tip sprigs regularly to encourage branching. Harvest sparingly in high heat. If dill deteriorates when heat comes, discard it and plant new seedlings in early September. Keep the flower heads picked until the end of the season. Dill may self-sow if the soil around the parent plants is cultivated and moist. To have dill seed for cooking, when the seedheads yellow or brown, but before they dry, shake the seeds into a paper bag and dry them on paper towels on screens.

Companion Planting and Design

Dill foliage lends grace to an herb garden, kitchen garden, or cutting garden. In choosing a place for dill, take into account that it may die out when high heat arrives. Dwarf dill varieties do well in containers.

Try These

'Dukat' or 'Tetra' dill have a delicate, rather sweet flavor and are slow to bolt. 'Bouquet' has especially large seedheads. 'Fernleaf' dill, an All-America Selections winner, is a lovely, blue-green, 18-inch dwarf with excellent flavor. 'Mammoth' is an aromatic 4- to 6-foot dill for pickling.

Lavender

Lavandula angustifolia

Botanical Pronunciation
luh-VAN-dew-luh an-guss-tih-FOE-lee-uh

Other Name
English lavender

Bloom Period and Seasonal Color
June, may repeat in August; lavender, deep purple, pink, white

Mature Height × Spread
1½ to 3 feet × 2 to 4 feet

Lavender's sweet, lasting scent has been a source of fragrance for thousands of years. It's a shrubby evergreen whose every part is intensely fragrant—flower spikes, stems, and needlelike, gray-green leaves. Lavender stems are harvested before the buds open, dried, and the buds are stripped and used to scent linens and lingerie, sleep pillows, and other tools of aromatherapy. The buds, dried or fresh, are also used to add a sweet mint-anise-rosemary flavor to *herbes de Provence*, honey, dessert butters, savory sauces, grilled fish and steaks, marinades for game, and to stews and soups. We plant lavender near roses and where it will sprawl across paths so we will brush against it often, releasing its wonderful aroma. Deer dislike it.

When, Where, and How to Plant

Lavender seed is very slow to germinate, and the seedlings are easily lost after transplanting. We recommend you set out container-grown plants. They can be planted in early spring, late summer, or early fall. Lavender requires full sun but can stand a touch of noon shade. It will grow in a large container on a patio, but isn't suited to indoor growing. Lavender does best in soil that has a pH above 6.0. It needs a well-drained site, and flourishes growing on a sandy southern slope. See "Soil Preparation and Improvement" in the introduction. Work the soil to a depth that is twice the height of the container to ensure good drainage. Set the plants 15 to 30 inches apart. Water well. Apply a 2-inch mulch starting 3 inches from the stem.

Growing Tips

To promote rapid, unchecked growth, for the first two or three weeks water often enough to sustain soil moisture. After that, water deeply every week or ten days unless you have a soaking rain. No fertilizer is needed.

Regional Advice and Care

In early spring to encourage new growth, prune 1 to 2 inches from the branch tips of established plants. Lavender often re-blooms in late summer if the first set of flowering stems has been deadheaded or harvested. Harvest lavender stems just before the buds begin to open, tie them in loose bunches and hang them upside down to air dry, then strip off the buds and store in a sealed container for later use.

Companion Planting and Design

Lavender grows well in a rock garden and makes a wonderful groundcover for sunny orchards. In ornamental gardens we plant 'Hidcote' for its deep purple flowers, and silvery little 'Munstead'.

Try These

The lavender we recommend as a dry perfume scent and for flavoring is the English type or true lavender, *Lavandula angustifolia* ssp. *angustifolia*. 'Lavender Lady' is a gray-green dwarf that blooms in late summer from spring-sown seed. The beautiful purple-pink French, or Spanish, lavender, *L. stoechas*, isn't reliably winter hardy in Zone 6 but it makes a pretty pot plant, and may winter over in Zone 8. Other great varieties are *L. intermedia* × 'Provence' and the dwarf *L. angustifolia* 'Blue Cushion'.

Mint

Mentha spicata spp. and cultivars

Botanical Pronunciation
MEN-thuh spy-KAY-tuh

Other Name
Spearmint

Bloom Period and Seasonal Color
Summer; purplish, white, pink, mauve, lilac

Mature Height × Spread
1 to 2 feet × 1 to 2 feet

The mints are upright or sprawling herbs 12 to 36 inches tall with intensely aromatic, crinkly green leaves (hairy in some species) that are pungent when brushed against. In summer, fuzzy mint-scented flower spikes appear. This species, *Mentha spicata*, has small, pointed, dainty leaves and a truly fine sweetish mint flavor. It is our choice for use as a culinary herb—for teas, juleps, vinaigrettes, lamb sauce, desserts (use fresh tiny tips), jellies, and soups. The fresh leaves decorate and flavor desserts and confections, Middle Eastern and Indian foods, are steeped for *digestif* teas, and dried in potpourris. Stepped on, mint sprawling onto a garden path becomes a carpet of magical fragrance. Bees graze mint diligently.

When, Where, and How to Plant

Mint spreads relentlessly, so gardeners are eager to share rooted divisions. But plant only a mint whose flavor you have tasted and like, or one you will use in bouquets. Garden centers offer many container-grown varieties. You can plant rooted mint at almost any season in full sun or in filtered or bright shade. It is invasive (in fact, very invasive) so unless you are planting in poor or clay soil, confine the roots to a large bottomless plastic pot or coffee tin and plant the container. Mints do best in slightly acidic soil, pH 5.5 to 6.5, but any well-drained soil will do. Space the plants 12 to 15 inches apart. Water well. The sprawling mints get muddied during rainstorms, so stake a few branches to have clean leaves available for cooking. Apply a 2-inch mulch starting 3 inches from the stem.

Growing Tips

To get the plants off to a good start, for the first two or three weeks water often enough to sustain the soil moisture. Water the small-leaved mints when you water the flowerbeds. Usually no fertilizer is needed.

Regional Advice and Care

Harvest only sparingly in summer's high heat. Shear mint to keep it looking neat and to produce fresh new growth. Mint growing in a container should be divided every year or two in the spring or early fall. Six-inch tip cuttings root readily in damp potting soil, sand, or water.

Companion Planting and Design

Centuries of growing mint has resulted in more than 500 species and cultivars. They are diverse in appearance and aroma and make an interesting collection for garden hobbyists. As an edger along walkways and in containers, we like the beautiful, variegated pineapple mint, *M. suaveolens* 'Variegata'; the flavor is negligible but this mint is somewhat less invasive than other species.

Try These

We grow a few spearmint plants to use fresh to flavor food and to dry for making mint tea. And, because we love the aroma of mint in bouquets, we let *M. arvensis*, which has broad, hairy leaves, grow wild in our kitchen flowerbed.

Parsley

Petroselinum crispum

Botanical Pronunciation
pet-roe-seh-LYE-num KRIS-pum

Other Name
Italian parsley

Bloom Period and Seasonal Color
Summer; grown for foliage only

Mature Height × Spread
1 to 1½ feet × 1 to 1½ feet

We plant three parsleys: curly parsley, flat-leafed or Italian parsley, (which are varieties of *Petroselinum crispum*), and Chinese parsley, (*Coriandrum sativum*, more often called cilantro now). All three are low, very green, leafy plants. Curly and flat-leaved parsley are pungent, winter-hardy biennials. Their earthy carrot/celery flavor blends other flavorful ingredients. Rich in chlorophyll, they kill odors and sweeten the breath. Curly parsley is the most beautiful for garnish and the quickest to mince. Flat Italian parsley, *P. crispum* var. *neapolitanum*, is more richly flavored. Cilantro is a cold-tolerant annual that grows to a foot or two in a season. It adds a unique flavor to Latin and Oriental recipes. Its dried ripe seed is the ancient Asian spice called coriander, which imparts a sweet lemony flavor and a hint of sage.

When, Where, and How to Plant

Parsley is a biennial, living two years. It stays green through our winters, flourishes mightily through most of spring, then when heat comes it quickly goes to seed. To have a steady supply, plant two or three parsley seedlings in early spring, and the following fall plant a new batch near the existing plants. Discard older plants when they bolt—or let them grow their greenish flower heads and enjoy watching the butterflies flock to them. (Planting time for cilantro seedlings is after the air warms.) All three do best in full sun in well-drained neutral soil, between pH 6.0 to 7.0. See "Soil Preparation and Improvement" in the introduction. Plant holes 8 to 12 inches deep and set the plants 8 to 10 inches apart. Water well. Provide a 2-inch mulch.

Growing Tips

To promote rapid, unchecked growth, water often for the first two to three weeks. Keep plants well watered. Parsley likes a little plant food.

Regional Advice and Care

Parsley can be harvested as soon as the plants have grown a substantial number of stems. Use scissors to harvest the outer stems and make the cut at the base. Never take more than one-quarter to one-third of one plant at a time. When curly and Italian parsley are growing lushly, harvest, mince, and freeze some for winter use. Sometimes butterfly caterpillars feed on parsley.

Companion Planting and Design

From an ornamental point of view, the parsleys can be planted wherever a low-growing mound of bright green is desirable. Curly parsley makes a handsome edging for bright red geraniums, and it thrives in window boxes and large containers. We like to keep a little bouquet of red geraniums and curly parsley in the kitchen.

Try These

'Clivi' is a mossy, dwarf curly parsley to use in window boxes. 'Krausa' parsley is a curly variety we like for flavor. 'Triple Curled' is a thickly ruffled parsley. 'Giant Italian' is a 3-foot, deep green parsley with a full, mellow flavor excellent fresh or dried. (Cilantro labeled "slow bolt" is best for foliage. If you'd like to grow your own coriander seeds, plant varieties called just "coriander.")

Rosemary

Rosmarinus officinalis

Botanical Pronunciation
roz-muh-RYE-nus uh-fiss-ih-NAY-lus

Bloom Period and Seasonal Color
Summer; pale lavender-blue flower spikes

Mature Height × Spread
2 to 6 feet × 2 to 8 feet

An age-old symbol of remembrance and beloved of bees, rosemary is a shrublike perennial that has gloriously aromatic, needlelike, gray-green leaves. Evergreen in Zone 8, in Zones 6 and 7 it may be wintered indoors and sometimes grows well enough to be trained as a Christmas tree topiary. The pungent needles impart a sweet, hot, piney, nutmeg flavor used to flavor many foods—polenta and potatoes, fruit, cookies, breads and biscuits, grilled meats, and fish. Olive oil infused with rosemary makes a delicious dipping and sauté oil. Rosemary is the base for many men's colognes and for potpourris. A circlet of rosemary branches makes a great base for an herb wreath. Sprigs of rosemary add aroma to bouquets of fresh flowers.

When, Where, and How to Plant

In Zones 6 and 7, rosemary is grown as an annual but in Duck, North Carolina, Zone 8, it has naturalized in the sand at the Viette beach house. To germinate, the seeds need nights at 75 degrees Fahrenheit, and can take three months to sprout. We recommend starting with a container-grown plant. Plant rosemary in full sun after danger of frost. A native to the Mediterranean, it withstands high heat and drought once established, and can be grown where it will be neglected. Rosemary does best in well-drained soil, acid or neutral. See "Soil Preparation and Improvement" in the introduction. Work the soil 8 to 12 inches deep and set baby plants 6 to 8 inches apart, shrub sizes 12 to 24 inches apart. Water well. Provide a 2-inch mulch starting 3 inches from the stem.

Growing Tips

To promote rapid, unchecked growth, water often enough to sustain the soil moisture for the first two or three weeks. Water established plants only during droughts.

Regional Advice and Care

Harvest 1- or 2-inch sprigs from young branch tips often to encourage bushiness. Before winter, pot the plant in sandy, humusy soil and bring it indoors to a sunny window; water regularly but don't keep the soil moist. Mist several times each week. Rosemary will last longest in bright light in a room kept at 50 degrees Fahrenheit. Put the plant out in the spring after all danger of frost is past.

Companion Planting and Design

Rosemary is a good bonsai and pot plant, and specimen to place near entrances, windows, and garden seats where you can enjoy its fragrance. In Zone 8 gardens it grows into an aromatic evergreen.

Try These

For flavoring, we recommend the species *Rosmarinus officinalis*. The hardiest rosemary is 'Arp', which is said to withstand winters as far north as New Jersey. Ornamental rosemaries that are lovely in the garden, though not the best for cooking, include *R. officinalis* 'Benenden Blue', which has handsome blue flowers; 'Lockwood de Forest', which has brighter leaves and bluer flowers; 'Kenneth Prostrate' and 'Huntington Carpet', which are superior creeping forms; and yellow-leaved 'Golden Rain'.

Sage

Salvia officinalis

Botanical Pronunciation
SAL-vee-uh uh-fiss-ih-NAY-liss

Bloom Period and Seasonal Color
Midsummer; violet, blue, white

Mature Height × Spread
1½ to 2½ feet × 1½ to 2½ feet

Common sage is a small, beautiful woody perennial whose grayish leaves have the texture of crepe. Some colorful varieties are beautiful enough to be grown as ornamentals. The leaves impart a subtle flavor—sweet pine, camphor, and citrus. Minced fresh sage is used to flavor bread, pasta sauces, and with roasted pork, chicken, and vegetables. Dried sage enhances fatty meats and is used in stuffing for poultry. The flavor of fresh sage becomes more potent the longer it cooks—so use it with caution in delicate sauces. Sage stays fresh for a week sealed in a vegetable bag in the crisper. The leaves dry well in a microwave oven, on screens, or tucked into a wreath.

When, Where, and How to Plant
Set out container-grown plants or root divisions in early spring after all danger of frost is past. Sage does best in full sun, but tolerates afternoon shade. Provide very well-drained, ordinary, neutral soil, around pH 7.0. See "Soil Preparation and Improvement" in the introduction. Work the soil 8 to 12 inches deep and dig generous planting holes 2 feet apart. Water well. Stake stems that sprawl to avoid having to rinse the foliage, robbing it of some of its flavorful oils. Apply a 2-inch mulch starting 3 inches from the stem.

Growing Tips
For the first two or three weeks water often enough to sustain the soil moisture. Water deeply every week or ten days, unless you have a soaking rain.

Regional Advice and Care
The flower spikes are edible and removing them improves the appearance and growth of the plant. Harvest tender tip sprigs at will. In the fall, trim sage back to a tidy mound to avoid root rot—a problem where drainage is poor. Sage can be harvested sparingly in winter. To multiply your holdings, divide well-established older plants in spring or early fall. Sage can also be grown successfully indoors as long as it gets sun at least six hours a day and has proper drainage. The plant should be pruned to no more than 12 inches. If it starts to look leggy and the leaves grow pale and are thinly spaced, the plant isn't getting enough light.

Companion Planting and Design
For their texture and beauty, we plant colorful cultivars of *Salvia officinalis* toward the front of flowering borders and in the herb and the kitchen gardens. Sage is pretty in a planter; set it so it droops over the edge. Several varieties of sage grouped together are striking. Sage's camphor aroma is said to deter garden insects.

Try These
The species is best for flavoring food, but some of the more colorful sages also have flavor, though less than *S. officinalis*. 'Tricolor', the showiest, has leaves splattered with deep pink, silver-gray, cream, and purple. 'Icterina' has beautiful gray-green leaves broadly edged with gold.

Tarragon

Artemisia dracunculus

Botanical Pronunciation
ar-tuh-MEE-zee-uh druh-KUNK-you-lus

Bloom Period and Seasonal Color
Summer; whitish green florets

Mature Height × Spread
1 to 2 feet × 2 to 3 feet

Tarragon is a perennial that grows into a good-sized, rather weedy shrub in our region. The slim, delicately flavored leaves impart a heavenly aroma of sweet anise or sweet licorice and camphor. Unique, haunting, the flavor and scent are used in vinegars, dressings, French and Southern European dishes, and in potpourris. Tarragon is what gives Béarnaise sauce its flavor and it is an essential ingredient in *fines herbes* for stocks, broths, and Green Goddess salad dressing. It enhances mushrooms, chicken, and fish. There are two main tarragon groups, French and Russian. French tarragon has an addictive, haunting sweet aroma, and that's what makes the plant worth looking for. Taste before buying! Russian tarragon can grow to 5 feet tall and doesn't do much for food but it's handsome in the garden.

When, Where, and How to Plant

True French tarragon cannot be grown from seed, so buy a container-grown plant or rooted cutting that meets your taste test. It may not winter over in exceptional winters. One or two plants will satisfy your needs. Plant tarragon in mid-spring in full sun—it tolerates a few hours of afternoon shade. It can take a lot of heat and resists drought, so you can plant it where it may be neglected. Don't plant tarragon in a kitchen garden where rototilling might disturb it. Tarragon thrives in ordinary neutral soil between pH 5.5 or 6.0 to 7.0. Good drainage, especially in winter, is essential. See "Soil Preparation and Improvement" in the introduction. Dig planting holes 8 to 12 inches deep and 8 to 12 inches apart. Water well. Apply a 2-inch mulch starting 3 inches from the stem.

Growing Tips

Water often enough to sustain soil moisture for the first two or three weeks. Water established plants every seven to ten days, unless it rains.

Regional Advice and Care

Harvest tip sprigs often in spring to promote growth of tender branches—the leafy tips are the tastiest. Cut the plants back in the summer when they begin to flower in order to promote new growth. In time, tarragon's roots become crowded and tangled, resulting in a less productive plant. Renew your plant by dividing the clumps in the spring. Carefully separate 3-inch pieces with shoots intact and replant. Discard any woody roots.

Companion Planting and Design

For all of its elegant flavor, tarragon is not a very jazzy-looking plant. We recommend placing it in an out-of-the-way place in your herb garden surrounded by other tall, more interesting looking plants. It's useful as a filler in a flower border or a container garden.

Try These

We grow the species for flavoring, and two of its aromatic cousins for their appeal in the garden and in bouquets. One is true wormwood, *Artemisia absinthium*, and the other is southernwood, *A. abrotanum*, a beautiful foliage plant with finely divided scented leaves.

Thyme

Thymus spp. and hybrids

Botanical Pronunciation
TYE-mus

Other Name
French thyme

Bloom Period and Seasonal Color
Early summer; pale pink, white, lilac, purple

Mature Height × Spread
2 to 12 inches × 2 to 3 feet

The thymes are small prostrate evergreen perennials with graceful trailing branches 6 to 10 inches long. The tiny, dark green leaves have a sharp aroma, and an earthy mint taste. The flavor combines well with bay leaf, parsley, and onion. The leaves are used dried or fresh in stuffings for pork and lamb, and in salads, soups, stews, Creole dishes, and gumbos. Parisians sprinkle thyme on steaks before broiling. The leaves are so small they don't need to be minced, just bruised to release the flavor. Herb fans brew thyme to make an herbal tea. To dry thyme for storing, pick tip sprigs, air dry them on screens until crisp, then strip off the leaves, and bottle and cap them. The thymes are excellent basket and container plants.

When, Where, and How to Plant
For an early crop, in mid-spring set out container-grown thyme. Plant it in full sun for the best flavor. A little noon shade can be helpful in the hottest parts of our region but the plant dies out if it doesn't have enough sun. Thyme tolerates considerable drought and abuse, so it can be planted where it is likely to be neglected. It does well in ordinary soil that has a pH above 6.0. See "Soil Preparation and Improvement" in the introduction. Provide a well-drained site and generous planting holes 8 to 12 inches deep and 12 inches apart. Water well. Mulch the area 2 inches deep.

Growing Tips
For a week or two after planting, promote rapid growth by watering often enough to sustain soil moisture. After the first few weeks, water deeply during droughts.

Regional Advice and Care
Harvest thyme sparingly in summer's high heat. Every year in early spring, shear established plants back mercilessly, and fertilize them with a handful of a slow-release fertilizer. To multiply your holdings, divide mature plants in spring or early fall.

Companion Planting and Design
Two or three thyme plants will likely meet your needs for thyme. The good culinary thymes make good edgers. Thyme's trailing stems and white-splashed pineapple mint are beautiful together in a hanging basket with white petunias and pink geraniums. Creeping thyme, *Thymus serpyllum*, is tough enough to be walked on and can be used between flagstones. Colorful when in bloom, varieties of the larger flowered subspecies *T. serpyllum* ssp. *serpyllum*—white-flowered 'Albus', crimson 'Coccineus', and red 'Splendens'—are suitable groundcovers for sunny slopes and are attractive planted where they will trail over garden walls. For edging, we plant varieties whose leaves are splashed silver or gold; the names usually include the words "argenteus" or "aureus."

Try These
The sweetest culinary thymes are *T. vulgaris* and its cultivars, such as 'Wedgewood English', an excellent taller form, and 'Orange Balsam', which has a hint of citrus. We also grow lemon thyme, *T. citriodorus*, and caraway thyme *T. herba-barona*.

ORNAMENTAL GRASSES

FOR THE MID-ATLANTIC

Windblown, untamed, graceful, 1 to 12 feet tall and more, the ornamental grasses are the signature plants of today's naturalistic landscaping, and they need little maintenance. The sight and sound of wind whispering through tall grasses is refreshing on a hot summer day—a country sound very welcome in a city garden. Airy, luminous seed heads develop late in the season and remain lovely through fall and early winter.

The low-growing ornamental grasses add texture to the front of flower beds and to pocket wild gardens. Those 6 feet tall or more can replace a high-maintenance espalier fronting a masonry wall. Planted among native trees and shrubs, grasses become part of a handsome low-maintenance screen. The mid-height ornamental grasses are the natural transition plants to woodland or water and, in combination with native wildflowers, make a beautiful flowering meadow. The recommended ratio for a meadow garden is one-third flowers to two-thirds ornamental grasses for sunny places, and one-third grasses and two-thirds flowers for shade.

The first consideration in choosing a grass is how the end-of-season height and width of the plant will fit the site. The very tall grasses must be featured as specimens and nearby plantings chosen to complement them. Then consider the overall form. Some grasses clump, some mound, some fountain. Chinese silver grass is very erect, maiden grass arches, while pennisetum fountains. The texture of the leaves and their color is important—fine, coarse, bold, bluish, greenish, reddish, gold, striped, variegated. For contrast, combine both fine- and coarse-textured grasses. When you have thought all that through, then you can consider which of the flower heads you are going to fall in love with. Grouping many plants of a few varieties is more effective than planting a few of many.

Author Carole Ottesen classes the grasses into cool-season and warm-season plants, and it's a useful concept. The cool-season grasses shoot up in late January or February, so they're cut back in late winter. Their early growth makes them the best choice when you want a grass that will be highly visible, the main show, all year-round. The warm-season grasses begin to grow later, so you can wait until early spring to cut them back. A warm-season grass is a good choice when you have in mind combining grasses and flowers: interplant them with big early spring-flowering bulbs that will bloom after the grasses' annual haircut and hide the bare crown while the grass is growing up. The grass will soon grow tall enough to hide the ripening bulb foliage.

Planting and Growing

Like the perennial flowers, the ornamental grasses begin to fill out the second year. They may be planted in early spring, summer, or early fall. At garden centers they are sold in containers; mail order suppliers may ship some ornamental grasses bare root. These plants must be soaked thoroughly before planting. Most of the ornamental grasses thrive in acid to neutral soil that is one-half to one-quarter humus, and most need a well-drained site. See "Soil Preparation and Improvement" in the introduction. Set the crowns ½ to 1 inch higher than the soil surface. Surround the plants with 1 to 2 inches of mulch.

The annual haircut is just a matter of shearing low-growing grasses and new plantings of the big grasses. When a big grass begins to mature, simplify the annual haircut by using sisal twine to rope the leaves together all the way to the top so that it ends up looking like a telephone pole. Then saw the top off a few inches above the crown. (If you use a chain saw take care not to catch the twine in the teeth!) For low-growing grasses, cut off the leaves and stalks a few inches above the crown.

Most ornamental grasses need annual fertilization. The time for fertilizing is when signs of new growth appear. Apply a slow-release organic fertilizer. In prolonged droughts, water slowly and deeply.

Other Options

In addition to the grasses recommended in this chapter, we like:

Dwarf pampas grass, *Cortaderia selloana* 'Pumila'

Korean feather reed grass, *Achnatherum brachytricha*
    (formerly *Calamagrostis arundinacea*)

Leather leaf sedge, *Carex buchananii, C. morrowii* 'Goldband'

Ravenna grass, *Saccharum ravennae* (formerly *Erianthus ravennae*)

Ornamental grasses can feel both formal and informal, depending on the setting.

Blue Fescue

Festuca glauca

Botanical Pronunciation
fess-TEW-kuh GLAW-kuh

Other Name
Blue sheep's fescue

Bloom Period and Seasonal Color
Tan flower heads mid- to late spring; season-long blue foliage

Mature Height × Spread
8 to 12 inches × 12 to 18 inches

Blue fescue forms low rounded tufts or hummocks of slender metallic blue-green blades that are evergreen in most areas of the Mid-Atlantic. It's a cool-season grass, that is, it starts to grow soon after the January haircut, which is all the maintenance it needs, and it blooms in mid- to late spring. The flowers are loose, lacy panicles on stems that reach well above the foliage. The contrast between the relatively small, stiff clump and the thin, gracefully arching and gently swaying flower stalks is charming. It's widely used in perennial borders where it adds a welcome blue accent. The genus includes familiar lawn grasses as well as big, handsome ornamentals.

When, Where, and How to Plant

Set out dormant, container-grown plants as soon as the ground can be worked in late winter. Plant blue fescue in full sun or in very bright shade. Without enough light, the blue will be less intense. Avoid damp spots. The foliage has a bluish gray, waxy coating that protects it from excessive water loss through transpiration, and wet feet (soggy roots) can cause problems. Blue fescue thrives in a range of soils from pH 5.5 to 6.5. It develops the bluest color in soil that is not especially fertile, and on the dry side. See "Soil Preparation and Improvement" in the introduction. Provide roomy planting holes and set the plants an inch above the soil level about 2 feet apart. Water well. Mulch 2 inches deep around and between the plants.

Growing Tips

Water a new planting every week or two for the first season. The plant is fairly drought resistant, so once it is established local rainfall should be enough to keep it growing except during our mid- and late-August droughts. Blue fescue grows rapidly during cool weather, but in hot, dry periods it sulks. Do not try to force growth by watering or fertilizing. Wait for cool weather, and it will revive.

Regional Advice and Care

Allow the seedheads to ripen and stand through fall and winter. Toward the end of January, prune the plant back to the crown. Replenish the mulch until the plants have spread widely enough to shade out weeds. This grass benefits from division every few years. You can divide and replant this grass in fall, but not in summer.

Companion Planting and Design

Blue fescue is attractive planted as edging for beds of shrubbery, walks, naturalized areas, and grass gardens. It is sometimes used as a groundcover, but we find the clumps too compact, and the foliage too stiff—it never seems quite comfortable in the role. It looks well, and grows well, with lavender, salvia, and Russian sage.

Try These

This one is definitely our favorite. 'Elijah Blue' has the most intense blue of all the fescues.

Blue Oat Grass

Helictotrichon sempervirens

Botanical Pronunciation
huh-lick-toe-TRY-kun sem-PUR-vur-enz

Other Name
Avena grass

Bloom Period and Seasonal Color
Blue-gray inflorescences turn to tan in summer;
metallic blue leaves all season

Mature Height × Spread
2 to 3 feet × 2 to 2½ feet

This is a lovely steely blue grass that's a little taller than blue fescue, and it maintains its color through late winter. A cool-season grass, it starts growing very quickly after its early spring haircut, forming compact spiky tufts of striking silvery blue-green leaves. In May, delicate, golden, oat-like flowers sway far above the foliage on graceful erect or arching stems that extend 1 feet or more beyond the foliage, swaying and bobbing in the wind. In summer, the blue-gray flower heads turn a bright tan that contrasts beautifully with the foliage. It's a good specimen for open situations, terraces, and rock gardens.

When, Where, and How to Plant
As soon as the ground can be worked in early spring, set out container-grown plants or rooted divisions. Plant blue oat grass in full sun or in part sun. Without enough light, the blue will be less intense. Avoid damp spots. In Zone 8, our southern shore region, plant blue oat grass in high, bright shade such as there is under tall pines; it doesn't tolerate high temperatures combined with strong sun and drying winds. Blue oat grass thrives in rich soil and succeeds in a wide pH range from acid 3.0 to neutral 7.0. See "Soil Preparation and Improvement" in the introduction. Provide roomy planting holes and set the plants an inch above ground level and about 2 feet apart. Water well. Mulch 2 inches deep around and between the plants.

Growing Tips
Water a new planting every week or two for the first season. Once established, local rainfall should be enough to keep blue oat grass growing except during our mid- and late-August droughts.

Regional Advice and Care
Allow the spikelets to ripen and stand through fall and winter. In late January, prune the plant back to the crown. Trim the plant back earlier if storms flatten the flower stems, or if it becomes less appealing. Replenish the mulch in late winter until the plants have spread widely enough to shade weeds out. You can divide and replant this grass in fall, but not in summer. Dig the crown, cut it apart, and replant the pieces.

Companion Planting and Design
Blue oat grass has many uses in the home landscape. Planted toward the middle of a large perennial border, it makes a colorful textural accent and it is beautiful massed and naturalized. We've seen it combined very effectively in wild gardens near the shore with silvery plants like artemisia, nepeta, and stachys.

Try These
Plant the species.

Chinese Silver Grass

Miscanthus sinensis and cultivars

Botanical Pronunciation
miss-KAN-thuss sye-NEN-siss

Other Name Eulalia

Bloom Period and Seasonal Color
Pale pink flower clusters in late summer; fading with foliage to silver and gold in fall

Mature Height × Spread 3 to 8 feet × 3 to 5 feet

Chinese silver grass is one of the most desirable and versatile of the big landscape grasses, a 3- to 8-foot grass to use boldly in big spaces. Beautiful in fall and winter, it is a warm-season grass that grows slowly in spring and then rapidly, producing robust, open, upright clumps of gracefully arching leaves that develop into dense, effective screening. In late summer and fall, silky, silvery, pale pink flower clusters open on panicles up to 1 foot long. With cold weather, the foliage and the plumes turn to silver and tan. Long grown in Japan and China, beloved of the Victorians, who called it eulalia, the species has given rise to many cultivars considered the most beautiful of the ornamental grasses.

When, Where, and How to Plant

Set out container-grown plants as soon as the ground begins to warm. Most Chinese silver grass cultivars grow best in six or more hours of direct sun, but some, including the lovely cultivar 'Gracillimus', or maiden grass, make do with three to four hours of direct sun. Given a constant supply of moisture, *Miscanthus* thrives, but established plantings sustain modest growth in drier soil. *Miscanthus* species are not particular as to pH, and adapt to reasonably fertile soil. See "Soil Preparation and Improvement" in the introduction. Provide generous planting holes and plant with 3 to 4 feet between the centers. Water well. Mulch 2 inches deep.

Growing Tips

Water a new planting every week or two for the first season. Water during droughts until the plants are fully matured. Established cultivars can do with less moisture—the leaves roll if they need more.

Regional Advice and Care

This warm-season grass starts its growth when winter is over, so wait until early spring to cut it back to the crown. Replenish the mulch. To multiply, divide before new growth begins. Lift and carefully use an axe to cut the crown apart, giving each section at least one growing point.

Companion Planting and Design

Some cultivars are planted as specimens, others as transitional plants by water features. We think it's most beautiful growing in groups.

Try These

For the smaller home garden we recommend 5- to 6-foot maiden grass, *M. sinensis* 'Gracillimus', which has narrow arching leaves; 5- to 7-foot 'Cabaret', whose broad leaves have silver stripes; 5- to 6-foot 'Cosmopolitan', whose wide leaves have broad white stripes; and 4-foot 'Morning Light', which has narrow green leaves with a white midrib and a silvery look. In larger landscapes we like 6- to 8-foot zebra grass, 'Zebrinus', a striking upright grass gold-banded horizontally, and refined 7- to 8-foot 'Silver Feather' ('Silberfeder'), which bears beautiful silver plumes. Giant silver grass, *M. floridulus*, is a wide-leaved coarse species 8 to 12 feet tall that fills with silvery light when the wind catches it.

Feather Reed Grass

Calamagrostis × acutiflora
'Karl Foerster', spp., and cultivars

Botanical Pronunciation
kal-uh-muh-GRAHSS-tiss uh-kew-tih-FLORE-uh

Bloom Period and Seasonal Color
In spring purple-tinted flower heads, changing to tan; after frost, foliage fades to gold, platinum

Mature Height × Spread
5 to 6 feet × 20 inches

The feather reed grass 'Karl Foerster', named a Perennial Plant Association Plant of the Year, is an upright cool-season grass that shoots up after its winter haircut, and remains attractive through hot summers. The seeds are sterile, so it never is invasive. Most of the spring the plant is a solid mass of medium to dark green foliage. By the time the late-blooming daffodils have gone it is 4 feet tall and producing pale, feathery, bronze-purple, foot-long panicles of florets that stand straight up on wiry green stems and gradually turn tan colored. With the coming of frost, the foliage fades to gold and platinum and, unless winter storms flatten the stems, it remains really beautiful until it is cut back.

When, Where, and How to Plant
Set out dormant, container-grown plants as soon as the ground can be worked in late winter. It requires full sun; without enough light the flower heads will flop over. A pH range of between 6.0 and 7.0 suits feather reed grass. It grows well in dry or wet soil and isn't particular as to fertility. See "Soil Preparation and Improvement" in the introduction. Provide generous planting holes and set the plants an inch above ground level and about 2 feet apart. Water well. Mulch 2 inches deep around and between the plants.

Growing Tips
If the plants are in dry soil, water every week or two for the first month, or until you see signs of vigorous growth. After that, water moderately.

Regional Advice and Care
Allow the seedheads to ripen and stand through fall and winter. Toward the end of January, cut the plant back to its crown. Trim it earlier if storms flatten the flowering stems. Replenish the mulch. Feather reed grass grows rapidly during cool weather, but in hot, dry periods it may sulk. Do not try to force growth by watering or fertilizing. The plants will not need dividing for eight to ten years or more. When they do, dig the crowns, and chop them apart with an axe. You can divide and replant this grass in spring, but not in summer or fall.

Companion Planting and Design
In a smaller landscape, we like this grass in mass plantings. It's beautiful as a specimen or a hedge against a masonry wall and also lovely interplanted among shrubs and evergreens. Its meadowy autumn golds are beautiful backing black-eyed Susans, sedum 'Autumn Joy', pale and dark purple asters, and boltonia, and fronting taller varieties of *Miscanthus*.

Try These
In a very small garden, a good choice would be *C. × acutiflora* 'Overdam', which has arching, white-striped foliage about 1 foot high. Its flowers are 3-foot pink plumes that age to gold. It requires some shade in hot regions.

Fountain Grass

Pennisetum alopecuroides

Botanical Pronunciation
pen-ih-SEE-tum al-loe-peck-yer-ROI-deez

Other Name
Chinese pennisetum

Bloom Period and Seasonal Color
Rose-tan to maroon foxtails in summer; fading with foliage to a silvery wheat

Mature Height × Spread
2 to 4 feet × 2 to 4 feet

Fountain grass is a beautiful, medium-tall, finely textured grass that produces dense, graceful clumps of cascading foliage. A warm-season grass, it begins its growth at tulip time and is considered by many to be the best ornamental grass for use in perennial gardens. When fountain grass begins to fade in fall, it still maintains a real presence in the garden. In summer, flowering stems rise topped by slender, cascading rose-tan to maroon foxtails that nod and toss in the slightest breeze. Exceptionally graceful and beautiful in flower, it also is lovely in winter when it blanches to the color of silvery wheat. Fountain grass sprawls, so it needs space all around. A single plant makes an impressive show and a trio is spectacular.

When, Where, and How to Plant

Set out container-grown plants in mid-spring. Fountain grass will be fullest and most colorful growing where it receives at least six hours of sun daily; in warm Zone 8, it succeeds in bright shade. A pH range between 6.0 to 7.0 suits it well. It thrives in a site with good drainage and moist, fertile soil. See "Soil Preparation and Improvement" in the introduction. For a groundcover, space the plants 2 feet apart; to grow fountain grass as a specimen, allow 3 feet all around. Set the plants an inch or so above ground level. Water well. Mulch 2 inches deep around and between the plants.

Growing Tips

Water a new planting every week for the first season. Once established, local rainfall should be enough to keep fountain grass growing except during droughts. But if it goes dry it will be less beautiful.

Regional Advice and Care

Allow the seedheads to ripen and stand through winter—in a moist situation they may self-sow. Wait until late winter to cut the plant back to ground level. Trim it back earlier if it becomes less appealing. Replenish the mulch in late winter. Divide and replant this grass in spring before heat comes. Dig the crown, cut it apart, and replant. Fountain grass is considered winter hardy where temperatures do not fall below 5 degrees Fahrenheit; if your winter wind-chill factor goes below that, protect the plants with a cover of evergreen branches or leaves.

Companion Planting and Design

Fountain grass is beautiful naturalized with asters, black-eyed Susans, sedums, and small flowering trees. You can use it in gardens of large perennials for texture and color. Position it so the new growth will camouflage yellowing bulb foliage and fill spaces left empty as poppies and other spring perennials go by.

Try These

'Little Bunny' is the smallest cultivar, a graceful little fountain grass 12 to 18 inches tall with green foliage and tan-gold foxtails; it can be used as a groundcover. Oriental fountain grass, *Pennisetum orientale*, is a dainty form 18 inches high, which is grown as an annual in Zones 7 and 8.

Hakone Grass

Hakonechloa macra

Botanical Pronunciation
ha-koe-ne-KLOE-ah MAY-krah

Other Name Japanese forest grass

Bloom Period and Seasonal Color
Late summer to early fall pinkish seedheads;
foliage turns pinkish red, then bronze, then tan

Mature Height x Spread
1 to 2 feet x 2 to 3 feet

Zones 6 and 7

This is an elegant Japanese grass just 2 feet high whose glossy foliage falls in graceful cascades and comes in fresh greens and gold and in many shades and variegations. The glossy, rather soft leaves grow upright, then fall gracefully forward in a rushing water effect. It does best in a shaded location but can handle sun, especially the green varieties, if the site includes late afternoon shade. The plants are slow-growing the first season but in two or three years in moist fertile soil they make lush mounds. Pinkish seedheads form in later summer. In cold weather, the leaves turn pinkish red, then bronze, then tan and last until cut down in early spring. In May, fresh foliage appears.

When, Where, and How To Plant
You can plant from mid-spring to early summer. The best site has afternoon shade, but this grass will do well in full shade and the green-leaved forms succeed even in full sun. The soil needs to be moist where there is a lot of sun, but the grass will tolerate dry soil in shady spots. Before planting, fluff the soil 10 to 12 inches deep. Clay soils will need to be amended with a half portion of compost or leaf mold. Set the crown just above the soilline. A mulch is beneficial, but keep it at least 3 inches from the crown.

Growing Tips
To encourage growth, provide fertile soil, and water weekly the first year. After the grass is growing well, water only during long, dry spells or if the plant shows signs of wilting. The plant grows fairly slowly, so it needs little annual fertilizing.

Regional Advice and Care
Hakone grass may survive in Zone 5 if it is growing near a source of heat; a stone wall that gets a lot of sun, for example. It is safe in Zones 6 and 7. If a plant shows signs of dying from the center outward, dig it up, divide the healthy sections into individual plants and replant. Cut the plants back to 2 or 3 inches after the foliage dies down. Rabbits love it in spring. Well-grown plants are expensive, but worth the cost.

Companion Planting and Design
Plant alongside a shaded woodland path, with low-growing hostas and ferns, and coral bells, coleus, or big wax begonias. It can be used as groundcover under trees, and succeeds for a time in flower pots.

Try These
The species has shiny, bright green leaves that look well with ferns and other forest plants. *Hakonechloa macra* 'Aureola' glows golden green in the shade. 'All Gold' is all gold! The beautiful variegated white-streaked 'Albo-striata' can be hard to find but is worth looking for.

Northern Sea Oats

Chasmanthium latifolium

Botanical Pronunciation
kaz-MAN-thee-um lat-ih-FOE-lee-um

Other Name River oats

Bloom Period and Seasonal Color
Green seedheads in summer, changing to pink and copper

Mature Height × Spread
1 to 3 feet × 1 to 3 feet

This is a beautiful tall woodland grass that grows in narrow, upright clumps and produces fresh green leaves that, like bamboo leaves, are held perpendicular at intervals on stiff wiry stems. It is a warm-season grass. Though northern sea oats reach maximum size when they are growing in full sun, they also flourish in semi-shade at the edge of woodlands and in the shadow of tall buildings. The flower heads are eye-catching spikelets of flat fruits with oat-like heads. As much as an inch wide and an inch long, they are green in summer and gradually mature to shades of pink and copper. Spangled over wiry drooping stems that stand well above the foliage, they rustle and shimmer in a breeze.

When, Where, and How to Plant

Set out container-grown plants of this warm season grass in mid-spring as the ground begins to warm. It will be fullest and most colorful growing where it receives at least six hours of sun daily. It thrives in partial shade, but the less light it receives the more it will sprawl. A pH range between 6.0 to 7.0 suits it and it does best where the soil has sustained moisture without being soggy. It does, however, tolerate dry soil. See "Soil Preparation and Improvement" in the introduction. If the soil is sandy, work in 25 percent compost, peat moss, chopped leaves, or other organic material. Provide generous planting holes 2 to 3 feet apart. Set the plants about an inch above ground level and water well. Mulch 2 inches deep around and between the plants.

Growing Tips

To encourage rapid growth, water a new planting every week the first season. Once established, local rainfall should be enough to keep northern sea oats growing except during droughts, but it spreads most quickly if it doesn't dry out.

Regional Advice and Care

Allow the seedheads to ripen and stand through fall and winter. This warm-season grass will start new growth only when the cold has ended, so wait until late winter to cut the plant back to the crown. Trim the plant back earlier if storms flatten the stems, or it becomes less appealing. Replenish the mulch in late winter until the plants have spread widely enough to shade out weeds. Sea oats self-sows in the right environment, so you may have to rogue out the volunteers.

Companion Planting and Design

Northern sea oats is an excellent transitional plant that can be positioned to create screening. It looks best planted in groups, even massed. Ornamental plants that flourish in the same environment include Japanese anemone, lobelia, and toad lily. Sea oats are especially lovely growing on a slope where the seedheads can catch the light and be seen against a darker background.

Try These

Plant the species.

Switchgrass

Panicum virgatum 'Heavy Metal'

Botanical Pronunciation
PAN-ih-kum vur-GAY-tum

Bloom Period and Seasonal Color
In summer, pink inflorescences; flowers and foliage turn gold in fall and winter

Mature Height × Spread
4 to 5 feet × 2 to 3 feet

North American switchgrass, a prairie native, is an upright, narrow, arching, clump-forming warm-season grass that lifts a mist-like ethereal cloud of pale blooms on 3- to 6-foot stalks in summer. The inflorescences are spikelets on long open panicles held high above the foliage. With frost the foliage turns a warm gold; that color and its handsome structure remain until cut back. In the garden, we plant the 4- to 5-foot-tall cultivar 'Heavy Metal', whose leaves are a beautiful metallic blue-green; its flowers are tinged pink and the upright structure is useful for introducing contrast into the garden. The species itself occurs naturally in most of the country and is an excellent choice for naturalizing.

When, Where, and How to Plant
Switchgrass develops from rhizomatous roots and spreads quickly. Set out container-grown plants or root divisions in mid-spring or early fall. It will be most colorful where it receives direct sun. Though it thrives with fairly constant moisture, switchgrass is so deeply rooted it can withstand drought, as well as high heat and bitter cold. Any well-worked soil will do, and it is tolerant of sandy soils. See "Soil Preparation and Improvement" in the introduction. Provide generous planting holes and space the plants 16 to 18 inches apart. Water well. Mulch 2 inches deep around and between the plants.

Growing Tips
Water a new planting every week or two the first season. Switchgrass does best in moist soil, so even after the plants are established and spreading, water when late-summer drought stresses your flowers, maintaining soil moisture at the roots even if the surface is dry between waterings.

Regional Advice and Care
This warm-season grass will start new growth only when winter is over, so wait until early spring to cut the plant back to 4 to 5 inches above the crown. Fertilize with a light application of slow-release organic fertilizer. Replenish the mulch in late winter until the plants have spread widely enough to shade out weeds. To multiply, divide the plants in early spring before new growth begins. Lift and gently break or cut the clump apart, giving each section a few growing points.

Companion Planting and Design
Naturalize switchgrass with flowers that stand some neglect, such as daffodils, foxtail lilies, species tulips, Joe-pye weed, black-eyed Susan, asters, boltonia, and sedums. It is attractive planted as a specimen, and quite beautiful set out in large sweeps in transitional spaces.

Try These
'Heavy Metal' is one of the most beautiful of the grasses that add a strong blue accent to the landscape—and you can plant it where the drainage isn't very good, a definite advantage! 'Rehbraun' is an excellent green foliaged cultivar with leaves that turn reddish brown in late summer.

PERENNIALS

FOR THE MID-ATLANTIC

Perennial flower and foliage plants give our gardens continuity. Annuals live one season. Some perennials come back for just a few years, but many live ten to fifteen, and peonies can go on for more than 100 years. When we're planning a garden, our first selections are hardy perennial flowers whose sequence of bloom will carry color through the bed all season long. Within most species' stated bloom period, you can find varieties that come into flower early, midseason, or late. To avoid late spring frostbite in cool regions, choose late-blooming varieties of spring-flowering species; where frosts can come early in fall, choose early-blooming varieties of perennials that bloom in late summer. Most hardy perennials are resistant to frosts unless temperatures go below freezing, 32 degrees Fahrenheit.

Once we've chosen the flowers for a garden, we look for foliage plants that will complement or contrast with the flowers. Colorful foliage—silver, blue, yellow, or red—placed to reinforce, or to contrast with, the colors of nearby flowers, add depth to the design. Think of the effect of spiky globe thistle and furry lamb's ears. Two lovely blue foliage plants are the blue-green rue 'Jackman's Blue' and blue oat grass. Variegated foliage lightens the greens. At a distance, white variegated foliage appears jade green or soft gray; yellow looks like a splash of sunshine or a flower. We add ferns for the romance they lend to shaded spots. And ornamental grasses tall and small that dance, whisper, and bring sound and movement as well as contrasting texture to the garden.

In a large mixed border we include the big leaves and striking architectural forms of a few bold-foliaged perennials, like the big hostas, brunnera, and rodgersia. Giant tropical foliage plants—dwarf canna and the hardy banana—add a hint of mystery. These "tender perennials" won't winter over, but the effect they create is worthwhile. We also like to set two or three dwarf needled evergreens in strategic places. Their solid forms and strong color anchor flowerbeds in early spring and, with the ornamental grasses, they maintain a sense of life when the garden falls asleep.

Finally, we look for places to tuck in a few aromatic herbs and very fragrant flowers. Low-growing, fuzzy, white-splashed pineapple mint and silver variegated thyme lighten the bed and release their fragrance as you brush by. Aggressive plants like the mints can be set out in buried containers. Some flowering bulbs and many important perennials have fragrant varieties. The most fragrant of the spring flowers are the hyacinths. The Oriental lilies, especially pure white 'Casa Blanca', spread a fantastic perfume. 'Myrtle Gentry' is a scented peony. Many tall bearded irises are fragrant, as are some daylilies including 'Fragrant Light'.

A perennial bed planted with *Stachys byzantina*, *Geranium* 'Johnson's Blue', iris, *Trollius* x *cultorum* 'Golden Queen', and *Lupinus*.

When, Where, and How to Plant

If you are interested in experimenting with a flowering meadow or a wild garden, you'll need hundreds of plants. Try your hand at starting the perennials indoors from seed. (See "Starting Seeds Indoors," in the introduction.) Plants that are the species, rather than an improved or named variety, will come true from seed. But when you want named varieties, we strongly recommend you choose container-grown perennials grown from root divisions and rooted cuttings. Here's why: the named varieties (hybrids and cultivars) are superior flowers selected from among thousands planted. Growers propagate them from cuttings or root divisions and so they bloom true to the parent plants. André's motto is, "plant less and grow the best." Buy one plant, divide it into three plants, repeat for three years and you will have twenty-seven plants, in five years 243 plants, ad infinitum . . . so a perennial bed of the best can be inexpensive.

Perennials in 1-quart containers planted in the spring produce some blooms the first season; those sold in 2- to 3-gallon containers will make a bigger show. Most container-grown plants can be set out spring, summer, or fall. In the spring, growers ship some perennials bare root—astilbes, for instance. These often flower fully only the second or third season. A perennial that blooms early in the spring—columbine, for example—gives the best show its first year when it is planted the preceding late summer or early fall.

In clay and sandy soil the surest way to provide soil in which perennials will thrive for many years is to create a raised bed. In the "Soil Preparation and Improvement" section of the introduction you'll find instructions for creating a raised bed and for bringing the soil to a pH of 5.5 to 7.0, the range for most flowers. André's recipe for a raised bed includes long-lasting organic fertilizers. See page 222 for more information on fertilizers.

The spacing of perennials depends on the size the mature plant will be; we've offered suggestions with each plant. Always provide a generous planting hole, one twice the width and as deep as the rootball. Before you plant a container-grown perennial, unwind roots that may be circling the rootball, or make shallow vertical slashes in the mass, and cut off the bottom ½-inch of soil and rootball. Soak the rootball in a big bucket containing starter solution. Then set the plant in the hole, fill the hole with soil, and tamp firmly. Water slowly and deeply, then mulch around the planting following our suggestions in the introduction. Staking protects very tall flowers like lilies in a storm. But most others, if correctly fertilized and given plenty of space all around, won't need it. Tall, weak growth is often the result of force-feeding with non-organic fertilizers. Wide spacing also improves air circulation, reducing the risk of disease and mildew! Water a new planting slowly and deeply, every week or ten days for a month or so unless you have soaking rains. And water any time the plants show signs of wilting.

Care

After summer, we like to leave in place seed-bearing perennials with woody upright structures, like black-eyed Susans, because they look interesting in winter, and to feed the birds. Some self-sow and will refurnish the planting. In late fall, we clear away collapsed foliage that will grow slimy after frost. When you remove dead foliage, cut it off, don't pull it off because that may damage the crown beneath. In late winter or early spring, after the soil has dried somewhat, it is time to clear away the remains of last year's dead foliage; watch out for tender burgeoning new stems while raking through perennials such as lilies. Every year in spring, and again in September to October, we fertilize established perennial beds, not individual plants, by broadcasting a slow-release organic fertilizer in sunny areas, and a similar fertilizer for acid-loving plants in shaded areas.

Dividing for Productivity

To remain productive and showy, some perennials should be divided and replanted every four or five years. Dividing also gives you plants for the development of new gardens and to give away as gifts. On the plant pages that follow we explain when each is likely to need dividing. But the perennials themselves indicate when the time has come: the stems become crowded and leggy, the roots become matted, and there are fewer and smaller blooms. As to timing, the rule of thumb is to divide spring-flowering perennials a month before the ground will freeze in the fall, or before new growth begins in early spring; divide autumn-flowering perennials, such as chrysanthemums, in spring before any sign of growth appears. More specific instructions are given with each plant.

Other Choices Worthy of Consideration

The perennials described in this chapter are the best of the best for Mid-Atlantic gardens. Other perennials that we think very highly of include:

Adam's needle, *Yucca filamentosa* 'Bright Edge'

Bellflower, *Campanula carpatica*, *C. persicifolia*, *C. poscharskyana*

Blazing star, gayfeather, *Liatris spicata* 'Kobold'

Brunnera, Siberian bugloss, *Brunnera macrophylla*

Butterfly weed, *Asclepias tuberosa*

Candytuft, *Iberis sempervirens*

Catmint, *Nepeta* x *faassenii*

Foxglove, *Digitalis* spp. and hybrids

Geranium, Cranesbill, *Geranium* spp. and cultivars

Goatsbeard, *Aruncus dioicus*

Goldenrod, *Solidago* spp. and hybrids

Heliopsis, *Heliopsis helianthoides* cultivars

Lungwort, *Pulmonaria* spp. and hybrids

Meadow rue, *Thalictrum* spp. and hybrids

Mist flower, hardy ageratum, *Conoclinium coelestinum* (formerly *Eupatorium coelestinum*)

Southernwood, *Artemisia abrotanum*; silver king artemisia, *A. ludoviciana* var. *albula*

Speedwell, *Veronica* spp. and hybrids

Spurge, *Euphorbia epithymoides*, *E. dulcis*, *E. griffithii*

Stokes' aster, *Stokesia laevis*

Tickseed, *Coreopsis* spp. and cultivars

Crape myrtle underplanted with variegated Solomon's seal, hostas, and foxglove.

Astilbe

Astilbe × arendsii, spp. and hybrids

Botanical Pronuncition
uh-STILL-bee ah-RENDZ-ee-ee

Bloom Period and Seasonal Color
Late spring and early summer; creamy white, pale pink, lilac, coral, red

Mature Height × Spread
1 to 5 feet × 1 to 2 feet

The shade-loving astilbes are beautiful plants whose flowers are tall, graceful plumes composed of masses of small florets in mostly pastel shades. The deeply cut, fernlike, green or bronzed foliage is attractive both before and after flowering; with the years, plantings spread to make large, dense mats. Cut, the flowers are lasting, and they dry well. Although most astilbes flower from June through the middle of July, you can achieve a lasting show of color by planting early, midseason, and late bloomers. For instance: plant the white early-blooming favorite 'Deutschland', red 'Fanal', and pink 'Europa', with mid-season pink 'Ostrich Plume' ('Straussenfeder'), and late bloomers such as the lilac 'Superba' and mauve-pink 'Pumila'.

When, Where, and How to Plant
Catalogs ship bare-root astilbe crowns in early spring. Follow their planting instructions and be patient. For a quick show, set out container-grown astilbe plants in mid-spring or late summer. Astilbe grows best in light shade in well-drained, rich, moist humusy soil. In full sun, it can succeed if the soil never dries out. Although *Astilbe chinensis* tolerates drought, most astilbes need adequate moisture, but they suffer if soil is soggy in winter. Slightly acidic pH is best. See "Soil Preparation and Improvement" in the introduction. Follow the planting instructions at the beginning of this chapter, spacing the plants about 18 inches to 3 feet apart, according to the size of the variety. Water well. Mulch 2 to 3 inches deep starting 3 inches from the crown.

Growing Tips
Water astilbes deeply every week to ten days unless you have a soaking rain. The keys to success—particularly in the warmer reaches of the Mid-Atlantic—are sustained moisture and summer mulches. Fertilize the bed between late winter and early spring, and again in September to October, with a slow-release organic fertilizer for acid-loving plants. In spring, replenish the mulch.

Regional Advice and Care
We don't deadhead since the drying flower spikes are attractive. You can divide astilbe crowns every three years if you wish, between early spring and August.

Companion Planting and Design
Astilbes are excellent fillers for the middle or back of the border and lovely edging a woodland path, stream, or pond. Massed, astilbes in a range of colors make a lovely low tapestry of color. In summer and early fall the little Chinese astilbes, *A. chinensis* 'Pumila', raise mauve-pink flower heads; they spread rapidly by underground stolons and are very attractive as edging or groundcover in part shade.

Try These
Our favorite is little *A. simplicifolia* 'Sprite', a Perennial Plant Association Plant of the Year. It has much-divided, bright green foliage, masses of light pink florets borne on slightly pendulous panicles, followed by attractive rust-colored seedheads. The total height of the plant is 12 to 18 inches. It begins blooming in midsummer and continues for several weeks.

Balloon Flower

Platycodon grandiflorus 'Mariesii'

Botanical Pronunciation
plat-ee-KOE-dun gran-dih-FLORE-us

Other Name
Chinese bellflower

Bloom Period and Seasonal Color
Early summer to early fall; blue

Mature Height × Spread
1 to 2 feet × 2 to 3 feet

Old-fashioned balloon flower is a graceful, easy perennial, one of the best summer bloomers. This outstanding 1- to 2-foot-tall variety produces distinctive balloon-shaped buds along wandlike stems that open to starry flowers up to 2 inches across. There are double varieties. An excellent cut flower, fresh or dried, it blooms freely from early summer to early fall and has glossy foliage. In a test conducted in Zones 7 and 8 over a five-year period, both at the shore and 600 feet from the ocean, the balloon flower gave an excellent performance. It was grown in pure sand with Osmocote® and fertilized once yearly. The plantings were deeply watered three times each month, June through October, but not at all November through May.

When, Where, and How to Plant

Sow balloon flower seeds following the instructions on the seed packet in early to mid-spring, mark the place, and be patient. Balloon flower is one of the last plants to come up from seed. For more immediate results, set out container-grown plants or root divisions any time after the ground can be worked in spring. Balloon flower succeeds in full sun in the cooler regions of Zone 6, and in semi-sun in Zones 7 and 8. It needs well-drained soil, tolerates almost any pH, and does well in dry city conditions and by the shore. See "Soil Preparation and Improvement" in the introduction. If you are setting out container-grown plants, follow the planting instructions at the beginning of this chapter, spacing the plants about 2 feet apart. Water well. Provide a permanent 2-inch mulch starting 3 inches from the crown.

Growing Tips

Water new plants deeply every week the first season unless you have a good soaking rain. Balloon flower is drought resistant, so once it's established, local rainfall will be enough to keep it growing. Fertilize the bed between late winter or early spring, and again in September to October, with a slow-release organic fertilizer for acid-loving plants. In spring, replenish the mulch.

Regional Advice and Care

Deadhead to promote flowering. Balloon flower rarely needs dividing.

Companion Planting and Design

Use balloon flower to keep blue in the perennial bed all summer. We use it in place of the somewhat similar campanula, which fails regularly in our hot summers.

Try These

We are very taken with 6- to 12-inch-high dwarf balloon flower, *Platycodon grandiflorus* 'Sentimental Blue', which is perfect for a rock garden or the front of the flower border. Others we like are *P. grandiflorus* 'Apoyama', which bears violet flowers on plants 10 to 15 inches tall, and is very attractive planted with herbs. The Fuji series, a Japanese strain, is one of the best for the cutting garden; the cut flowers are long-lasting if the stems are seared before they're put in water.

Bleeding Heart

Dicentra spp. and cultivars

Botanical Pronunciation dye-SEN-truh

Bloom Period and Seasonal Color
Spring, or summer to fall, depending on the species; *Dicentra spectabilis*: cherry red and white; *D. formosa* and *D. eximia*: pink, cultivars white

Mature Height × Spread
D. spectabilis: 2 to 4 feet × 1½ to 3 feet
D. formosa and *D. eximia*: 9 to 24 inches × 12 to 18 inches

The bleeding hearts are old-fashioned, shade-loving plants named for the shape of the blossom—pretty pink, white, or red heart-shaped flowers that dangle from arching stems above beautiful lacy foliage. The loveliest flower is borne by the Asian species *Dicentra spectabilis*, a shrublike, spring-flowering perennial that grows to 36 inches across and bears up to twenty or more arching racemes from which dangle perfect little pink or white hearts. It is long-lived, a true aristocrat, though the foliage dies back when heat comes. The native fringed, or wild, bleeding hearts, *D. formosa* from the western U.S., and *D. eximia* from the eastern U.S., are smaller ever-blooming species that flower throughout the summer and until frost; they are a better choice where summers are really hot.

When, Where, and How to Plant
The best time for planting bleeding hearts, container grown, is just as active growth begins in early spring. Bright shade is ideal. In cool areas where soil moisture is retained evenly, bleeding hearts accept some exposure to full sun. They do best in well-drained, rich, moist, humusy soil in the pH range of 5.0 to 6.0. See "Soil Preparation and Improvement" in the introduction. Follow the planting instructions at the beginning of this chapter. Space planting holes for old-fashioned bleeding hearts 2 feet apart; space holes for wild bleeding hearts 15 to 18 inches apart. Water well. Provide a permanent 3-inch mulch starting 3 inches from the crown.

Growing Tips
Water bleeding hearts deeply every week to ten days for a month or so unless you have a soaking rain. The keys to a long bloom period—particularly in the warmer reaches of the Mid-Atlantic—are sustained moisture and mulch. Fertilize the bed between late winter and early spring, and again in late September to October, with a slow-release, organic, acid fertilizer. In spring, replenish the mulch.

Regional Advice and Care
When the foliage of the old-fashioned species looks ragged, cut the plant back to the ground. Cutting flowering stems of wild bleeding heart that have finished blooming prolongs flowering; wait for several killing frosts before cutting back the foliage entirely. In spring, if late frosts threaten, cover bleeding hearts with frost cloth, old blankets, or burlap. The roots are brittle, so divide bleeding hearts only if needed. Established plants resent being disturbed but with care they can be successfully divided in early spring.

Companion Planting and Design
Delightful massed in shady gardens, especially *D. spectabilis*, among ferns, hostas, and Solomon's seal, with wildflowers, and in rock gardens.

Try These
For its lasting foliage, we recommend *D. formosa*. Our favorite cultivars are 12-inch white 'Aurora'; 15-inch pink 'Bountiful'; 15-inch deep pink 'Luxuriant'; and *D. spectabilis alba*, a lovely white.

Blue False Indigo

Baptisia australis

Botanical Pronunciation
bap-TIZZ-ee-uh aw-STRAY-liss

Other Name
Plains false indigo

Bloom Period and Seasonal Color
Mid-spring; indigo blue

Mature Height × Spread
3 to 4 feet × 2 to 4 feet

Blue false indigo is a bold, 3- to 4-foot plant that in early spring produces multiple stems of beautiful gray-green foliage. By mid-spring, the foliage is topped by 1- to 2-foot flowering spikes that are a magnificent indigo-blue. The flowers last about a month. The leaves and the individual blossoms resemble those of the pea vine but they are much larger, showier, and more substantial. Handsome blue-black seedpods, 1 or 2 inches long, follow the flowers and usually remain handsome until at least the first hard frost. They're lovely in dried arrangements. *Baptisia* is a long-lived perennial—a little slow to get under way but it seems to go on practically forever. And it's a great indigo-blue flower for climates too hot to grow delphinium. A related species, *Baptisia pendula*, has white flowers, and a cross between the two, called 'Purple Smoke', has purplish flowers and lavender-gray stems.

When, Where, and How to Plant
Blue false indigo seeds are fresh when they first start to rattle around in the pod; plant fresh seeds in late summer if you want to start from scratch. Setting out root divisions of young plants in early spring is recommended because blue false indigo is slow to establish itself and doesn't transplant easily. *Baptisia* does best in full sun, but it can take a little filtered shade and still be productive. In partial shade it probably will require staking, or support from a peony ring. It tolerates drought but cannot stand soil that is soggy in winter. Blue false indigo thrives in humusy, somewhat acidic soil, with a pH range 5.5 to 6.5, but can tolerate higher pH. See "Soil Preparation and Improvement" in the introduction. Follow the planting instructions at the beginning of this chapter, spacing the plants about 3 feet apart. Water well. Mulch 1 inch deep starting 3 inches from the crown.

Growing Tips
Water new plants deeply every week to ten days the first month or so unless you have a soaking rain. Fertilize the bed between late winter and early spring, and again in September to October, with a slow-release, organic, acid fertilizer. In spring, replenish the mulch.

Regional Advice and Care
If you cut the plant back by one-third after flowering, it will fill in a few weeks later and become a handsome background "shrub" for the flowerbed. But you lose the seedpods. Removing spent flowers may encourage a few more blooms, but we like to let the end-of-season flower spikes remain for a fall and winter show. Cut blue false indigo to the ground when frosts blacken the foliage. You needn't divide it for ten years or more unless you want to multiply your holdings.

Companion Planting and Design
Blue false indigo's medium-tall mound of foliage and its indigo-blue flowers create strong vertical lines at the middle or back of a large flowering border. It's one of those very substantial plants used to anchor other flowers, and an excellent meadow plant.

Try These
Plant the species.

Chrysanthemum

Dendranthema spp. and hybrids

Botanical Pronunciation
den-DRAN-thuh-muh

Bloom Period and Seasonal Color
Nippon daisies bloom from September or October until frost; Shasta daisies bloom in early summer; hardy mums bloom September and October; in white and many colors

Mature Height × Spread
Nippon Daisies–3 to 5 feet × 3 feet
Shasta Daisies–2 to 4 feet × 3 to 4 feet
Garden Mums–15 inches to 3 feet × 3 to 5 feet

For André, fall is not about potted mums sold for instant fall color. It's about pumpkins and gourds, ornamental grasses, trees and shrubs changing color, berries and witches and goblins, Halloween and Thanksgiving—and *real* chrysanthemums. For wherever color will be needed in September and October, André plants long-lived hardy mums like 'Ryan's Pink', the semi-double pink 'Mei-Kyo', 'Pumpkin Harvest', pale pink 'Venus', and 'Viette's Apricot Glow'. For summer bouquets, the Viettes plant green-eyed Nippon daisies, *Nipponanthemum nipponicum* (formerly *Chrysanthemum nipponicum*), and sparkling white Shasta daisies, *Leucanthemum × superbum* (formerly *C. maximum*). Nippon daisies are great border flowers with handsome rhododendron-like foliage. Shastas are big, beautiful, single or double daisies. For edging, plant 12-inch-tall *Dendranthema pacificum*, a groundcover mum whose leaves are edged thinly with silver.

When, Where, and How to Plant

Set out container-grown plants in early spring, in summer, or in early fall. Nippon daisies and single-flowered Shastas need full sun; Shasta doubles do well in light shade. The hardy mums tolerate some drought and cannot stand soil that is soggy in winter. A wide range of soil types are suitable but a slightly acidic pH is best. See "Soil Preparation and Improvement" in the introduction. Follow the planting instructions at the beginning of this chapter, spacing the plants about 2 feet apart. Water well. Mulch 2 inches deep starting 3 inches from the crown.

Growing Tips

For a month or so after planting, water deeply every week to ten days unless you have a good soaking rain. Fertilize the bed with a slow-release organic fertilizer for acid-loving plants between late winter and early spring, and again in early summer. Replenish the mulch.

Regional Advice and Care

After the first flush of bloom, deadhead Shastas back to the nearest side buds; when these have bloomed, cut the plants down to the basal foliage, which will remain attractive until frost. Mums need to be divided every two or three years to remain fully productive; the best time is early spring or after the plants become dormant in fall.

Companion Planting and Design

Nippon and Shasta daisies are handsome in perennial beds and flowering borders. For edging, plant the beautiful 12-inch high groundcover mum, silver-edged *D. pacificum*. It spreads rapidly to make a 3½ foot mat, and bears very small tansy-like flowers in October. For glorious fall color, interplant perennials with hardy garden mums for September to October color.

Try These

André's favorite Shasta daisies are 2-foot 'Switzerland', a big, long-lived beautiful Viette introduction that blooms in June and July; and long-blooming 'Ryan's White', which flowers from June to September. 'Becky' is another good single Shasta.

Columbine

Aquilegia spp. and cultivars

Botanical Pronunciation
ack-wih-LEE-jee-uh

Bloom Period and Seasonal Color
Mid-spring to early summer; white, yellow, blue, rusty pinks, lavenders, purples, reddish orange, bicolors

Mature Height × Spread
1 to 3 feet × ½ to 1 feet

    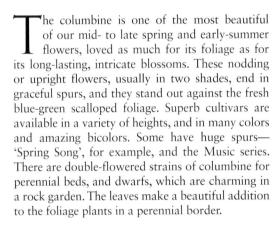

The columbine is one of the most beautiful of our mid- to late spring and early-summer flowers, loved as much for its foliage as for its long-lasting, intricate blossoms. These nodding or upright flowers, usually in two shades, end in graceful spurs, and they stand out against the fresh blue-green scalloped foliage. Superb cultivars are available in a variety of heights, and in many colors and amazing bicolors. Some have huge spurs—'Spring Song', for example, and the Music series. There are double-flowered strains of columbine for perennial beds, and dwarfs, which are charming in a rock garden. The leaves make a beautiful addition to the foliage plants in a perennial border.

When, Where, and How to Plant
Fresh seed gathered from plants and sown in late spring or early summer produces plants the following year. For bloom this year, in early spring set out container-grown plants or root divisions any time after the ground can be worked. In cool areas, you can plant columbine in the fall. Columbines succeed in sun in areas where the climate is moderate, and prefer some noon shade in warm regions. They do well in shade gardens in Washington, D.C. *Aquilegia* needs well-drained, rich, evenly moist soil. See "Soil Preparation and Improvement" in the introduction. Follow the planting instructions at the beginning of this chapter, spacing the plants 12 to 15 inches apart in groups of at least 3 to 5. Taller varieties may need staking. Water well. Mulch 2 inches deep starting 3 inches from the crown.

Growing Tip
Water new plants deeply every week to ten days for a month or so unless you have a soaking rain. Fertilize the bed between late winter and early spring, and again in late September to October, with a slow-release organic fertilizer for acid-loving plants. Replenish the mulch.

Regional Advice and Care
After the flowers have bloomed, cut the foliage way back, almost to the crown; it will grow back and make a beautiful low foliage filler for the rest of the season. Columbines generally live only four or five years, and need no dividing. They often self-sow; dig out those you don't want and transplant elsewhere. Leaf miners are the biggest concern.

Companion Planting and Design
The columbines do well in part shade, so they are often naturalized along sun-dappled paths through woodlands. The old-fashioned garden columbine, *Aquilegia vulgaris*, granny's bonnet, is a favorite cottage garden flower. The native eastern wild columbine, *A. canadensis*, can be resistant to the leaf minor that defaces the foliage of less hardy breeds; it self-sows so it's a good choice for naturalizing.

Try These
Among our favorites are varieties of *A. flabellata*, the fan columbine, which grows to 8 to 10 inches, needs no staking, and is longer lived than other species. 'Nora Barlow' is a beautiful dark pink and white, double-flowered columbine.

Coneflower

Rudbeckia fulgida 'Goldsturm'

Botanical Pronunciation
rud-BECK-ee-uh FULL-jih-duh

Other Name
Black-eyed Susan

Bloom Period and Seasonal Color
Summer into fall; dark gold with a brown eye

Mature Height × Spread
1½ to 2½ feet × 1½ to 2 feet

The showy perennial 'Goldsturm' is probably the finest of the yellow black-eyed Susan types. André's father, nurseryman Martin Viette, imported it from Germany many years ago and André still loves it. It blooms freely throughout the midsummer and well into fall on compact, bushy plants 18 to 30 inches high. The ray florets are deep yellow and the cone-shaped centers bronze-black. The foliage stays in good condition no matter how hot it gets. 'Goldsturm' is such a superior performer it was chosen as a Plant of the Year by the Perennial Plant Association. It self-sows aggressively so it's a good choice for wild gardens. Removing spent blooms early in the flowering season encourages repeat flowering. The flowers dry well. Leave a few for the birds, for winter interest, and to reseed.

When, Where, and How to Plant

You can plant coneflower from seedlings started indoors, or as seed in the open garden, any time after the ground can be worked in spring. But you will have bigger plants sooner if you set out container-grown plants or root divisions (friends often have coneflowers to share). *Rudbeckia* withstands high heat and thrives in full sun; in bright or partial shade it blooms well but tends to grow toward brighter light. A well-drained, light, and fertile soil is best, pH 5.0 to 6.5. See "Soil Preparation and Improvement" in the introduction. Follow the planting instructions at the beginning of this chapter, spacing the plants 8 to 12 inches apart. Water well. Mulch 2 inches deep starting 3 inches from the crown.

Growing Tips

Water a new planting deeply every week to ten days the first season unless you have a good soaking rain. Coneflower is drought resistant, so once it's established, local rainfall will be enough to keep it growing. Fertilize the bed between late winter and early spring, and again September to October, with a slow-release, organic, acid fertilizer.

Regional Advice and Care

After the first flush of bloom, deadhead to the next pair of buds. The cut stems last a few days in water. The rhizomatous plants spread, creating large colonies. Divide the planting in early spring every four years to keep the bed full and flowery.

Companion Planting and Design

'Goldsturm' self-sows and is a good naturalizer. A very tough plant that glows gold throughout the summer, it's an excellent edger for stands of ornamental grasses, for meadow gardens, and for hot, sunny flower borders. Let the sooty black seedheads stand when flowering begins to wind down as cold weather approaches, and you will be providing food for birds, and adding interest to the garden in the winter months.

Try These

We like 'Goldsturm'; Mark's 12- to 18-inch *Rudbeckia fulgida* Viette's Little Suzy®, whose foliage turns mahogany in cold weather; and 6- to 7-foot *R. nitida* 'Herbstsonne', beloved of Monarchs.

Coral Bells

Heuchera spp. and hybrids

Botanical Pronunciation
HEW-kur-uh

Other Name
Alumroot

Bloom Period and Seasonal Color
May to July; coral, deep red, pink, white

Mature Height × Spread
12 to 24 inches × 18 to 20 inches

In late spring and early summer, coral bells' dainty, eye-catching panicles of tiny bell-shaped flowers sway on 1- to 2-foot wiry stalks arching high above the foliage. The Bressingham hybrids bloom in shades of coral to deep red, pink, and white. The leaves of the species are low-growing, evergreen, dark green scalloped clusters that remain attractive most of the year. But these days the excitement generated by *Heuchera* has to do with cultivars with colorful foliage. *H. micrantha* 'Palace Purple' was named Plant of the Year by the Perennial Plant Association. It introduced a *Heuchera* planted primarily for its foliage. 'Palace Purple' has ivy-shaped leaves that are mahogany-red above, beet red below, and is especially handsome with the tans and reds that dominate in the fall. The flowers are off white.

When, Where, and How to Plant
Set out container plants or root divisions anytime after the ground can be worked in spring. Plants that are still near-dormant or just beginning to grow will give the best performance. 'Palace Purple' can stand more direct sun in the cool reaches of Zone 6, but it needs noon protection from hot sun in Zones 7 and 8. *Heuchera* is fairly drought resistant, but the leaves scorch if the plant dries out. It needs well-drained slightly acidic soil, pH 5.5 to 6.5. See "Soil Preparation and Improvement" in the introduction. Follow the planting instructions at the beginning of this chapter, spacing the plants 12 to 18 inches apart. Water well. Mulch 2 to 3 inches deep starting 3 inches from the crown.

Growing Tips
For the first month or so, water new plants deeply every week to ten days unless you have a good soaking rain. Since *Heuchera* is fairly drought resistant, water when you water the other perennials. Fertilize the bed between late winter and early spring, and again in September to October, with a slow-release organic fertilizer for acid-loving plants.

Regional Advice and Care
In cold climates, mulch with branches of evergreens after the first solid frost. Deadhead if you want to prolong the flowering. If your main interest is the foliage, removing the flowers before they grow makes for a better-looking plant. In late summer, cut off leaves that are less than perfect and allow the new foliage to develop and stay for winter. Divide every four or five years in early spring.

Companion Planting and Design
Coral bells' foliage is low to the ground, so the plant is used at the front of a flower border, or to edge a path, whether the plant is being grown for its foliage or its flowers.

Try These
'Palace Purple' is our favorite for foliage, but *H. villosa* 'Purpurea' comes close. July to October, blush pink bells sway above the glowing purple foliage. 'White Cloud' blooms May to July. 'Cathedral Windows' and 'Pewter Veil' are choice, as are many of the newer varieties.

Daylily

Hemerocallis spp. and cultivars

Botanical Pronunciation hem-ur-oh-KAL-iss

Bloom Period and Seasonal Color
June through September; near white, creamy yellow, orange, gold, purple, pink, fiery red, lavender, bicolors

Mature Height × Spread
Standards: 1 to 5 feet × 2 to 4 feet
Miniatures: 12 to 14 inches
(some reach 40 inches) × 1½ to 2 feet

Daylilies, André's favorite summer flower, bloom July through August in the gardens surrounding the Viette home in the Shenandoah Valley, and thousands more flower in the trial fields below the nursery. Enhanced performance has given rise to a whole new breed of these easy-care, long-lived flowers. The blossoms range from 2 inches to huge 8-inch trumpets. Large-flowered daylilies typically open one to three blossoms per stem every day; the miniatures open three to seven blossoms per stem every day. The daylilies classed as tetraploids have intense color, heavily textured petals, and strong stems—'Viette's Cranberry Red' and 'Viracocho' are examples. Those labeled as diploids are showy and daintier—'Stella de Oro', the miniature famous for its everblooming quality, is a diploid.

When, Where, and How to Plant
Plant in spring. Soak tuberous roots for two to six hours before planting. You can plant container-grown daylilies anytime, but early spring is best. Daylilies are adaptable. They will bloom most fully in full sun but also bloom well in bright shade. They thrive in clay, loam, or sandy soils, and tolerate heat, wind, cold, and seashore conditions. See "Soil Preparation and Improvement" in the introduction. If you are planting bare-root plants, fan the roots out in the planting hole, and set the crown so it is about 1 inch below the soil surface. Plant container-grown daylilies following the planting instructions at the beginning of this chapter. Space daylilies 24 inches apart. Water well. Mulch with pine needles, pine bark, or hardwood bark 2 to 3 inches deep starting 3 inches from the crown.

Growing Tips
Water deeply every week for the first two weeks. Once the plants are growing well, water deeply in lasting droughts. In mid-fall and again in late winter fertilize established beds with a slow-release organic fertilizer. Maintain the mulch.

Regional Advice and Care
After a couple of hard frosts, remove the foliage. Divide in mid-spring or early fall every four to five years.

Companion Planting and Design
With daylilies André likes *Rudbeckia*, ornamental grasses, sunny *Heliopsis* and *Helianthus*, *Crocosmia*, and poppies. Other good companion plants are fall-blooming asters and mums that take over as the daylilies begin to fade away.

Try These
For a long season of bloom, look for "rebloomer" daylilies, which flower early and again in late summer or early fall, or from summer into frost, such as 'Happy Returns'. For a small garden, André recommends little 'Stella de Oro' that bears somewhat fragrant 2¾-inch gold flowers with green throats. A three-year-old plant produces literally hundreds of blooms. Among daylilies with a marked fragrance are 'Fragrant Light', 'Hyperion', 'Lemon Cap', and the species *H. citrine*. The daylilies billed as evergreen are most successful in the frost-free areas of the South.

Globe Thistle

Echinops ritro 'Taplow Blue'

Botanical Pronunciation
eck-ih-NOP-sis RYE-troe

Bloom Period and Seasonal Color
June to August; steely blue

Mature Height × Spread
3 to 4 feet × 2 to 3 feet

When you are looking for a plant that will add texture and variety to the perennial border, consider the globe thistle. It is a stately, erect, thistlelike plant, 2 to 4 feet tall with big, beautiful spiny leaves that are gray-green and hairy on the underside. The foliage is spectacular, reason enough for growing the plant. From June through August the globe thistle raises handsome, spiky, perfectly round flower heads that last for a couple of months. An added benefit is that they attract goldfinches and nocturnal moths. The flower heads of 'Taplow Blue' are steely blue, and about 2 inches across. They add interesting texture and color to arrangements of fresh flowers, dry easily, and look great in dried winter arrangements. 'Taplow Blue' is the most popular of the cultivars.

When, Where, and How to Plant

Set out container-grown plants in spring. Globe thistle blooms fully given six hours of full sun, and benefits from afternoon shade, especially in warmer regions. Echinops is not particular as to soil pH, as long as the soil is well drained. It spreads in moist, rich soil, which may or may not be a blessing. See "Soil Preparation and Improvement" in the introduction. Follow the planting instructions at the beginning of this chapter, spacing the plants 20 to 24 inches apart. Water well. Mulch 2 to 3 inches deep starting 3 inches from the crown.

Growing Tips

Water new plants deeply every week or ten days for the first month or so unless you have a soaking rain. Established globe thistles tolerate drought. Fertilize the bed between late winter and early spring, and again in late September to October, with a slow-release organic fertilizer for acid-loving plants. Maintain the mulch.

Regional Advice and Care

To encourage reblooming, deadhead flowering stems back by one-third or half to a pair of basal leaves; if cut back twice they often bloom a third time. At the end of the season, leave the flower heads for the birds. In early spring, cut back to the crown. Division is usually not needed—and difficult—but can be successfully undertaken in early spring. If you let the flower heads remain over the winter, globe thistle may self-sow.

Companion Planting and Design

The globe thistles are handsome massed in a wild garden, and fronting tall shrubs. We grow a stand with ferns, astilbe, and Japanese iris as a backdrop to rocks encircling a small water garden. Attractive companion plants are ornamental grasses, Siberian iris, peonies, yucca, and coneflowers.

Try These

'Taplow Blue' is a favorite. The flower heads produced by 'Veitch's Blue' are a deeper blue than 'Taplow Blue'. If flowers are your main interest, this one is also a good choice because it often reblooms.

Hosta

Hosta spp. and hybrids

Botanical Pronunciation HOSS-tuh

Other Name Plantain lily

Bloom Period and Seasonal Color Summer to early fall; white, lavender, purple flowers, foliage may be green, chartreuse, blue, blue-green, gold, or white or gold variegated

Mature Height × Spread
2 to 36 inches × 2 to 60 inches

The hostas are clump-forming foliage plants—the finest of all foliage plants for shaded places. From low mounds of bold leaves, hostas raise slender flower stems studded with bell-like blooms in summer. The flowers of some are fragrant. Newer cultivars, like 'Aphrodite', have remarkably beautiful double flowers. There are dwarfs 2 inches across, giants 5 feet across, leaves that may be narrow or broad, smooth textured, quilted, puckered, or semi-twisted. The colors range from rich or muted shades of blue-green to yellow-white. The countless colorful variegations light up dim corners. There are green leaves with narrow or broad, white or gold edges, or interior splotches, and yellow-green leaves with dark green splotchings and edgings. Deer, alas, love hostas as much as we do, as do voles. Plant hostas with Soil Perfector® (from Espoma) to prevent losing them to these short-tailed little field mice.

When, Where, and How to Plant

Catalogs ship hostas bare root in early spring but they're slow to develop. Container-grown plants can be set out anytime after the ground has warmed. Hostas thrive in filtered light; yellow foliaged and variegated forms tolerate more sun. Where there are late frosts, hostas are safer under tall trees. Adaptable as to pH, hostas need well-drained, moist, humusy, fertile soil. See "Soil Preparation and Improvement" in the introduction. Follow the planting instructions at the beginning of this chapter, setting the plants an inch or two below ground level. Space small-leaved varieties 18 to 24 inches apart, and large-leaved forms 24 to 36 inches apart. Water deeply, and mulch well.

Growing Tips

Water a new planting every week or ten days for a month or two unless you have a good soaking rain. Maintain soil moisture for the first two or three years; established plants tolerate drought. Don't overdo; moisture encourages slugs. In early spring and mid-fall, fertilize with a slow-release, organic, acidic fertilizer.

Regional Advice and Care

In fall clean the beds since fallen leaves can harbor slugs. If late frosts threaten, cover hostas with frost cloth, old blankets, or burlap. Harvest the flowers for bouquets. Hostas need three years to mature and the older they get the more impressive they become. Divide them if you wish in early spring or fall. In prolonged rainy weather, slugs attack hostas—sprinkle diatomaceous earth, silica gel, or slug bait around the plants. You also can trap them with small saucers of beer.

Companion Planting and Design

Mass hostas using a single type in a woodland garden. Or, combine contrasting colors and sizes. Small white variegated hostas make a neat edging for shaded paths. The hostas start up rather late, so they're good companion plants for spring bulbs.

Try These

André was one of the original charter members of the American Hosta Society. He loves all hostas, especially big, bold 'Sum and Substance', 'Blue Mammoth', which is 4 feet wide, and perfumed *Hosta* 'Fragrant Bouquet', and *H. plantaginea*.

Japanese Anemone

Anemone spp. and hybrids

Botanical Pronunciation
an-eh-MOE-nee

Other Name
Windflower

Bloom Period and Seasonal Color
August to September; white, pink, deep rose

Mature Height × Spread
2 to 5 feet × 1½ to 3½ feet

Fall-flowering anemones are late summer and early fall's most beautiful tall flowers. Low, attractive clusters of divided leaves that are crimson on the reverse side appear first. Then multi-branched stems develop, and toward late summer the plants climb to 2 to 3 feet higher and for many weeks silvery buds open to airy flowers 2 to 3 inches in diameter. The single-flowered types have five rounded petals surrounding a central heart of bright yellow stamens. There are also doubles. *Anemone hupehensis* is covered in fall with attractive seedheads rather like cotton balls. The stems withstand whipping winds. *A.* × *hybrida* varieties are larger and more beautiful, and have been bred to many forms and colors, but they don't have the cottony seedballs.

When, Where, and How to Plant
Plant a container-grown Japanese anemone after the ground has warmed in spring—April in Zone 8, mid-May in Zones 6 and 7. In the warmer areas Japanese anemone does best in morning sun or all-day bright shade. The Japanese anemone needs well-drained soil, and does well in a pH of 5.5 to 6.0. See "Soil Preparation and Improvement" in the introduction. Follow the planting instructions at the beginning of this chapter, spacing the plants at least 24 inches apart. The tallest cultivars will need staking. Water well. Mulch 2 inches deep starting 3 inches from the crown.

Growing Tips
For the first month to six weeks, water a new plant every week to ten days unless there's a soaking rain.

Established clumps are fairly drought resistant, but best results are obtained when plants are well watered during dry periods. Fertilize the bed between late winter and early spring with a slow-release organic fertilizer for acid-loving plants. Replenish the mulch.

Regional Advice and Care
Deadhead to keep the plant attractive. When the foliage dies down, cut the plant back to the crown. In Zone 6, it's a good idea to cover hybrids with a winter mulch. These plants need two or three seasons to become established and resent disturbance; divide every ten years to refresh the clump.

Companion Planting and Design
The Japanese anemones are lovely growing at the edge of a woodland with ferns, hostas, and epimediums. We've seen white Japanese anemones blooming as follow-on plants in a bed for spring bulbs with a formal gray stone wall in the background, and that was quite a sight! Anemones are lovely backed by a tall ornamental grass.

Try These
The heirloom variety 'Honorine Jobert' is a gleaming white, single-flowered anemone 3 to 4 feet tall. 'Margarette' is smaller and produces masses of double or semi-double, bright rose-pink blooms on stems 2 to 3 feet tall. 'Queen Charlotte' is an exquisite pink semi-double.

Lamb's Ear

Stachys byzantina

Botanical Pronunciation
STAY-kiss biz-un-TYE-nuh

Other Name Woolly betony

Bloom Period and Seasonal Color
Silvery foliage all season long; in summer, violet or white flower spikes

Mature Height × Spread
6 to 15 inches × 12 to 24 inches

Lamb's ear is included in flowering borders for the unusual texture and the striking silvery light it brings to the dominant greens. The plant develops a mound of long, oval, semi-evergreen leaves that are so furry they invite stroking, and so luminous they catch moonlight. From midsummer until frosts, lamb's ears produces fuzzy, semi-upright spikes of small flowers that are usually violet or white. Most gardeners remove the flowering spikes as they begin to develop to keep the mound low, and the focus on the leaves. The plant has been a favorite long enough to have acquired a number of common names, including lamb's tongue and lamb's tails, which describe the shape of the leaves.

When, Where, and How to Plant
Set out container plants or root divisions in early spring or in early fall. Lamb's ears grows well in full sun in cool Zone 6, but in hot zones 7 and 8 it can do with protection from noon sun and from hot late afternoon sun. It is not particular as to soil pH, but requires a very well-drained site and light, fertile, humusy soil. See "Soil Preparation and Improvement" in the introduction. Follow the planting instructions at the beginning of this chapter, spacing the plants 12 to 24 inches apart and 1 inch above ground level. Water slowly and deeply. Mulch an inch deep with something fine textured, like cocoa hulls or pine needles, starting 3 inches from the outer leaves.

Growing Tips
Water a new planting three times during every thirty days, slowly and deeply. Lamb's ears tolerates drought once established, but wetting the foliage, especially in hot weather, may encourage disease. Avoid overhead sprinkling and frequent shallow watering.

Regional Advice and Care
Remove the flower spikes to keep the plants tidy; if you let the flowers open and go to seed that will cause the foliage to deteriorate. Cut out leaves and stems that are showing signs of rot. Leave healthy foliage in place for the winter, and remove it before growth begins in spring.

Companion Planting and Design
Lamb's ears is a good container plant, and gives pleasure wherever you plant it. It's a delight as an underplanting for sedums 'Ruby Glow' and 'Vera Jameson', and lovely nestled in fallen leaves. To make a show, you need to plant lamb's ears in groups of at least three plants. The leaves dry well and can be included in tussie mussies and dried wreaths.

Try These
André loves 'Big Ears' ('Helen von Stein'), whose silvery leaves are twice the size of other varieties and better able to withstand heat and humidity. The non-flowering 3- to 6-inch high 'Silver Carpet' spreads rapidly and is choice for cooler regions.

Marsh Rose Mallow

Hibiscus moscheutos and hybrids

Botanical Pronunciation
hye-BISS-kiss moss-KEW-tus

Other Name
Swamp rose mallow

Bloom Period and Seasonal Color
Midsummer to frost; red, white, pink, bicolors

Mature Height × Spread
3 to 8 feet × 2 to 5 feet

The most familiar hibiscus used to be the tropical *Hibiscus rosa-sinensis*, a gorgeous funnel-shaped flower that lasts just a day. And the lovely old-fashioned rose-of-Sharon, shrub althea, *H. syriacus*, is a woody flowering plant or small tree described in the chapter on Shrubs. But in recent years, the huge blooms of the marsh rose mallow have captured the imagination of gardeners. It's a shrubby perennial that in midsummer bears funnel-shaped flowers 7, 10, and 12 inches across. In late spring, the plant's new growth shoots up 3 to 8 feet. The canes eventually sprawl but the plant does not need staking—just lots of sprawl space. When in bloom, it's eye-catching even at some distance. The dried pods are handsome.

When, Where, and How to Plant

Set out container-grown or dormant roots (bare root) in early spring in full sun; in part shade, it won't produce as many big flowers. Rose mallow does well in moist situations, and in a wide range of soils. It does best where the pH is between 5.5 and 7.0. See "Soil Preparation and Improvement" in the introduction. Follow the planting instructions at the beginning of this chapter; provide a hole twice the size of the rootball and deep enough to set the crown 2 inches below the soil surface. If you plant more than one, space plants on 4- to 5-foot centers. Rose mallow doesn't have to be staked, but it benefits from the support of a wall or a fence corner where it also gets air. Water deeply. Mulch 2 to 3 inches deep with pine needles or decayed leaves starting 3 inches from the crown.

Growing Tips

Water a new plant deeply every week to ten days for the first season unless you have a good soaking rain. Rose mallow resists some drought once it's established, so local rainfall should be enough to keep it growing. Fertilize the bed in fall and again between late winter and early spring with a slow-release, organic, acidic fertilizer.

Regional Advice and Care

The blooms, like tropical hibiscus, last a day then turn to brown mush. Removing them keeps the plant more attractive. Late in the season, we allow seedheads to form and stay on the plant through winter. Cut the stems to the ground in early spring and in late spring new stems will appear. To keep the plant groomed, author Tracy DiSabato-Aust recommends cutting the stems back by half when they are 18 inches high.

Companion Planting and Design

Rose mallow is handsome in a corner, and beautiful blooming through and over a low metal fence.

Try These

The flowery red 'Lord Baltimore' strain has beautifully lobed leaves; light pink 'Appleblossom' has deeper rose margins; 'Turn of the Century' is a pink-on-white bicolor; and the pink-and-white bicolor 'Kopper King' has copper foliage.

Monarda

Monarda didyma

Botanical Pronunciation
muh-NAR-duh DID-ih-muh

Other Name
Bee balm

Bloom Period and Seasonal Color
July and August; scarlet, pink, cerise, red, white, violet

Mature Height × Spread
2 to 5 feet × 2 to 3 feet

We call it "monarda" now and grow modern varieties with perennials and in wild and meadow gardens for their beauty and long season of bloom. But in the past, monarda was called "bee balm" and grown primarily for its herbal properties. (It was also known as "bergamot" and "Oswego tea.") The tips of young shoots were—and still are—used as garnishes for drinks and salads. An herb tea was, and is, made of the pointed, bright green leaves, which have the scent of mint-bergamot. Middling tall, the attractive globelike flowers are made up of whorls of shaggy tubular petals surrounded by red-tinted bracts. They bloom throughout the summer on stiff stems above neat plants and are wildly attractive to hummingbirds, butterflies, and bees. Monarda is a native American plant. It makes an excellent cut flower.

When, Where, and How to Plant

Set out container plants or root divisions in spring, summer, or fall. Monarda blooms fully in direct sun, or with afternoon shade, even in cooler regions. It thrives in well-drained, moist, humusy soil that is slightly acidic, pH 5.0 to 6.5. See "Soil Preparation and Improvement" in the introduction and follow the planting instructions at the beginning of this chapter. The plant is susceptible to mildew so plant it where it has plenty of space and good air circulation all around; it will fill its space quickly. Water well. Mulch 2 to 3 inches deep starting 3 inches from the crown.

Growing Tips

Water new plantings of monarda deeply every week to ten days for a month or so unless you have a soaking rain. Maintain soil moisture during dry spells. Fertilize the bed between late winter and early spring with an organic slow-release fertilizer at the rate of 4 pounds per 100 square feet. In spring, replenish the mulch.

Regional Advice and Care

Deadheading lengthens the period of bloom. If the plant shows signs of mildew after flowering, cut the stems back to just above the fresh new foliage at the base. Monarda spreads thanks to creeping stems that can quickly fill a considerable area; planting it in 3- to 5-gallon containers keeps it under control. You can divide the planting every two to three years in late summer; just pull individual rooted stems from the center of the clump and replant them with space all around.

Companion Planting and Design

Monarda provides splashes of subtle color throughout midsummer. We like it in perennial borders, meadow and wild gardens, anywhere that we get to see the wildlife it attracts in action. It's a good cut flower, but when you are harvesting bee balm, watch out for bees who may think it belongs to them.

Try These

We recommend mildew-resistant varieties, such as 48- to 60-inch 'Jacob Cline', which has large, dark red flowers; 30- to 48-inch 'Marshall's Delight', a compact pink-flowered variety; and an exciting newer dwarf, 10- to 12-inch 'Petite Delight', which has lavender-pink flowers.

Oriental Poppy

Papaver orientalie

Botanical Pronunciation
puh-PAY-vur or-ee-en-TAL-ee

Bloom Period and Seasonal Color
Spring and early summer; red, orange, salmon, pink, white, bicolors

Mature Height × Spread
1 to 4 feet × 1 to 3 feet

Poppies come in all sizes. Silky, shiny, and colorful, they're a mainstay of sunny gardens everywhere. The stars of the poppy domain are the big, crinkled-silk Oriental poppies. A spangle of these brilliant, beautiful blossoms lifts a garden from ordinary to extraordinary. The blossoms measure 5 to 10 inches across, and they unfold in spring and early summer in vibrant colors and color combinations. The petals of some are splotched at the base in a contrasting color, usually black or mahogany, and others have contrasting edges. Though the wiry stems bend to even a little wind, the flowers withstand storms of amazing proportions. The fuzzy pods are attractive in dried arrangements. The deeply cut foliage dies after the flowers have bloomed and new foliage appears in the fall.

When, Where, and How to Plant

Set out sturdy container-grown plants in early spring. Poppies need full sun, but can be productive in filtered shade. In Zone 8 they succeed in bright shade under tall trees. Poppies tolerate a range of soils, pH 6.0 to 7.5, as long as it is well-drained, deeply dug, light, somewhat sandy, but humusy enough to hold moisture. See "Soil Preparation and Improvement" in the introduction. Follow the planting instructions at the beginning of this chapter. Set the crowns 1½ inches below the soil level and space the plants about 2 to 3 feet apart. Water deeply. Mulch 2 to 3 inches deep starting 3 inches from the crown.

Growing Tips

Maintain moisture during the growing and flowering period, but don't force watering during the dormant period that follows. When the foliage begins to re-grow in the fall, fertilize with a slow-release, organic, acidic fertilizer. In late winter, replenish the mulch.

Regional Advice and Care

The big, decorative seedheads should be removed: it's better for the plant. When poppies die the foliage deteriorates; allow it to yellow and brown, then gently remove it from the crown. Oriental poppies have a fleshy taproot that is difficult to dig and transplant. They're very long lived and rarely need dividing; the best time to dig a poppy is after it becomes dormant. These are gorgeous cut flowers and will last longer if you sear the bottom of the stem with a hot flame before putting it into water.

Companion Planting and Design

Don't plant poppies with flowers requiring moist soil in summer. Since the Orientals are unsightly as the foliage is dying, they belong toward the back of the border, fronted by plants that will grow big as they fade away—dahlias, asters, chrysanthemums, for example.

Try These

Oriental poppies are cold hardy but difficult south of Zone 7. The most beautiful and easy to grow are 'Cedar Hill', light pink; 'Maiden's Blush', pale salmon pink; brilliant 'Raspberry Queen'; and fringed 'Turkenlouis', a fiery orange red.

Peony

Paeonia spp. and cultivars

Botanical Pronunciation
pee-OH-nee-uh

Bloom Period and Seasonal Color
Spring; white, shades of pink and rose, coral, deep crimson, bicolors

Mature Height × Spread
1 to 3 feet × 1 to 3 feet

There are two types of peonies—the familiar herbaceous perennials, and woody forms that are classed with shrubs. The herbaceous peonies often outlive the gardeners who plant them. The showy flowers bloom in April and May for four to six weeks, producing huge heads of crinkled silk—single, semi-double, fully double—that make awesomely luscious bouquets. The doubles are the most popular, but interest is growing in the exotic single-flowered and Japanese peonies. Peonies must have a chilling period at below 40 degrees Fahrenheit to flower. The best bets for Zone 8 are herbaceous types that flower early and in midseason, and the Japanese and single herbaceous peonies.

When, Where, and How to Plant

In our area, we plant container-grown peonies between early September to early December. They require a minimum of six hours of the strongest sun and are most successful in well-drained, fertile, humusy, neutral or slightly alkaline soils, pH 6.0 to 7.5, but tolerate mildly acidic soils. See "Soil Preparation and Improvement" in the introduction. Do not use barnyard or composted manure with peonies. Provide a hole 24 inches wide and 18 inches deep and follow the planting instructions for container-grown plants at the beginning of this chapter. Space peonies 36 inches apart. Water well. Do not mulch.

Growing Tips

Water plants every week or ten days for the first month or so, unless you have a soaking rain, then water as needed. Water established peonies during droughts. In fall and in early spring, fertilize the bed with a slow-release organic fertilizer.

Regional Advice and Care

Remove invasive groundcovers and weeds by hand. Harvest slow-to-open side blooms; they may open in vase water. In early September to October, cut the stems to the ground and burn them. That's the moment to divide or transplant peonies. Provide each piece of the crown with three to seven eyes, and plant so the eyes are 2 inches below ground level. Transplanted peonies need a year or two to re-establish themselves.

Companion Planting and Design

Plant peonies in groups of four to eight in lawns, and in groups of two or three to anchor large flowering borders. In snow country they are planted in rows to hedge walks, and even driveways, because the foliage dies away in fall, leaving space for snow removal.

Try These

Peonies were the favorite flowers of André's father, the late nurseryman Martin Viette. A world-famous peony grower, he once won seventeen out of nineteen blue ribbons at the International Peony Show. André still grows Martin Viette's favorites—here they are in the order of his preference: 'Gay Paree', 'Sword Dance', 'Sea Shell', the Lobata hybrids, 'Jan Van Leeuwen', 'Tomate Boku', 'Nick Shaylor', and fragrant 'Philippe Revoire'.

Perennial Salvia

Salvia × sylvestris 'May Night'

Botanical Pronunciation
SAL-vee-uh sill-VES-tris

Bloom Period and Seasonal Color
June to August; midnight blue

Mature Height × Spread
1 ½ to 2 feet × 1 to 1 ½ feet

This perennial salvia is a tough plant that winters over even in Zone 3. Square-stemmed like its kissin' cousin *Salvia splendens*, described in the chapter on Annuals, perennial salvia has a whole other look, more that of a small upright shrub with dark green, pointy leaves. The slim flowering spikes of 'May Night' ('Mainacht') are a rich, wonderful, midnight violet-blue. Growing in full sun, the flower spikes rise straight up like a candelabra and they bloom for weeks, followed by reddish bracts that are attractive in their own right. In less light, 'May Night' grows taller and sprawls so widely you'd hardly recognize it. Deadheading extends the flowering period. 'May Night' was chosen as Plant of the Year by the Perennial Plant Association.

When, Where, and How to Plant

Set out container-grown plants anytime; set out rooted divisions in early to mid-spring or late summer. Salvia needs full sun to stay trim looking, but while it sprawls widely in partial shade, it still blooms well. Perennial salvia is tolerant as to pH, but needs a site that is well drained and soil that is fertile and humusy. See "Soil Preparation and Improvement" in the introduction. Follow the planting instructions at the beginning of this chapter, spacing the plants 24 to 30 inches apart. Water well. Mulch 2 to 3 inches deep starting 3 inches from the crown.

Growing Tips

For the first two months, water newly planted perennial salvia every week to ten days unless you have a soaking rain. Then, water only as needed.

Fertilize the bed between late winter and early spring with a slow-release, organic, acidic fertilizer at the rate of 4 pounds per 100 square feet. In spring, replenish the mulch.

Regional Advice and Care

Deadhead down to a pair of lateral leaves, and perennial salvia reblooms beautifully. André has seen salvia rebloom three and four times when the flowers are deadheaded right after blooming. If the plant falls open and gets stringy looking after blooming, you can cut it down to the crown and it will usually re-grow and, depending on your climate, may have time to re-bloom. After such radical treatment it's a good idea to fertilize the plant and make sure the soil doesn't go dry. Dividing, which isn't often necessary, is best undertaken in early spring.

Companion Planting and Design

Perennial salvia is the perfect plant for the middle of the border between airy summer flowers like boltonia, sturdy yarrow, and dainty coreopsis 'Moonbeam'. We like it anchoring clumps of flowers with light variegated foliage.

Try These

'May Night' is André's favorite but there are other perennial salvias and more are coming because it is a very useful border plant. 'Rose Wine' is the rose-pink version of 'May Night'. And now there's a white perennial salvia that comes to us from Germany called 'Snow Hill' that makes a striking plant in part shade.

Phlox

Phlox paniculata cultivars

Botanical Pronunciation
FLOCKS puh-nick-you-LAY-tuh

Other Name
Summer phlox

Bloom Period and Seasonal Color
July to September; white

Mature Height × Spread
2 to 5 feet × 1½ to 3 feet

The full flower heads of *Phlox paniculata* filled old-time midsummer gardens with luscious pastels, and homes with their sweet scent. An American native, the species bears big, rounded heads of open-faced, silky-soft florets. This was the backbone of summer borders until its vulnerability to mildew—and a strong tendency to self-sow and come back in magenta—caused gardeners to forget about it. Now it's making a comeback in healthy and beautiful cultivars such as 'David', named a Plant of the Year by the Perennial Plant Association. It is praised for the bright white, delightfully fragrant flowers that bloom from mid-July to September. Its resistance to powdery mildew, according to PPA, is better than that of other phloxes.

When, Where, and How to Plant

Set out container-grown plants in early fall or spring. Phlox will bloom most fully in full sun, but also flowers in partial shade or bright filtered light. 'David' tolerates a wide pH range, but to be all it can be, it requires well-drained, moist, fertile soil rich in compost and humus. See "Soil Preparation and Improvement" in the introduction. Follow the planting instructions at the beginning of this chapter, spacing the plants 24 inches or more apart; good air circulation deters mildew. Water deeply. Mulch 2 inches deep starting 3 inches from the crowns.

Growing Tips

For the first two months, water new plantings weekly unless you have a soaking rain; keeping phlox growing is part of the program that keeps it healthy.

Maintain soil moisture to keep the plants growing lustily. Fertilize the bed between late winter and early spring with a slow-release, organic, acidic fertilizer.

Regional Advice and Care

To prolong the flower display, pinch back one or two weaker stems in each clump early on so secondary flowers will be growing as the main stems fade. Rogue out seedlings and remove seeded flower heads so the plants will bloom again and won't self-sow. Cut them down to the crown at the end of the season or in early fall, and destroy the stems. Keep them vigorous by dividing the crowns every three years in spring before growth begins. Discard the center of the crown and provide each piece with three to four vigorous shoots.

Companion Planting and Design

Plant phlox near asters that will come into bloom as the phlox flowers fade in late summer, or with fall-flowering Japanese anemone. In mid-fall, tuck in potted cushion mums in white and lavender.

Try These

In 1920 to 1922, Martin Viette hybridized 'Katherine', a light lavender-blue with white eyes. It was lost until the great horticulturist Fred McGourty found it in an old Connecticut garden. André has reintroduced it, and says it's still the best blue. 'Flamingo Pink' is one of the most mildew resistant. André also loves the little creeping phloxes *P. divaricata*, *P. stolonifera*, and the moss phlox, *P. subulata*.

Pinks

Dianthus spp. and hybrids

Botanical Pronunciation
dye-AN-thus

Other Name Miniature carnation

Bloom Period and Seasonal Color
Spring, summer, early fall; pink, red, salmon, white, yellow *(D. knappii)* often with a contrasting eye, bicolors

Mature Height × Spread
6 to 36 inches × 6 to 24 inches

Pinks are dainty members of the genus *Dianthus*, which includes carnations and sweet Williams. Annuals, biennials, and perennials, they are loved for their sweet, spicy clove scent. The perfume is strong in the big florists' carnations and in the little grass or cottage pinks that fill gardens with sparkling colors spring, summer, and fall. Pinks range in size from 6 to 36 inches and the fresh, grassy foliage, evergreen in most, is an all-season asset. Some we plant for the perfume, some for their colorful flowers, and some for both flowers and foliage. Many varieties of pinks will bloom for months if they are deadheaded, or sheared, after the first flush of bloom. There are double-flowered forms.

When, Where, and How to Plant

Flats of dianthus varieties and container-grown plants are available in early spring, in summer, and early fall. Full sun is best, but in Washington, D.C., pinks bloom in part sun too. They do best in well-drained, even sandy, soil whose pH is between 6.0 to 7.5. Excellent drainage in winter is essential. In unimproved clay and where humidity is high, the pinks are short-lived. See "Soil Preparation and Improvement" in the introduction, and for the pinks, be a little stingy with the humus. Annuals are often sold in flats; cut the plants apart with a sharp, clean knife for planting. For container-grown plants follow the planting instructions at the beginning of this chapter. Space pinks 12 to 15 inches apart and set them a little higher than the soil level. Water

well. Spread a light, fine mulch such as cocoa hulls 2 to 3 inches deep starting 3 inches from the crown.

Growing Tips

Water new plantings every week or ten days unless you have rain. Pinks are drought resistant once established and they don't like wet feet. Fertilize the bed between late winter and early spring with a slow-release organic fertilizer at the rate of 6 pounds per 100 square feet. Replenish the mulch.

Regional Advice and Care

After the first flush of bloom, deadhead or shear off the faded flowers. If the plants show brown tips in August, cut them off, and make sure the plants don't go dry. They will freshen when fall comes, and can go on blooming until frost. The little pinks divide and transplant easily in spring or early fall.

Companion Planting and Design

We use pinks as edgers, and position them where the fragrance is a frequent experience.

Try These

André recommends the cheddar pink, *D. gratianopolitanus* 'Bath's Pink', which can take a lot of heat. 'Tiny Rubies' is a very popular double-flowered, deep pink variety. The Zing series—'Zing Rose' for example—are 6- to 8-inchers that bloom all summer. The old-fashioned annual sweet William, a great cutting flower, is nicely scented too.

Purple Coneflower

Echinacea purpurea

Botanical Pronunciation
eck-ih-NAY-see-uh pur-PUR-ee-uh

Period and Seasonal Color
Late spring, early summer; magenta with orange cone

Mature Height × Spread
1½ to 5 feet × 1 to 2 feet

This big bold coneflower with huge, magenta, daisylike blooms is one of the showiest, toughest, and longest-lived natives for meadow gardens. It grows 1½ to 5 feet tall, and has coarse, dark green foliage. 'Magnus' was named a Plant of the Year by the Perennial Plant Association. Its petals sweep back from a deep orange-bronze cone and are a rich, dusky rose-purple. Purple coneflower blooms in late spring and early summer; deadheaded, it goes on intermittently into fall. There are white varieties but they don't have the eye-catching appeal of the purple. Purple coneflowers last well as cut flowers, and they dry easily and the cones look terrific in dried winter flower arrangements. Butterflies love purple coneflower.

When, Where, and How to Plant

To have plants the first season, set out container-grown plants or root divisions any time after the ground can be worked in spring. Purple coneflower really needs full sun, but it can take a little filtered shade and still be productive, especially in the warmer parts of the Mid-Atlantic. It tolerates drought and can't stand soil that is soggy in winter. The ideal soil is in the somewhat acid range, pH 5.5 to 6.0. Overfertilized soil makes for tall, leggy plants that need staking. See "Soil Preparation and Improvement" in the introduction, and reduce the fertilization recommendations by half. Follow the planting instructions at the beginning of this chapter, spacing the plants 18 to 24 inches apart. Water well. Mulch 2 to 3 inches deep starting 3 inches from the crown.

Growing Tips

The first six weeks, water purple coneflower weekly unless you have a soaking rain; given time to establish, it will tolerate drought. In reasonably fertile soil, spring fertilization may not always be necessary.

Regional Advice and Care

Deadheading prevents self-seeding and reverting to inferior forms. Whether you deadhead or not, new blossoms keep coming. Keep some stands of purple coneflower deadheaded, and allow some to form seedheads to feed the birds that relish the seeds; next year you can rogue out the self-sown plantlets that will appear in abundance in spring. When cutting bouquets, cut the stem just above the next flower bud so the stem can produce more blooms.

Companion Planting and Design

Purple coneflower is the backbone, showpiece, and eye catcher of a meadow garden! Lovely in groups of five to seven planted in the center or toward the back of a formal border, it keeps color throughout midsummer. Virtually pest- and disease-free and tolerant of considerable drought, purple coneflower is excellent for naturalizing.

Try These

For the cutting garden, plant 'Bright Star', which is a rosy pink coneflower with a copper center. 'Kim's Knee High' has done well. The cream-white varieties with orange centers, like 'White Lustre', are attractive growing with black-eyed Susans. 'Double Scoop Cranberry' is said to be hardy. 'Pink Passion' is a charming compact.

Red Hot Poker

Kniphofia uvaria

Botanical Pronunciation
nip-HOE-fee-uh

Bloom Period and Seasonal Color
Late spring and summer; yellow and red, cream, orange

Mature Height × Spread
3 to 4 feet × 2 to 3 feet

Now that we are eager for more drought-resistant plants, the red hot poker is getting the attention it deserves for its color, style, and for its ease of maintenance. In late spring and summer, eye-catching 3- to 4-foot flower spikes appear, yellow on the bottom and bright red on the top. They stand straight as a poker, several spikes per plant. The yellow lower portion of the "pokers" is where early-blooming florets are aging; the red at the top is where new florets are just opening. The arching sword-shaped, gray-green, semi-evergreen or evergreen foliage is attractive when new. There are many new cultivars, and they're more compact than the old-fashioned varieties and have attractive softer colors.

When, Where, and How to Plant
In the cool uplands, set out container-grown plants in early spring. In Zones 7 and 8, red hot poker can be set out in early fall. It can stand a lot of direct sun, but in the hotter regions it benefits from protection from noon sun. Good drainage for the planting site is essential. Red hot poker tolerates drought but can't stand soil that is soggy in winter and does best when it's not constantly buffeted by strong winds. It does best in neutral to alkaline soils, pH 6.0 to 7.5. See "Soil Preparation and Improvement" in the introduction. Follow the planting instructions at the beginning of this chapter, spacing the plants 24 inches apart. Water well. Mulch 2 inches deep starting 3 inches from the crown.

Growing Tips
Water new red hot poker plants every week unless you have a soaking rain. Once established they are tolerant of drought. Fertilize the bed between late winter and early spring, with a slow-release organic fertilizer at the rate of 6 pounds per 100 square feet. In spring, replenish the mulch.

Regional Advice and Care
Keep fading flower spikes removed until the end of the season. The plants rarely set seed. In spring before growth begins, cut the plants back to about 3 inches above the crown. Red hot poker dislikes being disturbed and rarely needs dividing. If you want to multiply your plants, divide in early spring.

Companion Planting and Design
Red hot poker is a flower for dry places, xeriscapes, and modernistic gardens fronting stark modern architecture.

Try These
We like 'Springtime', whose colors are coral and a muted yellow. The color of 2½- to 3½-foot 'Earliest of All' is a soft coral rose. 'Alcazar' is fiery red to tangerine.

Russian Sage

Perovskia atriplicifolia

Botanical Pronunciation
pur-OV-skee-uh at-rih-pliss-ih-FOE-lee-uh

Bloom Period and Seasonal Color
June through September; lavender blue

Mature Height × Spread
3 to 5 feet × 2 to 3 feet

Russian sage keeps a cloud of that coveted color, blue—a beautiful, soft, powdery lavender-blue—in the garden for a long time in summer and early fall, from July, August, and most of September. In Zone 8 it starts to bloom in June. Very tall, so airy they're cloudlike at a distance, the stems and the grayish foliage are topped by spikes of tiny florets in a lovely, subtle shade of blue. When the foliage is crushed, you get a whiff of the clean, warm scent of sage. In winter the branches are a cloud of silvery white. One of the most heat- and drought-resistant of all the perennials, Russian sage 'Blue Spire' was named a Plant of the Year by the Perennial Plant Association.

When, Where, and How to Plant
Set out container-grown plants anytime; set out rooted softwood cuttings in early spring or fall. Russian sage requires full sun to do its best, and a very well-drained site. It thrives in moderately fertile soil in the neutral range. See "Soil Preparation and Improvement" in the introduction. Follow the planting instructions at the beginning of this chapter, spacing the plants 24 inches apart. Water well. Mulch 2 to 3 inches deep starting 3 inches from the crown.

Growing Tips
For the first two months, water deeply and thoroughly every week to ten days, unless you have a good soaking rain, then water as needed.

Regional Advice and Care
Russian sage is a sub-shrub with a woody base. Cut the stems back to about 6 inches above the ground in the spring and new buds will start from these stems. In cooler regions, the stems may die to the ground; as long as your winters are no colder than Zone 5, the plant will likely re-grow. If unusually late frosts damage the stems, trim off the spoiled branch tips. In very warm areas where Russian sage blooms early, cutting the branches back by two-thirds after they have flowered will produce a new flush of bloom in fall. Russian sage hardly ever needs dividing.

Companion Planting and Design
We like Russian sage at the back of a perennial border in groups of three, backed by evergreens that will show off its winter color. It is beautiful massed with boltonia and ornamental grasses in naturalized settings. It's also a great shore plant.

Try These
André's choice is 'Filigran', which is just 2 to 3 feet tall and blooms from July to October.

Scabiosa

Scabiosa columbaria
'Butterfly Blue'

Botanical Pronunciation
skab-ee-OH-suh coll-um-BARE-EE-uh

Other Name
Blue pincushion flower

Bloom Period and Seasonal Color
May to October; blue

Mature Height × Spread
1 to 1½ feet × 1 to 1½ feet

Scabiosa, the "pincushion" flower, is an old-time favorite—and the blossoms do look like sweet little pincushions surrounded by curving petals. Actually, the blooms are domed heads composed of tiny flowers surrounded by leafy bracts. It's an excellent flower for cutting and for drying. 'Butterfly Blue' can take the cold all the way to Zone 3 and keep flowers into fall if it is consistently sheared or deadheaded. A heavy-blooming dwarf, it produces 2-inch flowers in amazing abundance from mid-spring until mid-fall. The color is beautiful, the plant itself a neat compact mound, and the masses of flowers are amazing. 'Butterfly Blue' was named Plant of the Year by the Perennial Plant Association.

When, Where, and How to Plant
In early spring set out container-grown plants or root divisions. In cooler regions, scabiosa does best in full sun, but in warm regions it flowers well with noon or afternoon shade. Scabiosa thrives in soil close to neutral, pH 7.0, and very well drained. Excellent drainage in winter is essential. See "Soil Preparation and Improvement" in the introduction. Follow the planting instructions at the beginning of this chapter, spacing the plants 15 to 18 inches apart. Water well. Mulch 2 to 3 inches deep starting 3 inches from the crown.

Growing Tips
For the first two months, water new plantings of scabiosa every week to ten days unless you have a soaking rain. Then, water only as needed. Fertilize the bed between late winter and early spring, and again in September with a slow-release, organic, acidic fertilizer. In spring, replenish the mulch.

Regional Advice and Care
In cool regions, provide a light, dry winter mulch of pine boughs or hay. Deadheading prolongs bloom, but is complicated by the fact that the fading blooms can be mistaken for the emerging flower buds. If the stems do not branch, just cut down to the crown. With time, scabiosa begins to put up just one central leader; when that happens, cut it down to the basal foliage. Before winter, cut back old flowering stems but leave the basal foliage in place; in spring before growth begins, remove dead foliage. Every three to four years, if the plants seem crowded, divide the crowns anytime in early to mid-spring until active growth begins. The flowers last longer harvested half open.

Companion Planting and Design
Plant scabiosa toward the front of the perennial bed with space all around.

Try These
'Butterfly Blue' is the best. Another lovely scabiosa is *Scabiosa caucasica*, which has very large flowers and is grown specifically for cutting. It has grayish ferny foliage and pale blue, white, or lavender flowers summer to frost. 'Fama' is the clear intense sky blue version, and 'Alba' is the white form. 'Pink Mist' is a lavender-pink version of 'Butterfly Blue'.

Sedum

Sedum spp. and hybrids

Botanical Pronunciation
SEE-dum

Other Name
Stonecrop

Bloom Period and Seasonal Color
Summer to fall; yellow, pink, white, red

Mature Height × Spread
1 to 24 inches × 1 to 2 feet

Indestructible, heat- and drought-resistant, sedums are valued for their succulent, evergreen foliage and for the beautiful fall flower color of some tall cultivars. The flowers are tiny, star-shaped and in taller forms cluster in showy flat-topped flower heads. The little ground-hugging sedums are used in rock gardens, between stepping stones, in wall crannies, and by steps. Taller types, like 'Autumn Joy', are considered by perennial experts including André Viette to be among the top fifteen perennials. Its jade green foliage is evergreen. In spring new stems rise, followed in early summer by fresh, apple green broccoli-like flower heads. These change to rich pink, then rose, salmon, bronze, and finally to rosy russet. *Sedum spectabile* 'Neon' has the brightest pink flowers. Deer sometimes eat sedum foliage but leave the flowers.

When, Where, and How to Plant

Set out container-grown plants in spring, summer, or fall. Plant root divisions anytime after the ground can be worked in spring, or in late summer. Many smaller sedums are invasive, and even tall varieties, if not deadheaded, self-sow. The plants flourish in full sun in cold Zone 6 and all the way to Zone 3; in warmer areas they are at their best during cool weather. The ideal soil is pH 6.0 to 7.5, very well drained, humusy, and fertile. Most seem to prefer dry soil, but tolerate moisture. See "Soil Preparation and Improvement" in the introduction. Follow the planting instructions at the beginning of this chapter, spacing the plants according to the size at maturity. Water well. Mulch 2 to 3 inches deep starting 3 inches from the crown.

Growing Tips

Sedum withstands heat and drought even in sand and by the sea. Watering if there's no rain is a good idea but necessary only until you see vigorous new growth. Sedums need average moisture during active growth but can stand a lot of drought later. Fertilize the bed between late winter and early spring, with a slow-release organic fertilizer and replenish the mulch.

Regional Advice and Care

Don't deadhead the taller sedums, like 'Autumn Joy'; the flowers change color as they go to seed and provide a beautiful color accent in the garden throughout fall and winter; cut them off just above the basal foliage in late winter. Divide clumps to multiply your holdings any time; to refresh the plants divide clumps in early spring every six to ten years.

Companion Planting and Design

The taller cultivars are superb growing with ornamental grasses in naturalized plantings that include *Rudbeckia* 'Goldsturm', purple coneflowers, and Russian sage.

Try These

'Autumn Joy' is the favorite. Another handsome sedum is 'Ruby Glow', a slightly smaller plant whose flower heads are iridescent ruby-red. *S. spurium* 'John Creech', an excellent evergreen groundcover, was introduced by André Viette, who named it for the horticulturist who first collected it.

Siberian Iris

Iris sibirica

Botanical Pronunciation
EYE-riss sye-BEER-ih-kuh

Bloom Period and Seasonal Color
Late spring; blue-purple, lavender, maroon, white, off pink, yellowish

Mature Height × Spread
24 to 36 inches × 12 to 18 inches

We love the Siberian irises—they're easy to maintain and have few problems. Breeders agree, and are enhancing the colors, range, and bloom times of these exceptionally graceful plants. Depending on the zone, Siberian irises bloom in late spring to early summer. Clusters of two or three flowers top tall slender stems above slim grassy leaves that turn lovely shades of rust in winter. The flowers stand a little taller than the bearded irises, from 24 to 40 inches, and come in as many colors and forms as anyone could want— from white to yellow, blues, some edged with silver, and there's a pansy purple with white lines. Some are ruffled, some have huge flaring blossoms. It's an excellent flower for cutting and very lovely massed in a large border. The dried pods are handsome.

When, Where, and How to Plant
You can plant container-grown Siberian irises anytime; growers ship rhizomes bare root in early spring. The irises are successful growing in full sun in cold wet climates; in warmer regions they tolerate light shade or late afternoon shade. They adapt to a pH of 5.0 to 7.5, but prefer moderately acidic soils. They tolerate poor, dry soil but bloom best in well-drained, rich, evenly moist garden loam with good drainage. Once established, they can stand some drought. See "Soil Preparation and Improvement" in the introduction. For container-grown plants, follow the planting instructions at the beginning of this chapter, allowing a good 18 inches between crowns. Plant rhizomes with the roots on the underside, and the tops just below the soil surface, and space them 18 to 24 inches apart

depending on the size of the iris; they soon grow into a solid, deep-rooted clump. Water well. Mulch 2 to 3 inches deep starting 3 inches from the outer edges of the planting.

Growing Tips
Water the planting every week for a month to six weeks, unless you have a soaking rain. Then, water as needed. Fertilize the bed between late winter and early spring with a slow-release organic fertilizer for acid-loving plants, 4 pounds per 100 square feet.

Regional Advice and Care
Deadhead, leaving one-third of the handsome seedheads in place to extend the plant's high season. Remove dead foliage in spring before growth begins. Divide and transplant Siberian iris late summer to early fall or in early spring. Get the rhizomes into the ground as soon as possible; keep them moist until planted.

Companion Planting and Design
One or two slim, elegant Siberian irises are beautiful beside a water garden and are among the few flowers allowed into a Japanese water garden. Clumps of Siberians add grace to mixed perennial borders. Siberian iris, *Sedum* 'Autumn Joy', and a bramble of coreopsis give the garden form while the earth rests.

Try These
Good cultivars include deepest purple 'Tealwood', yellow and white 'Butter and Sugar', and blue 'Ego'. 'Super Ego' is an excellent blue variety.

Solomon's Seal

Polygonatum spp. and cultivars

Botanical Prononciation
poll-ee-GON-uh-tum

Other Name
King Solomon's seal

Bloom Period and Seasonal Color
Mid- to late spring; creamy white flowers

Mature Height × Spread
1 to 6 feet × 1 to 6 feet

Solomon's seal is a superb flower and foliage plant for woodland gardens and naturalized corners of the landscape. The North American, Asian, and European species gardeners grow are graceful spring-bloomers that originated in damp light woodlands, so they're reliable performers for a shade garden. *Polygonatum biflorum*, a native aristocrat, is now propagated and sold by nurseries. In spring, rows of dangling bell-shaped green or cream-white flowers, usually in pairs, line the arching stems and are followed by blue-black berries. Pretty if not spectacular, and the flowers of some are fragrant. The foliage turns an appealing yellow-brown in fall and persists. Solomon's seal thrives in domesticity as long as it is provided with light and soil approximating its native haunts.

When, Where, and How to Plant

Set out nursery-grown root divisions in fall or spring; do not dig Solomon's seal growing in the wild as it is protected. *Polygonatum* volunteers in full sun where there is moisture in cool Zones 5 and 6, and in quite deep shade in woodlands, so it is adaptable. In regions where summers are very hot, a partially shaded site is best. Solomon's seal thrives in well-drained, deeply dug, rich, humusy, somewhat acidic soil, about pH 5.0 to 6.0. See "Soil Preparation and Improvement" in the introduction. Follow the planting instructions at the beginning of this chapter, spacing the plants 18 to 20 inches apart. Water well. Mulch 2 to 3 inches deep starting 3 inches from the outer stems.

Growing Tips

Keep the soil moist while the plant is establishing itself, and water deeply during droughts. Fertilize the bed between late winter and early spring with a slow-release organic fertilizer for acid-loving plants at the rate of 4 pounds per 100 square feet.

Regional Advice and Care

Once a planting is established you can dig and transplant the rhizomes while still dormant in late winter; divide the rhizomes with a knife, allowing each section at least one healthy bud. Set the rhizomes 2 to 3 inches deep with the bud facing upward in the direction in which you want the plant to grow.

Companion Planting and Design

Plant Solomon's seal along a woodland path with columbines, fragrant lily-of-the-valley, primroses, trilliums, and hostas. *P. commutatum*, a magnificent 6-footer at maturity, belongs in a large wild garden.

Try These

André's favorite is *P. multiflorum*, a beautiful, graceful, deep green, European Solomon's seal. Martin Viette introduced 30-inch *P. odoratum* 'Variegatum', a superb variegated Solomon's seal that is fragrant, to American gardeners just before World War II. André introduced the 6- to 90-inch dwarf species *P. humile*. It was a gift received from a friend.

Yarrow

Achillea spp. and hybrids

Botanical Pronunciation
ack-ih-LEE-uh

Other Name
Milfoil

Bloom Period and Seasonal Color
June through August; yellow, gold, off pink, cerise, red, rust, salmon, off white.

Mature Height × Spread
1 to 4 feet × 2 to 3 feet

Yarrow is a flower for all seasons and all locations, from the formal perennial border to the herb garden. From spring through midsummer, the large, flat-topped flower heads of modern cultivars stand in strong yellows, gold, off-pink, cerise, and off-white above woolly gray-green foliage 1 to 4 feet high. The ferny foliage of this ancient herb is strongly scented and makes a great filler. Yarrow is showy naturalized with ornamental grasses in meadow gardens, and a wonderful textural accent in perennial borders. The cut flowers are very long-lasting in fresh bouquets. They also dry quickly, preserve excellent color and much of their volume, and are a mainstay of winter arrangements.

When, Where, and How to Plant

In spring or late fall, set out container-grown plants or root divisions. Yarrow really needs full sun, even in hot regions. It is excellent for very well-drained sandy soils, and poor soils. Very rich or moist soils encourage lax growth and cause *Achillea millefolium* cultivars to become invasive. Yarrow handles drought but can't stand soggy soil, especially in winter. See "Soil Preparation and Improvement" in the introduction but halve the fertilization recommendations. Follow the planting instructions at the beginning of this chapter. Yarrow is a wide-spreading plant, so space the plants 18 to 24 inches apart. Water well. Mulch to keep weeds down 2 to 3 inches deep starting 3 inches from the crown.

Growing Tips

Yarrow requires watering for the first few weeks after planting; once it shows signs of vigorous growth, it should do well with ordinary rainfall. Fertilize the bed lightly between late winter and early spring, applying a slow-release organic fertilizer for acid-loving plants at the rate of 2 pounds per 100 square feet. In spring, replenish the mulch.

Regional Advice and Care

Prune spent flowers down to the first pair of buds, and these will bloom. Yarrow, especially fern-leaved yarrow, *A. filipendulina*, makes a delightful dried flower, so harvest the last round of blooms for winter bouquets. Before growth begins in spring, gently remove the dead foliage. Every four or five years—or if the plant becomes less productive—divide in early spring before growth begins.

Companion Planting and Design

Yarrow's beautiful ferny foliage adds texture to perennial beds and is very attractive in naturalized plantings.

Try These

Beautiful cultivars of fern-leaved yarrow, *A. filipendulina*, which has deeply divided silvery foliage, are golden 'Coronation Gold' and 'Moonshine'. Varieties of *A. millefolium*, a slightly smaller species that self-sows, come in many attractive shades: 'Cerise Queen' is cherry red; 'Paprika' is brick red; and 'Red Beauty' is rose red. André loves the newer 'Terra Cotta', which starts out peach colored and matures to a rich terra-cotta hue.

ROSES
FOR THE MID-ATLANTIC

The rose was designated the nation's floral emblem in 1987. Roses thrive here—and gardeners fall in love with the beautiful form and seductive fragrance of varieties like green-eyed white 'Madame Hardy' and David Austin's 'Graham Thomas'. Fall in love, but confine your passion to roses billed as "disease resistant." Those we recommend are resistant, as are those that received awards from All-America Rose Selections (now defunct) and the American Rose Society.

Planting and Pruning

For roses to produce a dazzle of flowers and fragrance, nearly all need eight hours of morning sun, or six hours of afternoon sun, all day sun, or very bright filtered light. They need a well-drained site, and for most a pH of between 5.5 and 7.0. See "Soil Preparation and Improvement" in the introduction. The key to success is thorough and deep soil preparation—deeply dug planting holes 24 inches wide and 24 inches deep, and humusy, fertile soil. André applies an organic fertilizer three times a year, in late winter or early spring, in early midsummer, and in early fall.

An Explorer tree rose underplanted with petunias, lobelia, and scaveola growing in a container.

You can plant a container-grown rose in early or late spring, in summer, or fall before Indian summer. If the rootball is encircled by roots, untangle them gently. If they can't be unwound, make four shallow vertical cuts in the wall of roots and slice off the matted roots on the bottom. Half-fill the planting hole with improved soil, and pack it down very firmly. Set the rootball into the hole so it is about an inch above the ground level. For grafted or budded roses, set the plant so that the bud union is 2 to 3 inches above ground level. Roses on their own roots do not have a bud union. Half-fill the hole again with improved soil, and pack it down firmly. Finish filling the hole with improved soil, and pack it down firmly. Make a saucer around the plant, and water it slowly and deeply. You plant bare-root roses the same way, but soak the roots for twelve hours before planting, and drape them over a firm mound in the center of the hole.

Deadheading and harvesting big-flowered show roses keeps them blooming. When cutting roses for bouquets, leave a five-leaf sprig on each shoot as a base for new flowering shoots. Make all pruning cuts ½ inch above an outside bud eye or sprig. Do not prune roses after the wood has hardened for the winter. Before growth begins in early spring, cut out diseased and damaged canes. Prune roses that

A rose arbor gives a focal point to a garden, inviting the guest to step into it.

bloom on new wood to the desired shape in early spring. Prune roses that bloom on wood from the previous season—some shrub and climbing roses—after they have flowered. Cut the oldest canes of recurrent bloomers back to two or three bud eyes, and remove twiggy ends. As new canes grow, tie them to fencing or trellising. To encourage growth of flowering laterals, cut side branches to short spurs.

Some roses, especially the hybrid teas and miniatures, may require winter protection. Cover the plants with pine boughs, or hill soil over the lower stems. Don't mulch with leaves or anything that creates a cozy habitat for field mice (voles); they'll girdle the roses and kill them.

Rose Problems

If you run into the *Rosa* genus' big three problems—Japanese beetles, blackspot, and powdery mildew—what we have learned may help. One way to deal with Japanese beetles is to spray plants under attack with rotenone, an okay spray. Another is to apply milky disease spores to the gardens and the lawn. Effective the second year, this natural deterrent kills the larvae. In early morning, the beetles are sluggish, and you can knock them into a pot of soapy water. Releasing native parasitic wasps and flies that go for the beetles helps. Do *not* crush the beetles as that releases pheromones that will draw more Japanese beetles to the garden.

For **blackspot**, which loves hybrid teas, floribundas, and grandifloras, try the spray recommended by Cornell University research: 1 tablespoon baking soda (sodium bicarbonate) and 1 tablespoon ultrafine horticultural oil to 1 quart water. And remove infected vegetation from the plant and the ground. **Powdery mildew** may be minimized by spraying with the Cornell University research solution. Ask your garden center about new, environmentally safe controls. **Deer**—well, sprays containing very bitter Bitrex® may keep deer away for a time. The only sure protection is to screen the bushes with chicken wire. It isn't noticeable at a distance. Or put up a 10-foot deer fence.

Climbing Rose

Rosa spp. and hybrids

Botanical Pronunciation
ROE-zuh

Other Name
Pillar rose

Bloom Period and Seasonal Color
Spring, summer, until frost; all colors except true blue

Mature Height × Spread
6 to 20 feet × 3 to 6 feet

The roses we call "climbers" put forth long canes that can be trained to cover an arch, an arbor, a trellis, a wall, a fence, or to climb a tree. "Training" means being tied—roses don't climb on their own. The showiest climbers are ramblers that bear clusters of small blooms on pliant canes that rise annually from the base. Climbers that are tall shrubs with stiff, not pliant, canes bear large flowers singly or in clusters. There are large climbing roses (CL) and miniature climbing roses (MCL). The large types are usually included as backdrops for rose gardens—trained to an arch, a pergola, or a wall. The miniatures require little space at the base and succeed in containers with winter protection; they are ideal for small condominium patios and porches.

When, Where, and How to Plant

Plant bare-root roses before the last frost in spring. Plant container-grown roses in early to mid-spring, summer, or early to mid-fall. Most roses need full sun, but climbers whose branches are in the sun will bloom with their roots in shade. Climbers attach themselves with their thorns but they must be trained (tied) in the direction they are to grow, unless climbing a tree. Plant a rose meant to climb a tree so prevailing winds blow the branches toward the tree. Leave 12 inches between a climber and a house wall, and provide a trellis for support. The ideal planting soil is well drained, fertile, humusy, with a pH between 5.5 and 7.0. See "Soil Preparation and Improvement" in the introduction. Follow the planting instructions at the beginning of this chapter. For grafted roses, set the plant so that the bud union is 2 to 3 inches above ground level. Water well. Apply a 3-inch mulch beginning 3 inches from the main stem.

Growing Tips

The first year, unless there's a soaking rain, in spring and fall pour a bucket of water slowly and gently around the roots every two weeks; in summer, water every week or ten days. Maintain the mulch throughout the summer. Apply a slow-release organic rose fertilizer in late winter or early spring, again in early midsummer, and again in early fall. Renew the mulch.

Regional Advice and Care

Every year, remove one of the oldest canes, and save two or three of the new canes for next year; five or six heavy canes is all a climbing rose can support.

Companion Planting and Design

A climbing, or pillar, rose can be trained into a 10- to 12-foot pillar. Climbing roses trained to grow horizontally along fences tend to flower more. To hide a climber's bare legs, plant a bushy companion, catmint or lavender for example.

Try These

For pillar roses with recurrent bloom, we recommend fragrant 'Golden Showers', an AARS winner; fragrant blush-pink 'New Dawn'; and 'White Dawn'. Very fragrant climbers include 'Don Juan', Golden Gate®, and 'Paul's Lemon Pillar'.

Garden Rose

Rosa spp. and hybrids

Botanical Pronunciation
ROE-zuh

Bloom Period and Seasonal Color
Recurrent all-season bloom; all colors except true blue

Mature Height × Spread
English Roses—3 to 5 feet × 2 to 5 feet
Polyanthas—1 to 4 feet × 1 to 4 feet
Floribundas—2 to 6 feet × 2 to 5 feet

The English roses, the polyanthas, and the floribundas (meaning many-flowered) are cluster-flowering garden roses whose beauty rivals hybrid teas. Modern disease-resistant plants, they produce blooms almost all season long and many are fragrant. The many-petaled David Austin English roses bear 2½- to 5-inch blooms that recall the full, fragrant roses our grandparents grew, but the shrubs are compact and easily managed. The polyanthas are 1 to 4 feet tall, and bear clusters of charming little seashell-like flowers under 2 inches across. The floribundas are 2 or 6 feet tall with 2- to 5-inch blooms, which, like the polyanthas, are borne in clusters. Some have blooms in the form of hybrid tea roses. In Europe, they landscape many roadsides and parks.

When, Where, and How to Plant

Plant bare-root roses before the last frost; plant container-grown roses in early to mid-spring or early to mid-fall. Most roses need full sun; when a rose can do well with less, it is stated in the grower's description. Leave 12 inches between a rosebush and a house wall because the ground there tends to stay dry even in hard rain. The ideal planting soil is well drained, fertile, humusy, with a pH between 5.5 and 7.0. See "Soil Preparation and Improvement" in the introduction. Follow the planting instructions at the beginning of this chapter. For grafted roses, set the plant so that the bud union is 2 to 3 inches above ground level. Water well. Mulch 2 to 3 inches deep starting 3 inches from the main stem.

Growing Tips

The first year, unless there's a soaking rain, in spring and fall slowly and gently pour a bucket of water around the roots every two weeks; in summer, water every week or ten days. Maintain the mulch throughout the summer. Apply a slow-release organic rose fertilizer in late winter or early spring, again in early midsummer, and again in early fall. Renew the mulch.

Regional Advice and Care

If an English rose sends out an excessively long shoot, cut it back hard anytime. As the buds swell in spring, prune English roses back by about a third of their height, and cut polyanthas and floribundas back one-third of their size. Remove the oldest flowering canes and leave the plants open in the center, creating a vase-shaped framework.

Companion Planting and Design

English roses are most effective planted in groups of three or more of one variety. The floriferous little polyantha roses grow into dense impenetrable low hedges, so you may need only one or two. The pretty, slightly fragrant, seashell pink 'The Fairy' makes a dense flowery hedge. A floribunda favorite for edging fences is 'Betty Prior', a vivid pink whose emerald foliage stays fresh all summer.

Try These

Among our favorite David Austin English roses are the pink Cottage Rose® and pristine white Fair Bianca®. In warm regions pink floribunda 'Gruss an Aachen' blooms in high shade.

Hedge Rose

Rosa spp. and hybrids

Botanical Pronunciation
ROE-zuh

Bloom Period and Seasonal Color
Spring, summer, until frost; white, all hues of pink, rose, red

Mature Height × Spread
3 to 7 feet × 3 to 8 feet

For hedging and impressive specimen planting, we recommend the repeat-blooming hedge and shrub roses, along with the old garden and rugosa roses (as well as the cluster-bearing polyanthas and floribundas described on preceding pages). Many varieties have flowers shaped like hybrid teas. The shrub roses and the old garden ("romantica") species are robust growers, and bear gorgeous flowers. The romantica species tend to bloom profusely but only in spring; modern shrub roses may repeat bloom. The modern rugosa, or Japanese roses, hybrids of *Rosa rugosa*, bear clove-scented single or double flowers in spring with some repeat blooming, followed in fall by colorful foliage and shiny coral-orange rose hips high in vitamin C. Tall, stiff, and spiny, they're effective as hedges and known for success by the sea.

When, Where, and How to Plant

Plant bare-root roses before the last frost; set out container-grown plants in early to mid-spring, summer, or early to mid-fall. They need full sun. Leave 12 inches between the bush and a house wall because the ground there tends to stay dry. The ideal planting soil is well drained, fertile, humusy, with a pH between 5.5 and 7.0. See "Soil Preparation and Improvement" in the introduction. Follow the planting instructions at the beginning of this chapter. For grafted roses, set the plant so that the bud union is 2 to 3 inches above ground level. Water well. Mulch 2 to 3 inches deep starting 3 inches from the main stem.

Growing Tips

The first year, unless there's a soaking rain, in spring and fall slowly and gently pour a bucket of water around the roots every two weeks; in summer, water every week or ten days. Maintain the mulch throughout the summer. Apply a slow-release organic rose fertilizer in late winter or early spring, again in early midsummer, and again in early fall. Renew the mulch.

Regional Advice and Care

As the buds swell in spring, remove diseased and damaged canes. Beginning the fourth season for a rugosa rose, in early spring, remove all canes that have flowered to encourage vigorous new growth.

Companion Planting and Design

If space allows, plant several different roses for a longer season of interest, including colorful hips in the fall.

Try These

'Madame Hardy', a fragrant old white rose with a green-button eye, is one of the world's most beautiful roses. For brilliant rose hips in fall, plant *R. rugosa* 'Alba', 'Rubra', and 'Belle Poitevine', which has almost double, pink flowers. The 5-foot light pink cultivar 'Fru Dagmar Hastrup' can be pruned repeatedly without diminishing the production of flowers. 'Thérése Bugnet' grows to 5 feet and bears large, flat, slightly fragrant deep pink flowers, with some repeat bloom. Almost thornless 'Linda Campbell' grows 5 to 7 feet and produces large clusters of crimson flowers in six to seven flushes of blooms.

Hybrid Tea Rose

Rosa hybrids

Botanical Pronunciation
ROE-zuh

Other Name
Large-flowered bush rose

Bloom Period and Seasonal Color
Spring, sporadically through summer;
many colors

Mature Height × Spread
2 to 6 feet × 2 to 6 feet

The hybrid tea roses are long-stemmed cutting flowers, with blooms that are large, high-centered, pointed, and semi- or double-flowered. The best, like the exquisite and enduring yellow-and-rose 'Peace', are perfumed. Most bloom in June, throw a few flowers throughout summer, and bloom well from September through October. Though the shrubs are leggy, need attention, and are not always hardy here, these are the most popular roses. The tea rose form appears in small polyantha roses, large-flowered floribunda roses, miniature roses, and climbing roses. To set the florist's single-stemmed, large-flowered hybrid tea rose apart, its classification has recently been changed to large-flowered bush rose; but time will pass before most nurseries and catalogs call them anything but hybrid tea roses.

When, Where, and How to Plant
Plant bare-root hybrid teas before the last frost; set out container-grown teas in early to mid-spring, summer, or before mid-fall. They need full sun. Leave 12 inches between the bush and a house wall because the ground there tends to stay dry. The ideal planting soil is well drained, fertile, humusy, with a pH between 5.5 and 7.0. See "Soil Preparation and Improvement" in the introduction. Follow the planting instructions at the beginning of this chapter. For grafted roses, set the plant so that the bud union is 2 to 3 inches above ground level. Water well. Mulch 2 to 3 inches deep starting 3 inches from the main stem.

Growing Tips
The first year, unless there's a soaking rain, in spring and fall slowly and gently pour a bucket of water around the roots every two weeks; in summer, water every week or ten days. Maintain the mulch throughout the summer. Apply a slow-release organic rose fertilizer in late winter or early spring, again in early midsummer, and again in early fall. Renew the mulch.

Regional Advice and Care
As the buds swell in spring, remove diseased and damaged canes and the oldest flowering canes, leaving an open structure of four to five strong canes 5 or 6 inches long with the uppermost buds pointing outward. Remove spent flowers, fallen petals and leaves, and suckers as they occur. Cut roses and spent blossoms at a point just above a five-leaf stem. Every seven to ten days, and after heavy rainfalls, apply an all-purpose rose spray that controls insects and disease.

Companion Planting and Design
Hybrid teas are most often grown in a bed of their own with lavender, or full-foliaged annuals, to disguise their legginess.

Try These
Some favorites that have fragrance are the outstanding pink 'Dolly Parton', 'Mr. Lincoln' (are considered by some as the best of the hybrid teas), two-toned pink 'Double Delight', 'Pink Promise', and 'Bewitched', known for its long vase life and 5-inch blooms.

KNOCK OUT®
Rose

Rosa 'Radrazz'

Botanical Pronunciation ROE-zuh

Bloom Period and Seasonal Color
Spring to frost; red, pink,
white, yellow

Mature Height x Spread
3 to 4 feet x 3 to 4 feet

The amazing, hardy, heat-resistant, disease resistant, extraordinarily flowery, low-maintenance, self-cleaning cherry red KNOCK OUT® rose was introduced at the turn of the century, and became the best-selling rose everywhere. It covers itself with blooms every five or six weeks from mid spring until hard frosts. New colors have been introduced so this gardener-friendly beauty is now available in pink, rainbow rose, blushing rose, and a sunny yellow. The Double KNOCK OUT® rose is the heaviest bloomer. The size is 3 to 4 feet wide by 3 to 4 feet tall. The plants can be kept smaller by pruning in late winter or early spring while the plants are still dormant. To keep the KNOCK OUT® rose blooming at full capacity, you will need to apply a rose fertilizer after each bloom cycle. Enjoy!

When, Where, and How To Plant
A container-grown KNOCK OUT® rose can be planted anytime in early or late spring, in summer, or fall before Indian summer. To produce a maximum number of blooms, nearly all need a site that provides eight hours of sun, or six hours of afternoon sun, all day sun, or very bright filtered light. It also needs well-drained soil and does best with a pH between 5.5 to 7.0. If the rootball is encircled by roots, untangle them gently then set the plant in its planting hole so it is about an inch above the soil level. Half fill the planting hole with improved soil, and pack it down very firmly. Water well. Mulch to within 3 inches of the stem.

Growing Tips
The first year, unless there's a soaking rain, in spring and fall pour a bucket of water around the roots every two weeks; in summer, water every week or ten days. Fertilize with a rose-specific product after each bloom cycle. Maintain the mulch throughout the summer.

Regional Advice and Care
Before winter cold sets in, apply a thick layer of mulch around the roots—about 3 inches from the trunk—to keep the ground evenly cold in winter and avoid a chance of frost heaving. In late winter to early spring, prune the bushes to keep the interior airy and the shape somewhat symmetrical. Every two or three years consider cutting the bushes back by one-third to encourage fresh new growth.

Companion Planting and Design
The pink ones are lovely interplanted with lavender, low-growing hostas, and low ornamental grasses, Mexican sage (*Salvia leucantha*), and underplanted with angelonia.

Try These
The cherry red double KNOCK OUT® rose is the best bloomer, and slightly hardier than other KNOCK OUT® roses. The Carefree™ series of shrub roses is another easy-to-grow group; light rose Carefree Beauty™ is fragrant. Another repeat-bloomer is 'Bonica', an easy-care landscape rose that bears 2½-inch, slightly fragrant, pale pink flowers.

Miniature Rose

Rosa spp. and hybrids

Botanical Pronunciation ROE-zuh

Bloom Period and Seasonal Color
Spring, or repeat bloom; white, all hues of yellow, pink through red

Mature Height × Spread
½ to 3 feet × 1 to 3 feet

The miniature roses are offspring of *Rosa rouletti* found growing in Switzerland, and 'Minima', a fairy rose, which blooms all season. Those sold as climbers can also be trained as tree form, basket, and container plants. The minis flower modestly from June to frost, and bear flowers less than 1¾ inches in diameter, often shaped like hybrid teas or cabbage roses. Too small to be effective as specimen plantings, they're delightful as edging plants and in rock gardens and containers. Miniature roses will bloom for a time indoors on very sunny windowsills. They also flourish in containers set in sun on patio or porch, but to be safe for the winter they need to be in a spot protected from the wind.

When, Where, and How to Plant
Miniature roses are usually sold growing in containers. They may be planted anytime in early to mid-spring, summer, or early to mid-fall. They produce the most blooms in full sun but will bloom in some shade. The ideal planting soil is well drained, fertile, humusy, with a pH between 6.5 to 7.0. Space the plants 2 feet apart. See "Soil Preparation and Improvement" in the introduction. Follow the planting instructions at the beginning of this chapter, but make the holes twice the width of the rootball and 12 inches to 15 inches deep. Set the roses so they are at ground level. For grafted roses, set the plant so that the bud union is 2 to 3 inches above ground level. Water well. Mulch 2 to 3 inches deep starting 3 inches from the main stem.

Growing Tips
The first year, unless there's a soaking rain, in spring and fall slowly and gently pour a bucket of water around the roots every two weeks; in summer, water every week or ten days. Maintain the mulch throughout the summer. Apply a slow-release organic rose fertilizer in late winter or early spring, again in early midsummer, and again in early fall. Renew the mulch.

Regional Advice and Care
Deadheading isn't necessary. As buds begin swelling in spring, remove dead, weak, and discolored canes and canes that cross. Trim all the branches back by about one-third, enough to maintain a pleasing form.

Companion Planting and Design
We like miniature roses as edging for beds of leggy shrub roses. Those sold as climbers make beautiful tree form roses and are lovely dripping from containers. Some of the very dense miniature roses make delightful edges for paths and driveways.

Try These
For fragrance, we recommend yellow 'Rise Shine', a recipient of the American Rose Society Award for Excellence. 'China Doll' makes a sweet 18-inch hedge covered with pink, semi-double blooms. For hanging baskets we like 'Red Cascade', a vigorous miniature with cascading branches, which also has an award for excellence from the ARS, and Starina®, a fragrant, orange-red miniature.

SHRUBS
FOR THE MID-ATLANTIC

Shrubs wed the other elements of the landscape to the buildings and the trees. Given a minimum of maintenance they provide flowers, foliage, fragrance, fruit, and interesting structures—pyramidal, columnar, arching, rounded, upright, or sprawling.

The leaf-losing flowering shrubs bring color to the garden early in the year. Forsythia turns to gold in March and the beautiful quinces follow. The spicily fragrant viburnums bloom later. In mid-spring, mature mock oranges perfume our gardens and the roses, described in the Roses chapter, come out full force. Summer has its stars, among them shore-loving hydrangeas, and butterfly bush—a prime attraction for these beautiful insects. Daphne fills summer afternoons with perfume. The foliage of some deciduous flowering plants also contributes to the beauty of the garden. When shrub borders are a mass of dark green in summer, the colorful foliage of *Weigela florida* 'Variegata' lightens the overall effect. In cold weather, spirea and the silver-backed leaves of willowleaf cotoneaster, *Cotoneaster salicifolius* 'Autumn Fire', take on a purplish cast that blends beautifully with autumn's russet tones. The structure of the deciduous shrubs is an important winter asset, especially very twiggy plants like the barberries.

Many beautiful broadleaved evergreens flourish here, and we recommend them highly because they not only add color, they add green to the garden at other seasons. Bright and beautiful azaleas and rhododendrons, some deciduous, some evergreen, peak in late April and early May. Evergreen mahonia's fragrant spring flowers are followed by blue berries that attract bevies of birds. In fall and winter nandina adds lipstick red berries and red-tipped leaves to perennial beds and shrub borders. The favorite hedge and accent plant in the Mid-Atlantic is English boxwood. It can be sheared for centuries, literally, so it's ideal for low hedges and to edge formal beds. Have a look some time at the most complete living collection of boxwood—at the U.S. National Arboretum in Washington, D.C. The needled evergreen shrubs we find most beautiful and valuable are included in the Conifers chapter.

When, Where, and How to Plant

When we are choosing shrubs, our first concern is whether the places we have in mind will suit them as they mature. To develop well, a shrub needs air and space. Small young shrubs may look cozy in a deep, airless corner but they become cramped as they mature, and might fall prey to certain insects and diseases under the stressful conditions. Light isn't usually a problem. Many are understory plants that developed in partial shade of taller trees, so they thrive in partial sun.

A lovely garden bench surrounded by boxwood provides a calm and serene spot in the garden.

Early spring and fall before Indian summer are the best planting seasons; early spring is best for shrubs that don't transplant easily. Container-grown plants can be set out anytime in spring, summer, or fall. Mail-order suppliers deliver some shrubs bare root and in time for spring planting—the roots need to be soaked six to twelve hours before planting. Young shrubs tend to be more vigorous than bigger, older plants that may have been in their containers for some time. Before buying a bargain plant, make sure the rootball has a healthy, earthy smell and is vigorous looking, not irretrievably locked in wound-around roots. When the color of a shrub's blossoms or its foliage is important to you, buy a plant whose flower or leaf color is evident at purchase.

A generous planting hole is the best send-off you can give a plant. Make the hole three times as wide and twice as deep as the rootball and plant the shrub so the crown will be an inch above the ground level. Loosen the soil on the sides, and blend the soil taken from the hole with the organic amendments described in "Soil Preparation and Improvement" in the introduction. Never replace existing soil with potting soil. Half-fill the bottom of the hole with the improved soil, and tamp it down to make a firm base for the shrub to rest on. Then proceed with the planting.

Before placing a bare-root shrub in its planting hole, make a firm mound in the center of the hole. Drape the plant roots over and around the mound and proceed with the instructions for planting a container-grown shrub. To free a containerized shrub, tip the container on its side and roll it around until the rootball loosens, or slit the pot open. If roots wrap a rootball, before planting make four deep vertical cuts in the sides

Berberis thunbergii 'Nana', *Juniperus conferta*, and *Betula platyphylla* var. *japonica* "Whitespire' provide a combination of forms and colors in a garden bed.

and slice the matted roots off the bottom 1 to 2 inches. Set the shrub in the hole and half-fill with amended soil. Tamp it down firmly. Fill the hole with improved soil and once more tamp it down firmly. Shape the soil around the crown into a wide saucer. Water the soil slowly, gently, and thoroughly with a sprinkler, a soaker hose, a bubbler, or by hand. You need to put down 10 to 15 gallons of water poured slowly from a bucket. Mulch newly planted shrubs 2 to 3 inches deep (for bigger shrubs) starting 3 inches from the stems. Replenish the mulch as needed to maintain it 2 to 3 inches deep.

Regional Advice and Care

For a shrub's first season, unless there's a soaking rain, in spring and fall slowly and gently pour two to three buckets of water around the roots every two weeks; in summer every week or ten days. Even after cold sets in, roots continue to develop, so during fall droughts continue the watering program sufficiently to keep the soil from drying out. Once established, most shrubs will require less extra watering than perennials; they slow their growth in high heat so they adapt unless forced by shallow watering and inappropriate fertilizing to grow when the weather isn't supporting growth. Fertilize shrubs twice a year. Late winter is the best time to apply the slow-release, natural, organic fertilizers we recommend (see page 222 in the appendix), but early spring is okay; repeat in fall. Avoid fertilizing flowering shrubs with chemical fertilizers shortly before blooming; that stimulates growth at a time when you want the plants to direct their energy into flowering. After the winter or early spring fertilization, renew the mulch. For shrubs that do best in a soil with a low pH, apply fertilizers for acid-loving plants. Nourish the soil as the forest does with fallen leaves—gather, shred, allow to age, and return them to the garden in the form of leaf mold or compost.

Pruning

You can reduce the amount of pruning your shrubs will need by selecting dwarf and slow-growing varieties. But even dwarfs grow, albeit slowly, and they need some pruning to maintain their size. Pruning—reducing leaf surfaces—limits the sugar synthesized and sent to the roots, and that limits next year's growth. Pruning also stimulates growth. Pruning young, just-developing shrubs when they are growing actively encourages growth and makes growth bushier. Fresh, young shoots that are cut back by half immediately begin to grow lateral shoots.

The season to prune flowering shrubs depends on their bloom habit: In late winter or early spring, well before growth begins, it is time to prune shrubs that bloom on the current season's wood. Prune a shrub that blooms in summer on current growth—butterfly bush for example—shortly before growth begins in spring. Those that bloom on last season's wood, such as azaleas, flowering quince, and forsythia, should be pruned as soon after their flowering period as possible, usually spring, because the next thing they do is to initiate buds for the following season. To encourage branching that produces more foliage in broadleaf evergreens like nandina, cut succulent new shoots in half while they are actively growing.

By pruning drastically in late winter you can rejuvenate leggy flowering shrubs that bloom on new wood. Make the cut 6 to 10 inches from the ground. To rejuvenate a multi-stemmed shrub, before growth begins in spring, take out one-third to one-quarter of the oldest of the branches and the suckers crowding young branches. Repeat the process for the next three to four years.

Other Shrubs Worthy of Consideration

Other beautiful shrubs that flourish here include:
Beautybush, *Linnaea amabilis* (formerly *Kolkwitzia amabilis*)
Bush cinquefoil, *Dasiphora fruticosa* (formerly *Potentilla fruticosa*)
Common privet, *Ligustrum vulgare*
California privet, *ovalifolium*
Golden privet, *Ligustrum* x *Vicary*
Japanese stewartia, *Stewartia pseudocamellia*
Korean stewartia, *S. koreana*
Prostrate broom, *Cytisus decumbens*
Scotch broom, *C. scorparius* 'Moonlight'
Warminster broom, *C.* x *praecox*
Spicebush, *Lindera benzoin*
Virginia sweetspire, *Itea virginica; I.* 'Henry's Garnet'

Blue Spirea

Caryopteris × *clandonensis*

Botanical Pronunciation
kair-ee-OP-tur-iss klan-dun-EN-siss

Other Name
Blue-mist

Bloom Period and Seasonal Color
Midsummer; shades of blue

Mature Height × Spread
1 to 3 feet × 3 to 6 feet

Blue spirea is a small, easy deciduous shrub or subshrub that in August produces spikes of airy flowers in delightful shades of blue. The long arching branches are covered with silvery foliage and the leaves, stems, and flowers are delicately aromatic. The plant grows quickly to 2 or 3 feet, and develops an open, airy, twiggy shape that is very appealing in flowering borders, and attractive edging walks and paths. The flowers bloom on new wood at or after midsummer when most other flowering shrubs have gone out of bloom, and they attract hordes of butterflies. Both foliage and flowers are used in bouquets, fresh and dried. This hybrid is superior to the common bluebeard, *Caryopteris incana*, and some first-rate cultivars are offered by nurseries and garden centers.

When, Where, and How to Plant

Container-grown blue spirea transplants easily in early spring or in early fall. The flowering will be best in full sun but it will also do well in part sun. Almost any soil will do as long as it is well drained, loose, or loamy, with enough humus to maintain moisture. See "Soil Preparation and Improvement" in the introduction, and the planting instructions at the beginning of this chapter. Provide a planting hole three times the width of the rootball and twice as deep. Set the shrub so the crown will be an inch or two above ground level. Shape the soil around the crown into a wide saucer. Water slowly and deeply. Apply mulch 3 inches deep starting 3 inches from the crown.

Growing Tips

The first year, unless there's a soaking rain, in spring and fall slowly and gently pour two to three buckets of water around the roots every two weeks; in summer, water every week or ten days. Maintain the mulch. Using a slow-release organic fertilizer, fertilize lightly in fall and again in late winter or early spring. Replenish the mulch.

Regional Advice and Care

The bluebeards bloom on new wood; to improve flowering, in spring, just as the buds are breaking, prune back to within an inch of the living wood growth that starts from the short woody branches at the base of the plant. Severe pruning in early spring improves the flowering.

Companion Planting and Design

Include blue spirea in your butterfly plantings. Its late blooming habit makes it an excellent addition to flowering borders.

Try These

We recommend 'Longwood Blue', a small blue spirea between 2 and 4 feet tall, for its heavy crop of deeper blue flowers and silver foliage; 'Dark Knight', a 2-footer with a spread of 1½ to 2 feet, for the very fragrant dark purple-blue flowers that attract butterflies and hummingbirds and silvery green foliage; 'Blue Mist', which grows 2 to 3 feet tall and wide, and has fringed blue flowers; and 'Worcester Gold', which has blue flowers and bright yellow to chartreuse foliage.

Boxwood

Buxus sempervirens and spp.

Botanical Pronunciation
BUCKS-us sem-PUR-vur-enz

Other Name
Box

Bloom Period and Seasonal Color
Spring blooms are insignificant; grown for evergreen foliage

Mature Height × Spread
5 to 15 feet × 5 to 15 feet

Boxwood is more than just a shrub to the Mid-Atlantic; it's a link to the clipped hedges that defined our ancestors' gardens and the great estates in their European homelands. It is the most popular subject for topiary. The trim hedges outlining the parterres at Versailles are clipped box. The species has dainty evergreen leaves, grows very slowly, is long lived, and can be clipped and pruned almost to any shape. Clippings are used to make Christmas roping and imitation Christmas tree topiaries. Historically, boxwood was used as edging and for tailored hedges. The most popular is English boxwood, *Buxus sempervirens* 'Suffruticosa', a slow-growing shrub with us since colonial times. Plants 150 years old have been kept to below 3 feet by pruning. The next most popular is 'Arborescens', tree boxwood.

When, Where, and How to Plant

Plant a container-grown boxwood in spring, summer, or fall. Transplant established box just before growth begins in mid-March, but spray it with wilt-proofing first. Mature plants thrive in full sun or light shade. Boxwood doesn't tolerate salt or wet feet; established plants tolerate some drought. They need well-drained, humusy, loose soil, pH 6.0 to 7.0. See "Soil Preparation and Improvement" in the introduction and instructions at the beginning of this chapter. Dig a hole three times the width of the rootball and twice as deep. Set the shrub so the crown will be an inch or two above ground level. Shape the soil around the crown into a wide saucer. Water slowly and deeply. Mulch 3 inches deep starting 3 inches from the crown.

Growing Tips

The first year, unless there's a soaking rain, in spring and fall slowly and gently pour two to three buckets of water around the roots every two weeks; in summer, water every week or ten days. Maintain the mulch to keep the temperature even around the roots. Using a slow-release organic fertilizer, fertilize lightly in early fall and again in spring. Replenish mulch as needed.

Regional Advice and Care

Shade newly transplanted boxwoods from summer sun. Boxwood's very fibrous roots are close to the surface, so weed by hand—not with a cultivator. Prune elongated shoots in late spring after new growth is complete to keep boxwood bushy and beautiful. To reshape overgrown shrubs, in February or early March, cut plants back to within 18 inches of the ground. They may take several years to fully recover. Deer avoid boxwood; chewing the leaves has killed some.

Companion Planting and Design

Boxwood thrives in city gardens and country estates. It is used with foundation plants, as a specimen, in group plantings, for hedges, and to edge knot gardens.

Try These

André recommends the species, and 'Arborescens' for shade; the 3 to 4 foot little-leaf boxwood, *B. microphylla*; and 'Kingsville Dwarf', a smaller variety. Where winters are hard, Korean little-leaf box, *B. microphylla* var. *koreana* is best; var. *japonica* is another good boxwood.

Butterfly Bush

Buddleja davidii, spp. and cultivars

Botanical Pronunciation
BUD-lee-uh duh-VID-ee-eye

Other Name Summer lilac

Bloom Period and Seasonal Color
August through September; species flowers are lilac; cultivars are white, pink, lavender, dark purple, purple-red

Mature Height × Spread
6 to 10 feet × 6 to 10 feet

Butterflies and hummingbirds—and bees—really do love this shrub, but that's not the only reason we recommend butterfly bush. The species grows to between 6 and 10 feet in a single season, and from July until frost produces slim arching canes that sweep the ground and in late summer are tipped with 4- to 10-inch spikes of delicately scented florets. The flowers are a rich source of nectar and a magnet for hummingbirds and bees as well as butterflies. The leaves range from green to gray-green to gray, and are narrow, 4 to 10 inches long, and silvery on the underside. Many beautiful cultivated varieties are available in a wide range or colors.

When, Where, and How to Plant
Container-grown butterfly bush transplants easily in early spring or in early fall. It flowers best in full sun but tolerates some shade. It thrives in humusy, fertile, well-drained soil with a pH of 5.5 to 7.0. See "Soil Preparation and Improvement" in the introduction, and the planting instructions at the beginning of this chapter. Provide a planting hole three times the width of the rootball and twice as deep. Set the shrub so the crown will be an inch or two above ground level. Shape the soil around the crown into a wide saucer. Water slowly and deeply. Apply mulch 3 inches deep starting 3 inches from the crown.

Growing Tips
The first year, unless there's a soaking rain, in spring and fall slowly and gently pour two to three buckets of water around the roots every two weeks; in summer every week or ten days. Maintain the mulch. Using a slow-release organic fertilizer, fertilize lightly in fall and again in late winter or early spring. After the winter fertilization, replenish the mulch.

Regional Advice and Care
To get the best flowering from butterfly bush, prune the shrub to 12 to 18 inches in early spring while the plant is still dormant. It blooms on new wood and will recover quickly.

Companion Planting and Design
For a small garden, dwarf butterfly bush is the better choice. *Buddleja davidii* var. *nanhoensis* 'Mongo', 'Petite Indigo', and 'Petite Plum' are 5-foot dwarfs with attractive grayish foliage; they are small enough to plant next to the kitchen steps where you can watch the butterflies. For a large garden, or for the back of a flowering border, consider *B. alternifolia*, a graceful 20-foot *Buddleja* with long, pendulous branches and flower spikes that are neat clusters of lilac-purple florets. It blooms early, in June.

Try These
The species offers a range of attractive colors we enjoy seeing planted together—'White Profusion', which bears white trusses 6 to 8 inches long; 'Pink Delight', whose trusses are up to 15 inches and a true pink; and 'Black Knight', which has very dark purple-violet flowers. 'Cran Razz' and Buzz™ 'True Blue' are excellent newer cultivars.

Camellia

Camellia japonica, spp. and hybrids

Botanical Pronunciation
kuh-MEEL-yuh juh-PON-ih-kuh

Other Name Japanese camellia

Bloom Period and Seasonal Color
In warm regions, fall and winter; in cold regions,
late winter and spring; flowers white to pink,
rose, crimson, purple-red, bicolors

Mature Height × Spread
4 to 15 feet × 3 to 10 feet

The camellia is a tall Southern belle with lustrous, olive green evergreen leaves and spectacular flowers that appear fall and winter in the Mid-Atlantic's warmest region, and in early spring in cooler areas. The blossoms are truly beautiful, sometimes fragrant, and many-petaled, semi-double, and double in many colors and bicolors. The widely grown Japanese camellia is a rather formal plant that bears flowers as much as 5 inches across in late winter and early spring. Temperatures below 32 degrees Fahrenheit can brown the buds and ruin the flowers. Select winter-hardy camellias with the assistance of staff at reliable local nurseries in your location, or check online.

When, Where, and How to Plant
Spring or fall, plant a dormant container-grown camellia in semi-sun, or in dappled or bright shade. In Zones 6 and 7, choose hardy camellias, and site them out of wind and direct western sun. Camellias prefer well-drained, humusy, acidic soil, pH 4.5 to 6.5. See "Soil Preparation and Improvement" in the introduction, and planting instructions at the beginning of this chapter. Provide a planting hole three times the width of the rootball and twice as deep. Set the shrub so the crown will be an inch or two above ground level. Shape the soil around the crown into a wide saucer. Water slowly and deeply. Apply mulch 3 inches deep starting 3 inches from the crown.

Growing Tips
The first year, unless there's a soaking rain, in spring and fall slowly and gently pour two to three buckets of water around the roots every two weeks; in summer every week or ten days. Maintain the mulch. Deadhead, including a couple of leaves below the flower to keep the shrub from growing straggly. In fall, make a light application of a slow-release organic fertilizer for acid-loving plants.

Care
Protect for winter with a 5- to 6-inch winter mulch and burlap barriers, or a spun polyester fabric wrap. Annual pruning is usually not needed. However, you can improve the flowering of a straggly camellia by shortening long shoots back to sturdy outward-facing side-shoots or buds after it has flowered. To rejuvenate older plants, remove one-third of the played-out branches before the shrub blooms every year for three years.

Companion Planting and Design
Camellias are used as foundation plants, grouped in a center island, planted as a flowering allée.

Try These
When cold cost the U.S. National Arboretum its large collection of camellias, 12-foot sasanqua camellia, *Camellia sasanqua*, survived and William Ackerman crossed it with hardy *C. oleifera*, the fragrant tea oil camellia. The hybrids are as pretty as the sasanquas and hardy in Zone 6, to -10 degrees Fahrenheit. The Ackerman hybrids have names like 'Winter's Charm'. However, even Ackerman hybrids suffer in exposed, windy areas, especially facing western sun.

Cotoneaster

Cotoneaster horizontalis and spp.

Botananical Pronunciation
kuh-toe-nee-ASS-tur hor-ih-zon-TAY-liss

Other Name
Rockspray cotoneaster

Bloom Period and Seasonal Color
Spring and summer; white or pinkish flowers; bright red berries; colorful fall foliage

Mature Height × Spread
2 to 3 feet × 6 to 8 feet

The cotoneasters are fine-textured, evergreen or semi-evergreen shrubs with layered branches and small white or pinkish flowers in spring and summer. The big show is the fall display of bright red or orange-red berries. There are tall and very low-growing members of the clan. Mid-sized rockspray cotoneaster, *Cotoneaster horizontalis*, is the most commonly planted species. It's a wide-spreading, semi-evergreen, tiered mound of branches that creates a herringbone pattern. The light pink flowers are followed in late summer by masses of persistent red fruits. The leaves are shiny dark green and usually turn scarlet-orange in the fall. Cotoneasters are good shore plants, and the fruits attract birds.

When, Where, and How to Plant

Set out a container-grown cotoneaster in early spring or early fall. It flowers well in full sun, four to six hours of sun, or all-day filtered light. Cotoneaster doesn't tolerate wet feet, but handles some drought. It succeeds in well-drained, humusy soil, acidic or alkaline. See "Soil Preparation and Improvement" in the introduction, and planting instructions at the beginning of this chapter. Provide a planting hole three times the width of the rootball and twice as deep. Set the shrub so the crown will be an inch or two above ground level. Shape the soil around the crown into a wide saucer. Water slowly and deeply. Apply mulch 3 inches deep starting 3 inches from the crown.

Growing Tips

The first year, unless there's a soaking rain, in spring and fall slowly and gently pour two to three buckets of water around the roots every two weeks; in summer, water every week or ten days. Maintain the mulch. In late winter or early spring fertilize with a slow-release organic fertilizer. Replenish the mulch. Fertilize again in fall.

Regional Advice and Care

Rockspray cotoneaster blooms on old wood. Minimal pruning is needed, and it's best undertaken after the berries are over. If the plant is growing against a wall, retain a few widely separated main branches and allow these to develop side branchlets. Keep an informal hedge in bounds by light selective pruning during the growing season. A formal hedge may be lightly sheared as needed.

Companion Planting and Design

Use cotoneaster for hedges and to clothe slopes, steps, and rocky places with attractive foliage, interesting branching, and bright berries.

Try These

In addition to the popular rockspray cotoneaster, for a groundcover in rocky places we recommend cranberry cotoneaster, *C. apiculatus*, which bears larger, bright red berries; creeping cotoneaster, *C. adpressus*, a very compact dwarf form; bearberry cotoneaster, *C. dammeri*, a low, prostrate evergreen groundcover; and spreading upright cotoneaster.

Deciduous Azalea

Rhododendron mucronulatum

Botanical Pronunciation
roe-doe-DEN-drun mew-kron-you-LAY-tum

Other Name
Korean azalea

Bloom Period and Seasonal Color
March and early April; rose-magenta

Mature Height × Spread
4 to 8 feet × 4 to 8 feet

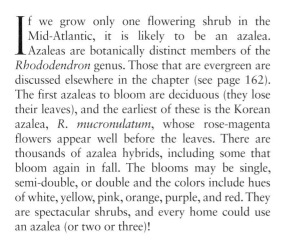

If we grow only one flowering shrub in the Mid-Atlantic, it is likely to be an azalea. Azaleas are botanically distinct members of the *Rhododendron* genus. Those that are evergreen are discussed elsewhere in the chapter (see page 162). The first azaleas to bloom are deciduous (they lose their leaves), and the earliest of these is the Korean azalea, *R. mucronulatum*, whose rose-magenta flowers appear well before the leaves. There are thousands of azalea hybrids, including some that bloom again in fall. The blooms may be single, semi-double, or double and the colors include hues of white, yellow, pink, orange, purple, and red. They are spectacular shrubs, and every home could use an azalea (or two or three)!

When, Where, and How to Plant
Azaleas are shallow-rooted and transplant well even when quite large. Plant a balled-and-burlapped azalea in early spring or early fall; plant a container-grown azalea in spring, summer, or fall. Azaleas do best in bright dappled light, but they tolerate full sun if the soil is moist. Provide soil that is well drained, rich in humus, and between pH 4.5 and 6.0. See "Soil Preparation and Improvement" in the introduction, and the planting instructions at the beginning of this chapter. Provide a planting hole three times the width of the rootball and the same depth. Set the shrub so the crown will be an inch or two above ground level. Shape the soil around the crown into a wide saucer. Water slowly and deeply. Apply mulch 3 inches deep starting 3 inches from the crown.

Growing Tips
The first season, unless there's a soaking rain, every two weeks in spring and fall slowly and gently pour two to three buckets of water around the roots; in summer every week or ten days. Maintain the mulch. Using a slow-release organic fertilizer for acid-loving plants, fertilize an azalea in late winter or early spring, and in the fall. Replenish the mulch.

Regional Advice and Care
To keep an azalea shapely, stimulate growth, and encourage the formation of flowering buds, after blooming prune the branches back to outward-facing buds.

Companion Planting and Design
We like deciduous azaleas with broadleaved evergreen shrubs—rhododendrons, mountain laurels, and evergreen azaleas. The Korean azalea is especially nice with early-blooming forsythia.

Try These
André's father Martin Viette's favorites were a white and 'Cornell Pink' Korean azalea. André recommends the showy, fragrant, pink royal azalea, *R. schlippenbachii*; the native, fragrant, white sweet azalea, *R. arborescens*, for its orange fall foliage; the native flame azalea, *R. calendulaceum*, for its showy flowers in shades of yellow, apricot, orange, and scarlet; and the pinkshell azalea, *R. vaseyi*, which is native to the Blue Ridge Mountains of North Carolina. And for their rhododendron-like blooms, try the Knap Hill and Exbury hybrids, and the Mollis group, *R. × kosteranum*.

Dwarf Burning Bush

Euonymus alatus 'Compactus'

Botanical Pronunciation
you-ON-ih-mus eh-LAY-tus

Other Name
Dwarf winged spindle tree

Bloom Period and Seasonal Color
Fall; glowing crimson foliage

Mature Height × Spread
8 to 10 feet × 8 to 10 feet

Dwarf burning bush is a member of the bittersweet family, a group that includes both leaf-losing and evergreen shrubs, small trees, and vines that have beautiful foliage and colorful fall fruits. Dwarf burning bush is a slow-growing shrub with outreaching branches, a compact version of the winged spindle tree, *Euonymus alatus*, whose flaming fall color rivals the sugar maple. When cold comes, every leaf on the winged spindle tree, and on the dwarf burning bush, turns a glowing rosy crimson before falling. The show is enhanced by small clusters of tiny fruits that turn lipstick red. The birds love the fruits and usually pick the branches clean. The word "winged" in the other common name refers to corky ridges edging the branches. The ridges are most pronounced in the tree, enough to have textural interest.

When, Where, and How to Plant

Container-grown *Euonymus* can be planted spring, summer, or fall. It succeeds even on dry, rocky slopes. The dwarf burning bush and the winged spindle tree color most brilliantly in full sun, but succeed in part sun or part shade. Any soil that isn't swampy will do, pH 6.0 to 8.0. See "Soil Preparation and Improvement" in the introduction, and the planting instructions at the beginning of this chapter. Provide a planting hole three times the width of the rootball and twice as deep. Set the shrub so the crown will be an inch or two above ground level. Shape the soil around the crown into a wide saucer. Water slowly and deeply. Apply mulch 2 inches deep starting 3 inches from the crown.

Growing Tips

The first year, unless there's a soaking rain, in spring and fall slowly and gently pour two to three bucketsful of water around the roots every two weeks; in summer every week or ten days. Maintain the mulch. Fertilize with a slow-release organic fertilizer for acid-loving plants in fall and again in late winter or early spring. Replenish the mulch periodically.

Regional Advice and Care

Burning bush is most attractive when it is allowed to develop naturally with some thinning to keep the plant structure open. To keep a hedge of evergreen *Euonymus* to 4 to 6 feet, cut back branch tips of older wood in April or May.

Companion Planting and Design

Dwarf winged spindle tree is used in informal hedges and as a featured lawn specimen. On the grounds of the U.S. Capitol, winged spindle tree grows with evergreens, forsythias, and other shrubs, unnoticed until fall—then the color draws the eye for weeks.

Try These

While all *Euonymus* are subject to scale, there's very little problem with *E. alatus*, either the dwarf or the species. A cultivar of the European *Euonymus*, *E. europaeus* 'Aldenhamensis' bears bright pink capsules and is more fruitful than the species. *E. fortunei*, the wintercreeper *Euonymus* planted for its silver-veined foliage, is a beautiful groundcover or vine, but it has too many problems.

Dwarf Fothergilla

Fothergilla gardenia

Botanical Pronunciation
fah-thur-GILL-uh GAR-den-ee-eye

Other Name Witch alder

Bloom Period and Seasonal Color
April to early May; white flowers; fall foliage is
yellow gold, orange, scarlet

Mature Height × Spread
2 to 4 feet × 2 to 4 feet

Fothergilla is native to the Alleghenies and is rated as one of the top ten to twenty native American shrubs. Like witch-hazel, to which it is related, fothergilla blooms early, has fragrant, somewhat similar blossoms, and the foliage colors brilliantly in fall. Dwarf fothergilla is a small bushy shrub, just as wide as it is high. In April and early May it bears rounded tufts of whitish bottlebrush flowers that have the sweet scent of honey. The flowers and the crinkly dark green foliage are reason enough to plant fothergilla, but the brilliant fall foliage is the star attraction. The leaves turn to yellow gold, orange, and scarlet, and usually with all three colors on the same bush.

When, Where, and How to Plant

Plant a balled-and-burlapped fothergilla in early spring or early fall. If it's container-grown, it can be planted spring, summer, or fall. Fothergilla flowers best and produces the brightest fall colors growing in full sun, but in hot areas it benefits from protection from noon sun in summer. To succeed, fothergilla must have soil with an acid pH, under 6.0. It is not suited to alkaline or limey soil. See "Soil Preparation and Improvement" in the introduction, and the planting instructions at the beginning of this chapter. Provide a planting hole three times the width of the rootball and twice as deep. Set the shrub so the crown will be an inch or two above ground level. Shape the soil around the crown into a wide saucer. Water slowly and deeply. Apply mulch 2 inches deep starting 3 inches from the crown.

Growing Tips

The first year, unless there's a soaking rain, in spring and fall slowly and gently pour two to three buckets of water around the roots every two weeks; in summer every week or ten days. Maintain the mulch. Using a slow-release organic fertilizer for acid-loving plants, fertilize lightly in fall and again in late winter or early spring. Replenish the mulch.

Regional Advice and Care

Before growth begins in spring, cut back to the ground old branches that are crowding others, taking care not to harm young shoots coming up from the base.

Companion Planting and Design

Fothergilla lights up shrub borders planted with azaleas, rhododendrons, and evergreens. We like to place them near the house and along paths where the sweet honey scent of their flowers can be appreciated.

Try These

Dwarf fothergilla is best for smaller gardens, but where there's space, choose larger, faster-growing *Fothergilla major*, which grows more upright and matures at 6 to 10 feet. Two newer cultivars are 'Snowday Blizzard' and 'Snowday Surprise'.

Evergreen Azalea

Rhododendron spp. and hybrids

Botanical Pronunciation
roe-doe-DEN-drun

Bloom Period and Seasonal Color
April to September; white, shades of coral, pink, rose, red, purple, bicolors

Mature Height × Spread
2 to 6 feet × 4 to 6 feet

Evergreen azaleas, like the deciduous azaleas described earlier in the chapter (see page 159), belong to the genus *Rhododendron*. The flowers of the evergreen azaleas are funnel-shaped rather than bell-shaped, like the leaf-losing azaleas, and the plant is smaller and more refined. The foliage of some varieties acquires a plum or maroon tint in fall and others turn to gold. You can have evergreen azaleas in flower from early spring to late summer. The hundreds of medium-tall *R. kaempferi* cultivars, which are hardy in Zones 5b to 9, are usually evergreen. An evergreen group that does well here is the Glenn Dale type, developed by B. Y. Morrison, first director of the U.S. National Arboretum. You can see hundreds of varieties in bloom there in May.

When, Where, and How to Plant

Azaleas are fibrous-rooted and transplant well even when quite large. The best times to plant them are early fall and early spring. An azalea tolerates full sun here as long as the soil is moist, but it will do best in bright, dappled light. Provide soil that is well drained, rich in humus (we add leaf mold to the hole), and between pH 4.5 to 6.0. See "Soil Preparation and Improvement" in the introduction, and planting instructions at the beginning of this chapter. Provide a planting hole three times the width of the rootball and the same depth. Set the shrub so the crown will be about an inch above ground level. Shape the soil around the crown into a wide saucer. Water slowly and deeply. Apply mulch 3 inches deep starting 3 inches from the crown.

Growing Tips

The first year, unless there's a soaking rain, in spring and fall slowly and gently pour two to three buckets of water around the roots every two weeks; in summer, water every week or ten days. Maintain the mulch. Using a slow-release organic fertilizer for acid-loving plants, fertilize in spring and again in fall. Replenish the mulch.

Regional Advice and Care

To maintain the shape of an azalea, as soon as it finishes blooming, prune the branches back to outward-facing buds. Shearing to remove flowering tips when the blooms fade improves the next season's flowering; pruning too long after flowering cuts off next year's blooms.

Companion Planting and Design

Evergreen azaleas are especially useful for fronting a border of rhododendrons, andromeda, mountain laurel, and deciduous azaleas.

Try These

In addition to the Glenn Dale evergreen azaleas, try the many-hued Gable hybrids, hardy even in Zone 5, and the hardiest of the Encore™ azaleas, Autumn Jewel™, Autumn Lily™, and Autumn Royalty™. The lavender Yodogawa azalea, *R. yedoense*, has fragrant double flowers and is hardy in Zone 5. The lovely Kurume azaleas, and vivid red 'Hinodegiri', are hardy in Zones 5 and 6.

Firethorn

Pyracantha coccinea

Botanical Pronunciation
pye-ruh-KAN-thuh kock-SIN-ee-uh

Bloom Period and Seasonal Color
Late spring; white flowers; bright orange or red berries in fall

Mature Height × Spread
6 to 18 feet × 6 to 18 feet

Firethorn, sometimes also called scarlet firethorn, is a big, thorny, wide-branching evergreen or semi-evergreen shrub that produces fine foliage and white, lightly scented flowers in mid-spring. It is grown primarily for the clusters of brilliant red-orange fruits that mature in the fall. These "berries" (actually, they are pomes, like apples) are mildly toxic; keep that in mind if you have children at home or visiting. Firethorn, true to its name, is a prickly plant that's often used as a barrier planting, such as a hedge. The species is susceptible to scale, but in recent years several improved varieties have been introduced. When you buy *Pyracantha*, insist on having a scale- and fireblight-resistant variety.

When, Where, and How to Plant

Firethorn transplants with difficulty, so plant a container-grown shrub in early spring before growth begins. Firethorn flowers best and produces the brightest fruits growing in full sun. However, like most shrubs, it succeeds with four to six hours of sun, or all-day filtered light. It thrives in any well-drained soil in a broad pH range, 5.5 to 7.5. See "Soil Preparation and Improvement" in the introduction, and planting instructions at the beginning of this chapter. Provide a planting hole three times the width of the rootball and twice as deep. Set the shrub so the crown will be an inch or so above ground level. Shape the soil around the crown into a wide saucer. Water slowly and deeply. Apply mulch 3 inches deep starting 3 inches from the crown.

Growing Tips

The first year, unless there's a soaking rain, in spring and fall slowly and gently pour two to three buckets of water around the roots every two weeks; in summer every week or ten days. Maintain the mulch. Using a slow-release organic fertilizer, fertilize lightly in the fall and again in late winter or early spring. Replenish the mulch.

Regional Advice and Care

Firethorn becomes very widespread if left unpruned. If you wish to maintain the shape of this spring flowering shrub, shortly after it finishes blooming, prune the branches back to outward facing buds. Flower buds—and the fruit—form on old wood; as you prune, keep in mind that the flowers you don't prune off will provide you with a lovely show of berries in the fall.

Companion Planting and Design

Firethorn can be used as a freestanding specimen, and in hedges, but is most striking espaliered against a blank masonry or wooden wall, or grown on a trellis where the asymmetrical branching and bright fall fruits stand out.

Try These

One we can recommend is 'Mohave', an upright shrub 10 to 12 feet tall that bears masses of bright orange-red berries. It isn't hardy near the West Virginia border, but 'Fiery Cascade', another resistant hybrid that bears an abundance of bright fruits, withstands winters even in Zone 6.

Flowering Quince

Chaenomeles speciosa

Botanical Pronunciation
kee-NOM-uh-leez spee-see-OH-suh

Other Name
Chinese flowering quince

Bloom Period and Seasonal Color
Early spring; white, peach, pink, coral, rose, orange, red, ruby-red

Mature Height × Spread
6 to 10 feet × 6 to 10 feet

Flowering quince in bloom is one of spring's most beautiful flowering shrubs. The blossoms appear to sprout from the bark, like apple blossoms, and are perfectly arranged on the branches. There are exquisite single or double flowering forms that come in white and many beautiful coral and rose-red shades. The shrub is broadspreading, and produces a twiggy mass of rather thorny branches, quite extraordinary trained as an espalier, a pruned hedge, or in a Japanese structured, stylized form. The branches are easy to force into early bloom and are remarkably lovely. The new foliage is red-rose-bronze that changes to glossy green leaves. The quince grown for making preserves is the common quince, *Cydonia oblonga*, a large shrub or small tree, but flowering quince also bears fruit—waxy, yellowish, 2-inch fruits that are fragrant.

When, Where, and How to Plant

Plant a balled-and-burlapped quince in early spring or fall. Plant a container-grown quince spring, summer, or fall. Quince does best growing in full sun but succeeds with four to six hours of sun, or all-day filtered light. It thrives with a pH of 5.5, but can succeed in a broad range of soil types and pH as high as 7.5. See "Soil Preparation and Improvement" in the introduction, and the planting instructions at the beginning of this chapter. Provide a planting hole three times the width of the rootball and twice as deep. Set the shrub so the crown will be an inch or two above ground level. Shape the soil around the crown into a wide saucer. Water slowly and deeply. Apply mulch 3 inches deep starting 3 inches from the crown.

Growing Tips

The first year, unless there's a soaking rain, in spring and fall slowly and gently pour two to three bucketsful of water around the roots every two weeks; in summer, water every week or ten days. Maintain the mulch. Using a slow-release organic fertilizer for acid-loving plants, fertilize lightly in fall and again in late winter or early spring. Replenish the mulch.

Regional Advice and Care

Quince flowers on wood grown the previous season and on a system of spurs. To keep the center open, when the blossoms fade and before May, cut back older canes and suckers to the ground. As new wood hardens in summer, remove branches that cross or are badly positioned, and thin out older woody spurs. After the leaves fall, take the main branches back to two or three buds.

Companion Planting and Design

Flowering quince branches develop an elegant asymmetrical sprawl that is attractive in an informal hedge. In spite of its beauty, flowering quince is a single season plant, and in a small landscape shouldn't be given space that could go to a plant with appeal in three or four seasons.

Try These

There are innumerable named varieties, such as 'Toyo Nishiki' and hybrids such as 'Cameo' and 'Jet Trail'. The single-flowered forms have a kind of purity common to all singles—more drama, perhaps. The double-flowered forms appeal to us less but that's not the common experience.

Forsythia

Forsythia × intermedia 'Spectabilis'

Botananical Pronunciation
for-SYE-thee-uh inter-ME-dee-a

Other Name
Border forsythia

Bloom Period and Seasonal Color
March and April; deep yellow flowers

Mature Height × Spread
8 to 10 feet × 10 to 12 feet

orsythia is the herald of spring everywhere. It pops a few golden blooms before the plum trees have even budded. Forsythia flower buds open before the leaves appear, covering the widespreading, arching branches with small, showy, vivid yellow flowers. The small blooms last well, as long as we don't have a heat spell. When the cold comes in fall, the leaves take on an orangey plum hue before they fall. This is a fast-growing arching shrub that roots where it touches the ground. It develops dense thickets unless it is pruned annually, and is used as a tall groundcover for slopes. Branches pruned in late winter as the buds swell are easily forced into bloom indoors.

When, Where, and How to Plant
Container-grown forsythia transplants easily spring, summer, and fall; a balled-and-burlapped shrub and rooted plantlets transplant best in very early spring or in fall after the leaves drop. Forsythia flowers best in full sun but blooms in part shade. It thrives in almost any soil that is well drained, loamy, and has enough humus to maintain moisture, with a pH range of 6.0 to 8.0. See "Soil Preparation and Improvement" in the introduction, and the planting instructions at the beginning of this chapter. Provide a planting hole three times the width of the rootball and twice as deep. Set the shrub so the crown will be an inch or two above ground level. Shape the soil around the crown into a wide saucer. Water slowly and deeply. Apply mulch 3 inches deep starting 3 inches from the crown.

Growing Tips
The first year, unless there's a soaking rain, in spring and fall slowly and gently pour two to three buckets of water around the roots every two weeks; in summer, water every week or ten days. Maintain the mulch. Using a slow-release organic fertilizer, fertilize lightly in fall and again in late winter or early spring. Replenish the mulch from time to time.

Regional Advice and Care
To keep forsythia in bounds, when it finishes blooming, prune the branches back to outward facing buds and remove the oldest canes down to the ground. Branches that touch the ground root over time and can be transplanted.

Companion Planting and Design
Fast-growing border forsythia is used for screening, in informal hedges, as tall groundcover, and as a bank holder. It can stand a lot of shearing, and it can be espaliered. It is attractive featured as a specimen in the middle of a large lawn, or in a group with evergreens and other flowering shrubs.

Try These
The named variety 'Lynwood' ('Lynwood Gold') is a more upright plant that has perhaps the most beautiful flowers—they're more open and slightly larger. 'Primulina' (which may be hard to find), has pale yellow flowers and golden fall foliage that turns to mahogany, was a favorite of André's father, Martin Viette. 'Spring Glory' is a sulfur yellow.

Glossy Abelia

Abelia × grandiflora

Botanical Pronunciation
uh-BEEL-yuh gran-dih-FLORE-uh

Other Name
Abelia

Bloom Period and Seasonal Color
June till frost; pink flowers, purplish foliage in fall

Mature Height × Spread
3 to 6 feet × 3 to 6 feet

Glossy abelia's great asset is a summer-long show of flowers. The plant is a rounded, multi-stemmed, semi-evergreen shrub 3 to 6 feet tall, with twiggy branches, dainty foliage, and small, slightly fragrant, funnel-shaped pink flowers. It comes into bloom in June or July and goes on blooming until frost. The leaves take on a purplish bronze cast in late fall and persist until early winter. There are many varieties. A tried-and-true favorite is 4- to 6-foot 'Edward Goucher', a dense, arching shrub with orange-throated, lilac-pink flowers. In warmer areas of the Mid-Atlantic, glossy abelia is an evergreen. In the cool uplands the leaves may eventually fall. Either way, the shrub's twiggy structure is an asset to the garden.

When, Where, and How to Plant

The time to plant a container-grown abelia is in the fall before Indian summer, and in early spring while the shrub is still dormant. Abelia flowers best growing in full sun. However, like most shrubs, it succeeds with four to six hours of sun, or all-day filtered light. The ideal soil is well drained, humusy, sandy, and in the acidic range, pH 5.5 to 6.5, but pH can be variable. See "Soil Preparation and Improvement" in the introduction, and planting instructions at the beginning of this chapter. Provide a planting hole three times the width of the rootball and twice as deep. Set the shrub so the crown will be about an inch or two above ground level. Shape the soil around the crown into a wide sauce. Water slowly and deeply.

Apply mulch 3 inches deep starting 3 inches from the crown.

Growing Tips

The first year, unless there's a soaking rain, in spring and fall slowly and gently pour two to three buckets of water around the roots every two weeks; in summer, water every week or ten days. Maintain the mulch. Using a slow-release organic fertilizer for acid-loving plants, fertilize lightly in fall and again in spring. Replenish the mulch.

Regional Advice and Care

Glossy abelia blooms on side branches of the previous year's growth, and on new wood, so in late winter prune back dead branch tips to outward facing buds. Prune winterkilled tips in early spring. Once the shrub has attained a size that is pleasing, you can keep it at that size by removing up to one-third of the branch tips in a year. Prune to restrict its size when flowering is over.

Companion Planting and Design

Abelia is used as a bank cover. 'Edward Goucher' makes an informal hedge and is handsome enough on its own to be a featured specimen.

Try These

For the foliage, André recommends Ruby Anniversary™ and the cultivar 'Prostrata', a compact, low-growing shrub with smaller leaves that turn burgundy-green in winter.

Hydrangea

Hydrangea arborescens
'Annabelle', spp., and hybrids

Botanical Pronunciation
hy-DRAIN-juh ar-bore-ESS-enz

Bloom Period and Seasonal Color
Mid- to late summer; white, shades of pink and blue

Mature Height × Spread
3 to 18 feet × 3 to 20 feet

Hydrangeas are fast-growing deciduous shrubs with cane-like branches, large handsome leaves, and a mid- to late summer show of often huge flower heads composed of dozens of florets. Hortensia, or mophead, types have rounded flower heads of basically sterile florets; lacecaps are composed of both showy (sterile) flowers around the outer edge, and tiny (fertile) florets in the center, and may be cone-shaped or flattened. Georgia Gold Medal Award-winning *Hydrangea arborescens* 'Annabelle' is a superb plant that blooms fully every year, with white flower heads up to 12 inches across that turn a beautiful pale green with age. The blossoms dry so easily you can't resist making winter arrangements with them. Another favorite is bigleaf hydrangea, *H. macrophylla*, which includes both lacecap and hortensia varieties in cream, rose, pink, and light or dark blue; color depends on soil acidity. It needs winter protection in Zone 6.

When, Where, and How to Plant
Plant container-grown hydrangeas in early spring. They bloom in full sun, and in bright or dappled shade; in hot areas they benefit from noon or afternoon shade. *H. arborescens* 'Annabelle' and *H. quercifolia* (oakleaf hydrangea) are tolerant of pH. *H. macrophylla* will color blue or pink according to soil pH; acidic soil ensures blue; pH 5.0 to 5.5 results in a soft blue; 6.0 to 6.5, or slightly higher, maintains pink. Hydrangeas need a well-drained site, and loose or sandy soil with enough humus to maintain moisture. See "Soil Preparation and Improvement" in the introduction, and the planting instructions at the beginning of this chapter. Provide a planting hole three times the width of the rootball and twice as deep. Set so the crown will be an inch or two above ground level. Shape the soil around the crown into a wide saucer. Water slowly and deeply. Mulch 2 inches deep starting 3 inches from the crown.

Growing Tips
The first year, unless there's a soaking rain, in spring and fall slowly and gently water two to three buckets around the roots every two weeks; in summer, water every week or ten days. Using a slow-release organic fertilizer, fertilize lightly in fall and again in late winter or early spring. Replenish the mulch.

Regional Advice and Care
H. arborescens flowers on new wood. To maintain flowering and form, cut the oldest canes between late fall and early spring; deadhead to prolong flowering. *H. macrophylla*, must be pruned in spring since it blooms on new growth from buds from the previous season. Cut back to a live bud.

Companion Planting and Design
Hydrangeas are great seashore plants. They deserve a bed of their own.

Try These
André recommends Incrediball® and improved 'Annabelle'. He likes the oakleaf hydrangea Gatsby's Moon™, a magnificent plant with cone-shaped flower heads in early summer and red-purple fall foliage. 'Limelight', 'Snowflake', a double-flowered form, and 'Snowqueen', which bears enormous flower trusses, are other favorites.

Japanese Andromeda

Pieris japonica

Botanical Pronunciation
pee-AIR-iss juh-PON-ih-kuh

Other Name Japanese pieris

Bloom Period and Seasonal Color
February to April; white flowers, pink buds on some varieties

Mature Height × Spread
9 to 12 feet × 6 to 8 feet

The andromedas are handsome evergreen shrubs that do well in sun to shade and the acidic soils that suit azaleas and rhododendrons. They're the first of the evergreen shrubs to bloom. In late winter and early spring they are covered with large clusters of waxy, creamy white buds that open into small urn-shaped flowers. The leaves are shiny green year-round, and the new foliage is a gleaming rose-bronze. Japanese andromeda is a beautiful species, whose branches cascade almost to the ground. The tips are dense with clusters of rather fragrant flowers in strands 3 to 6 inches long that last two to three weeks. The new foliage is bronze to wine-red, and very showy in the newer cultivars.

When, Where, and How to Plant

A young container-grown or balled-and-burlapped andromeda transplants easily in early spring. The andromedas are known as shrubs for shady places, two to six hours of sun a day, but some growers recommend full sun for modern hybrids. The ideal site is out of the wind, well-drained, with humusy, moist soil that is acidic, pH 4.5 to 6.0. See "Soil Preparation and Improvement" in the introduction, and planting instructions at the beginning of this chapter. Provide a planting hole three times the width of the rootball and twice as deep. Set the shrub so the crown will be an inch or two above ground level. Shape the soil around the crown into a wide saucer. Water slowly and deeply. Apply mulch 3 inches deep starting 3 inches from the crown.

Growing Tips

The first year, unless there's a soaking rain, in spring and fall slowly and gently pour two to three buckets of water around the roots every two weeks; in summer, water every week or ten days. Maintain the mulch. Using a slow-release organic fertilizer for acid-loving plants, fertilize lightly in fall and again in spring. Replenish the mulch.

Regional Advice and Care

Removing spent blooms when the plant is young encourages growth and flower production. Ideally, andromeda's cascading branches are allowed to develop naturally. Damaged wood should be pruned back in March before new growth begins.

Companion Planting and Design

Andromeda has a rather formal appearance and is an excellent foundation plant. We like it in shrub groups with rhododendrons and azaleas whose need for acidic soil it shares.

Try These

There are some beautiful named varieties of Japanese andromeda. Among our favorites are 'Flamingo', whose flowers are deep rose-red bells; the semi-dwarf 'Variegata', whose foliage is flushed pink when new, then margined with white; and 'White Cascade', which bears long, large panicles of pure white flowers that last weeks longer than the species. The native mountain andromeda, *Pieris floribunda*, is a better choice for naturalized situations and cooler, more exposed sites.

Japanese Aucuba

Aucuba japonica

Botanical Pronunciation
aw-KEW-buh juh-PON-ih-kuh

Bloom Period and Seasonal Color
March and April; nonshowy purple blooms

Mature Height × Spread
6 to 10 feet × 5 to 9 feet

Aucuba is a tall, beautiful, shade-loving, drought-resistant, broadleaved evergreen that makes a great foundation plant, screen, or hedge. Though it produces berries, the leaves are its glory—large, leathery, and bright green, they clothe the plant's many succulent branching stems, usually all the way to the ground. A planting becomes increasingly dense because shoots touching the ground root and produce new plants. Male and female flowers are produced on different plants. When pollinated by a male, a female aucuba produces large, persistent, red berries. The variety 'Variegata', the gold-dust plant, is a female plant whose leaves are beautifully marked with flecks of gold. A suitable pollinator is the male plant 'Maculata', which is handsomely blotched yellow-white.

When, Where, and How to Plant
Aucuba survives droughts, urban situations, is pest- and disease-resistant, and thrives even under heavy-rooted trees where grass won't grow. In Zone 6 it needs a location protected from freezing winds and western sun. Plant a container-grown aucuba in early spring or late summer. It thrives in partial shade and handles deep shade; direct sun facing south or west may result in leaf damage. Provide a site that is well drained, with humusy soil that has a high organic content so that the roots are kept moist. Aucuba is pH tolerant. See "Soil Preparation and Improvement" in the introduction, and planting instructions at the beginning of this chapter. Provide a planting hole three times the width of the rootball and twice as deep. Set the shrub so the crown will be an inch or two above ground level. Shape the soil around the crown into a wide saucer. Water slowly and deeply. Apply mulch 3 inches deep starting 3 inches from the crown.

Growing Tips
The first year, unless there's a soaking rain, in spring and fall slowly and gently pour two to three buckets of water around the roots every two weeks; in summer, water every week or ten days. Maintain the mulch. Using a slow-release organic fertilizer, fertilize lightly in fall and again in late winter or early spring. Replenish the mulch.

Regional Advice and Care
Late winter and late summer are the best seasons to prune aucuba. To control the shoots that sprawl outward from the central stems, cut them out below ground level; to control the height, cut the tallest stems back to just above a pair of leaves.

Companion Planting and Design
Groups of aucuba soften bare shaded walls and light up dim corners. You can use it as a background hedge for small flowering shrubs, such as azaleas, and for perennials. In cold regions, it is grown in tubs and used as a screen and background plant in patio and terrace gardens; it winters indoors successfully in a bright, cool room.

Try These
'Variegata' is our favorite, but we also like 'Crotonifolia', whose leaves are dusted with yellow spots.

Japanese Kerria

Kerria japonica 'Pleniflora'

Botanical Pronunciation
KAIR-ee-uh juh-PON-ih-kuh

Bloom Period and Seasonal Color
April to May; bright yellow

Mature Height × Spread
5 to 10 feet × 6 to 10 feet

Like forsythia, Japanese kerria covers itself for two or three weeks in April or May with small flowers as bright and cheerful as sunshine. There's one species in cultivation and it comes from Central and Western China, though we call it Japanese kerria. A 3- to 6-foot shrub that was once so popular you still find it in all the older parks in the East, it bears masses of little, flat-faced, five-petaled flowers. Sometimes it repeats its bloom in summer. The variety 'Pleniflora', which is taller than the species, is the best for landscaping. It's a tough, vigorous, upright, bushy plant that bears masses of double golden yellow flowers. Cut branches of kerria last well in a vase.

When, Where, and How to Plant

You'll find balled-and-burlapped kerria transplants well in early spring or early fall. Container-grown kerria can be planted spring, summer, or fall. Kerria blooms well in sun and in part shade, even in dry urban gardens. Light shade is the best situation in our hotter regions. Kerria also isn't difficult about soil—it will flourish in almost any well-drained soil that is moderately moist and fertile. See "Soil Preparation and Improvement" in the introduction, and the planting instructions at the beginning of this chapter. Provide a planting hole three times the width of the rootball and twice as deep. Set the shrub so the crown will be an inch or two above ground level. Shape the soil around the crown into a wide saucer. Water slowly and deeply. Apply mulch 3 inches deep starting 3 inches from the crown.

Growing Tips

The first year, unless there's a soaking rain, in spring and fall slowly and gently pour two to three buckets of water around the roots every two weeks; in summer, water every week or ten days. Maintain the mulch. Using a slow-release organic fertilizer, fertilize lightly in fall and again in late winter or early spring. Replenish the mulch periodically.

Care

Kerria tolerates summer heat and drought. To keep 'Pleniflora' shapely, as flowers fade, trim old flowering stems back to strong young shoots or to ground level. Remove suckers that rise around the variegated cultivar 'Picta'; they tend to revert to plain green.

Companion Planting and Design

A traditional wall plant in cottage gardens, kerria is attractive massed in naturalistic plantings, on slopes, anywhere you have room for a good-sized shrub and would like to see a sunny color in early spring and wonderful green foliage in summer heat.

Try This One

'Pleniflora' is our choice.

Lilac

Syringa vulgaris

Botanical Pronunciation
sur-ING-guh vul-GAIR-iss

Other Name
Common lilac

Bloom Period and Seasonal Color
May; white to lilac, blue, lavender, purple, pink,
wine-red

Mature Height × Spread
12 to 16 feet × 8 to 12 feet

Lilacs are multi-stemmed shrubs or small trees that bear panicles of single or double florets in late spring. The one most famous for fragrance is the 12- to 16-foot common lilac, *Syringa vulgaris*, which came to America with the colonists. It was being hybridized in France to improve the flowers by the late 1700s, so many of today's most beautiful double-flowered forms and unusual colors are known as French lilacs; not all are fragrant. If perfume is what you love, look for varieties advertised as very fragrant, like 'Charles Joly', a double-flowered form with deep wine-red flowers, and 'Ludwig Spaeth', a heavily fragrant, dark purple, single-flowered variety. Lilacs are subject to mildew, so look for cultivars advertised as mildew-resistant.

When, Where, and How to Plant

Lilacs transplant easily in early spring and in early fall. They succeed in open, airy sites in full sun or light shade. The ideal soil is well drained, moist, and neutral—pH 7.0 to 7.5; an annual sprinkling of wood ashes or lime keeps soil neutral. See "Soil Preparation and Improvement" in the introduction, and the planting instructions at the beginning of this chapter. Provide a planting hole three times the width of the rootball and twice as deep. Set the shrub so the crown will be an inch or two above ground level. Shape the soil around the crown into a wide saucer. Water slowly and deeply. Apply mulch 3 inches deep starting 3 inches from the crown.

Growing Tips

The first year, unless there's a soaking rain, in spring and fall slowly and gently pour two to three buckets of water around the roots every two weeks; in summer, water every week or ten days. Maintain the mulch. Using a slow-release organic fertilizer, fertilize lightly in fall and again in late winter or early spring. Replenish the mulch.

Regional Advice and Care

Established lilacs tolerate some drought. Deadhead to encourage flowering. Regularly prune out the oldest branches and all but two or three strong suckers. The taller lilacs can be pruned to grow as single-stem or multi-stemmed plants.

Companion Planting and Design

A staple of Victorian shrub borders, lilacs are now featured lawn specimens, or used in tall hedges, and in allées called "lilac walks." Smaller forms do well in containers.

Try These

André's favorites are fragrant ones, such as compact, mildew-resistant, very flowery, pale violet-purple Korean lilac, *S. meyeri* 'Palibin', which blooms before the leaves appear; the small pale flowered Persian lilac, *S. × persica*, which blooms in mid-May, a beautiful old hybrid; and the 20- to 30-foot Japanese tree lilac, *S. reticulata*, which blooms last with big plumes of creamy white florets (alas, sharply scented as a privet hedge). 'Ivory Silk' is a lovely cultivar that will grow in acidic soil. He also recommends the reblooming lilacs Bloomerang® and Bloomerang Purple®.

Mock Orange

Philadelphus coronarius
and spp.

Botanical Pronunciation
fill-uh-DEL-fus kore-uh-NAIR-ee-us

Bloom Period and Seasonal Color
May to June; white

Mature Height × Spread
6 to 10 feet × 8 to 10 feet

Mock orange is a big old-fashioned shrub with crisp white flowers whose beauty and perfume recall orange blossoms. It's a large, rather dull plant with stiff branches until May and early June when it opens clusters of five to seven beautiful little 1- to 2- inch pure white flowers that have showy golden anthers. The perfume of fully fragrant plants permeates a garden. The modern varieties with old-fashioned fragrance are preferred. One of the best is *Philadelphus × virginalis* with semi-double or double flowers, which will quite often bloom for a second time in the summer. 'Glacier' has double flowers. 'Minnesota Snowflake' is tall, a 9-foot plant with arching branches whose big double flowers are fragrant.

When, Where, and How to Plant
To guarantee your mock orange will be as perfumed as you hope, buy a container-grown plant already in bloom (and sniff it). Plant a container-grown mock orange in spring, summer, or fall. It will flower most fully in full sun, but can handle some shade during the day. Mock orange succeeds in nearly any soil, but does best in a moist, well-drained site, pH 6.0 to 7.0. See "Soil Preparation and Improvement" in the introduction, and the planting instructions at the beginning of this chapter. Provide a planting hole three times the width of the rootball and twice as deep. Set the shrub so the crown will be an inch or two above ground level. Shape the soil around the crown into a wide saucer. Water slowly and deeply. Apply mulch 3 inches deep starting 3 inches from the crown.

Growing Tips
The first year, unless there's a soaking rain, in spring and fall slowly and gently pour two to three buckets of water around the roots every two weeks; in summer, water every week or ten days. An established mock orange tolerates some drought. Maintain the mulch. Using a slow-release organic fertilizer, fertilize lightly in fall and again in late winter or early spring. Replenish the mulch.

Regional Advice and Care
The mock oranges flower on growth made on branches developed the previous year. Giving older branches a light annual pruning after they have bloomed helps keep mock orange productive and well shaped. Woody stems that are more than five years old should be removed in winter or early spring.

Companion Planting and Design
Mock orange is a big shrub that needs a large garden to show off its beauty. It's usually grown as a specimen plant in the middle of the lawn. It's also attractive in a border for big shrubs such as weigela, forsythia, spirea, and deutzia.

Try These
Among the most fragrant modern mock oranges are named varieties of *P. × lemoinei*, which André's father Martin Viette worked with, including 6- to 10-foot 'Innocence', which is single-flowered and perhaps the most fragrant, and 4-foot 'Avalanche', a very fragrant single-flowered form.

Mountain Laurel

Kalmia latifolia

Botanical Pronunciation
KAL-mee-uh lat-ih-FOE-lee-uh

Other Name
Laurel

Bloom Period and Seasonal Color
Spring; white, pink, red, bicolors

Mature Height × Spread
5 to 15 feet × 5 to 15 feet

The mountain laurel is a tall, exceptionally handsome evergreen shrub with shiny, leathery leaves that make beautiful Christmas roping. In mid- to late spring, mountain laurel bears clusters of white, pink, or red-variegated cup-shaped florets. The blooms of the species are pale pink; modern hybrids are showier, blooming in brighter pinks, reds, and bicolors. 'Elf' is a slow-growing smaller mountain laurel, which grows 4 to 6 feet tall eventually, and whose showy clusters of light pink buds open to white. The buds of 'Ostbo Red' are an intense crimson that open to pink. 'Bullseye' is one of several forms whose flowers are banded red inside. (By the way, every part of the plant is toxic to people but not to wildlife—deer will nibble leaves.)

When, Where, and How to Plant

In poor, dry soil and full sun, mountain laurel develops leaf spot and dies. Plant a container-grown laurel in the fall before Indian summer, or in early spring while the shrub is still dormant. It needs a half-day of sun or bright shade all day to flower well and does best in light, open woodlands. It needs well-drained soil, one-third to one-half humus or leaf mold, and pH 4.5 to 6.0. See "Soil Preparation and Improvement" in the introduction, and planting instructions at the beginning of this chapter. Provide a planting hole three times the width of the rootball and twice as deep. Set the shrub so the crown will be an inch or two above ground level. Shape the soil around the crown into a wide saucer. Water slowly and deeply. Apply mulch 3 inches deep starting 3 inches from the crown.

Growing Tips

The first year, unless there's a soaking rain, in spring and fall slowly and gently pour two to three buckets of water around the roots every two weeks; in summer, water every week or ten days. Maintain the mulch. Using a slow-release organic fertilizer for acid-loving plants, fertilize lightly in fall and again in late winter or early spring. Replenish the mulch as needed.

Regional Advice and Care

Remove flower heads as they fade. *Kalmia* recovers slowly from pruning, and it is unnecessary in healthy plants. To restore an overgrown mountain laurel, wait till flowering is over, and remove one or two of the less attractive branches each year over a period of three to five years.

Companion Planting and Design

Mountain laurel is used at the back of shaded shrub borders and is ideal for naturalizing at the edge of an open sunny woodland fronted by rhododendrons and azaleas. Nothing is more beautiful than a shaded bank on the edge of a woodland with well-grown, fully flowered mountain laurels in bloom.

Try This One

'Elf' is used as a landscape accent, to create an informal low hedge, and toward the front of an evergreen shrub border.

Nandina

Nandina domestica

Botanical Pronunciation
nan-DYE-nuh doe-MESS-tih-kuh

Other Name Heavenly bamboo

Bloom Period and Seasonal Color
May, pinkish buds, then white; September, bright red berries

Mature Height × Spread
6 to 8 feet × 5 to 6 feet

Nandina is a tall, airy, graceful, unbranched, semi-evergreen or evergreen shrub whose dainty painted leaves are edged and splashed with real red in winter. In spring it produces loose clusters of small whitish florets that are followed in fall by small, perfectly round, lipstick-red berries in beautiful drooping clusters—great for Christmas decorations! The clusters are shaped like bunches of grapes, and they last until mid-spring. The new leaves are copper-toned and turn bluish green as they mature. The species is native to China and Japan, and has been grown widely in the South where the leaves are reliably evergreen and the berries color well and stay on the bushes for months.

When, Where, and How to Plant

Plant a container-grown nandina in fall before Indian summer, or in early spring while the shrub is still dormant. Nandina produces its bright red fruits whether it is growing in full sun or part shade. The shrub flourishes in well-drained, moist, fertile soil, but it is tolerant of other situations and not particular about soil pH. See "Soil Preparation and Improvement" in the introduction, and planting instructions at the beginning of this chapter. Provide a planting hole three times the width of the rootball and twice as deep. Set the shrub so the crown will be an inch or two above ground level. Shape the soil around the crown into a wide saucer. Water slowly and deeply. Apply mulch 3 inches deep starting 3 inches from the crown.

Growing Tips

The first year, unless there's a soaking rain, in spring and fall slowly and gently pour two to three buckets of water around the roots every two weeks; in summer every week or ten days. Maintain the mulch. Using a slow-release organic fertilizer, fertilize lightly in fall and again in late winter or early spring. Replenish the mulch.

Regional Advice and Care

To keep the plant compact, every year in early spring, before your nandina blooms, cut crowded or gangling canes back all the way to the ground. If it's only partially cut back, they sometimes don't break into new growth.

Companion Planting and Design

Nandinas are excellent in a shrub border, as a hedge, in containers, and compete successfully with tree roots. Stems of nandina provide lasting greenery for bouquets.

Try These

A favorite nandina for the vivid red of its winter foliage is big 'Moyers Red'. 'Umpqua Chief' is another—a vigorous plant that makes a fine 5- to 7-foot hedge and has leaves that turn fully red in winter. A superior dwarfish cultivar is 'Harbour Dwarf', a graceful plant that forms a dense mound 12 to 24 inches tall. The foliage is touched with pink or bronze in spring, and turns reddish purple in the fall.

Oregon Grape Holly

Mahonia aquifolium

Botanical Pronunciation
muh-HOE-nee-uh ack-wih-FOE-lee-um

Bloom Period and Seasonal Color
April; yellow flowers late summer,
blue-black berries

Mature Height × Spread
3 to 6 feet × 3 to 4 feet

The mahonias are shade-loving broadleaved evergreen shrubs with shiny, spiny, holly-like leaflets and small yellow flowers. The new leaves of the very upright Oregon grape holly start out red-bronze-green in spring, are dark green in summer, and turn a beautiful bronze-plum in winter. It has another asset we value; in late winter and early spring, it bears clusters of small, sweetly scented, yellow flowers that are followed in summer by blue-black fruits. Another beautiful species thrives here, leatherleaf mahonia, *Mahonia bealei*. It's more massive, with arching stems and big, gorgeous, blue-green, toothed leaflets that hold their color all winter. In late February and early March, drooping clusters of very fragrant yellow flower spikes appear, followed by blue changing to grapelike blue-black fruits the birds adore.

When, Where, and How to Plant

Plant a container-grown Oregon grape holly in early spring while the shrub is still dormant. *Mahonia* does best in partial shade. Oregon grape holly can stand more sun, but prefers shade. Avoid dry, hot spots, and windy, unprotected locations. The mahonias require soils that are slightly acidic, pH 6.0 to 7.0, well drained, with enough humus to maintain moisture around the roots. See "Soil Preparation and Improvement" in the introduction, and planting instructions at the beginning of this chapter. Provide a planting hole three times the width of the rootball and twice as deep. Set the shrub so the crown will be an inch or two above ground level. Shape the soil around the crown into a wide saucer. Water slowly and deeply. Apply mulch 3 inches deep starting 3 inches from the crown.

Growing Tips

The first year, unless there's a soaking rain, in spring and fall slowly and gently pour two to three buckets of water around the roots every two weeks; in summer every week or ten days. Maintain the mulch. Using a slow-release organic fertilizer for acid-loving plants, fertilize lightly in fall and again in late winter or early spring. Replenish the mulch.

Regional Advice and Care

If Oregon grape holly gets straggly, when blooming is over cut the tallest stems back to the ground. To keep it from expanding, root out suckers as they arise. To keep leatherleaf mahonia fresh and productive, after it has bloomed cut the oldest canes back to the ground.

Companion Planting and Design

Use the upright Oregon grape holly as a textural backdrop for shaded shrub and perennial borders, to anchor corners, and to mark entrances. Massive leatherleaf mahonia is ideal anchoring a large shaded area planted in hellebores, rhododendrons, azaleas, and low-trailing evergreen groundcovers such as bearberry.

Try This One

For a smaller garden we recommend the dwarf form of the Oregon grape holly, *M. aquifolium* 'Compactum', which grows to just 2 or 3 feet tall and has very glossy leaves that turn to bronze in winter.

Purple Beautyberry

Callicarpa dichotoma

Botanical Pronunciation
kal-ih-KAR-puh dye-KAWT-oh-ma

Other Name Beautyberry

Bloom Period and Seasonal Color
June to August; pinkish lavender flowers;
deep lilac-violet berries in fall

Mature Height × Spread
2 to 5 feet × 3 to 5 feet

Purple beautyberry is a multi-stemmed shrub valued for its late season appeal. Beautyberry's flowering period is summer but its biggest contribution is for the beauty of the berries that follow the flowers in fall. The shrub has other assets, however—the long slender branches arch over gracefully and touch the ground at their tips, and in spring, medium gray-green leaves array themselves in tidy pairs all along the stems. The flowers are pinkish lavender and stand above the foliage, so the small, luminous lilac-violet fruits that follow are nicely displayed against the foliage. The fruit is very dependable and makes an appealing show. When the leaves turn purplish and fall off, the fruits really stand out.

When, Where, and How to Plant

Plant container-grown beautyberry in spring, summer, or fall. The berries will be most effective if the plant is growing in full sun but it can make do with less light and still be productive. Almost any soil will do as long as it is well-drained, loose, or loamy soil with enough humus to maintain moisture. See "Soil Preparation and Improvement" in the introduction, and the planting instructions at the beginning of this chapter. Provide a planting hole three times the width of the rootball and twice as deep. Set the shrub so the crown will be an inch or two above ground level. Shape the soil around the crown into a wide saucer. Water slowly and deeply. Apply mulch 3 inches deep starting 3 inches from the crown.

Growing Tips

The first year, unless there's a soaking rain, in spring and fall slowly and gently pour two to three buckets of water around the roots every two weeks; in summer, water every week or ten days. Maintain the mulch. Fertilize beautyberry in late winter or early spring, and again in the fall. Replenish the mulch from time to time.

Regional Advice and Care

In spring before growth begins, tip prune and thin, but if the shrub is old and woody, you can prune 6 to 12 inches; beautyberry produces its flowers and fruit on the current year's growth.

Companion Planting and Design

Beautyberry is attractive planted in a shrub border where the berries will add color and texture in fall.

Try These

Our favorite is purple beautyberry, but there are other valuable varieties. *Callicarpa bodinieri*, bodinier beautyberry, is popular in Britain where it grows to 6 to 10 feet and bears lavender flowers and glossy purple-blue fruits. The 6-foot-tall variety 'Profusion' is grown in Holland and imported into the U.S. *C. japonica* has lilac-violet berries and is rather similar to *C. bodinier* beautyberry but taller; the variety 'Alba' is a white-berried form that keeps producing fresh, clean, new flowers July to September. The native *C. americana* is a coarser shrub with larger berries.

Purple Japanese Barberry

Berberis thunbergii

Botanical Pronunciation
BUR-bur-iss THOON-burg-ee-eye

Bloom Period and Seasonal Color
Flowers are insignificant; new foliage is pinkish or reddish in late spring, paler red in summer, glowing orange, yellow, and scarlet in fall

Mature Height × Spread
3 to 6 feet × 4 to 7 feet

The barberries are low deciduous and evergreen shrubs whose twiggy branches are so thorny they make almost impenetrable hedges. Deciduous barberries, like *Berberis thunbergii*, have pinkish or reddish new leaves in late spring and glowing shades of orange, yellow, and scarlet in fall. The winter silhouette is very textural, a real asset. In mid-spring, they bear small, attractive yellow flowers rather hidden by the foliage, followed by red, purplish, or bluish black fruits in late summer. 'Atropurpurea' has reddish purple leaves, and 'Atropurpurea Nana' is its dwarf form. The named variety 'Crimson Pygmy' has better color than the species, and is often the first to leaf out in spring. It is a low-growing, dense, rounded plant 2 to 3 feet tall by 3 to 4 feet wide, whose foliage emerges a rosy crimson in spring, fades a little in summer, and turns dark crimson in the fall.

When, Where, and How to Plant
Plant a bare-root shrub while it is still dormant, anytime between late fall and early spring, before the buds start to break. A container-grown barberry can be planted in spring, summer, or fall. The barberries display the brightest fall color when growing in full sun. However, like most shrubs, they succeed with four to six hours of sun, or all-day filtered light. They do well in most any soil, but prefer soil that is slightly acidic, well drained, loose or loamy, with enough humus to maintain moisture. See "Soil Preparation and Improvement" in the introduction, and the planting instructions at the beginning of this chapter. Provide a planting hole three times the width of the rootball and twice as

deep. Set the shrub so the crown will be an inch or two above ground level. Shape the soil around the crown into a wide saucer. Water slowly and deeply. Apply mulch 3 inches deep starting 3 inches from the crown.

Growing Tips
The first year, unless there's a soaking rain, in spring and fall slowly and gently pour two to three buckets of water around the roots every two weeks; in summer, water every week or ten days. Maintain the mulch. Using a slow-release organic fertilizer for acid-loving plants, fertilize lightly in fall and again in late winter or early spring. Replenish the mulch.

Regional Advice and Care
Barberries bloom on old wood. Pruning to control the height or shape of a hedge should be undertaken shortly after the shrubs have flowered. You can remove up to one-third of the branch tips in a year.

Companion Planting and Design
The barberries are used a great deal for hedges because the spiny leaves and thorns are wicked enough to discourage pets and wildlife. And gardeners as well, should you forget to wear gauntlet-type garden gloves when handling barberries.

Try These
'Crimson Pygmy' is our favorite. 'Rose Glow' is an excellent reddish purple barberry that is a little larger. Another appealing variety is 3- to 4-foot 'Aurea', whose foliage is bright yellow.

Rhododendron

Rhododendron spp. and hybrids

Botanical Pronunciation
roe-doe-DEN-drun

Bloom Period and Seasonal Color
May to June; white, pink, rose, lavender, purple-red, yellow flowers may be flushed, splotched, or spotted

Mature Height × Spread
2 to 20 feet × 2 to 25 feet

In the Mid-Atlantic, these big shrubs with their huge, airy globes of exquisite flowers are among the most valued of spring- and early summer-flowering shrubs. Native species growing in the wild reach 20 feet and more, but in cultivation most reach 6 or 8 feet. Mature specimens of the popular large-leaved evergreen rhododendrons provide spectacular displays of their huge blossoms in mid-spring—providing you have planted a variety suited to your climate, your site, and your soil. The large-leaved evergreen rhododendrons you can count on to survive winters everywhere in the Mid-Atlantic are the Catawba rhododendrons, from *Rhododendron catawbiense*; the one yellow rhododendron, dwarfish *R. keiski*; our native rosebay rhododendron, *R. maximum*; and the 3-foot by 3-foot Yakushima rhododendron, *R. yakusimanum*.

When, Where, and How to Plant

Plant a balled-and-burlapped or container-grown rhododendron in early fall or in early spring. To be sure of the flower, buy one already blooming, or labeled with its cultivar name. Rhododendrons do best in the bright dappled light of tall trees with protection from high winds. Ideal soil is well drained, humusy, and acidic, pH 4.5 to 6.0. See "Soil Preparation and Improvement" in the introduction, and planting instructions at the beginning of this chapter. Dig the hole three times the width of the rootball and the same depth. Set the shrub so the crown will be an inch or so above ground level. Shape the soil around the crown into a wide saucer. Water slowly and deeply. Apply mulch 3 inches deep starting 3 inches from the crown.

Growing Tips

The first year, unless there's a soaking rain, in spring and fall slowly and gently pour two to three buckets of water around the roots every two weeks; in summer, water every week or ten days. Maintain the mulch. Apply a slow-release organic fertilizer for acid-loving plants lightly in fall and in late winter or early spring. Replenish the mulch.

Regional Advice and Care

As each flower truss withers, pinch or cut it off, taking care not to damage the tiny leaf buds just behind it. Prune a rhododendron after it has bloomed, removing individual branches that have grown ragged or as required to achieve the desired shape.

Companion Planting and Design

Use rhododendrons for the transitional area to a woodland, backing a border of acid-loving shrubs, for screening, and rural hedges.

Try These

Showy, large-leaved, super-hardy evergreen rhododendron hybrids that handle winters in our area include Catawba rhododendrons such as 5- to 7-foot bright red 'America'; compact 4- to 5-foot white 'Boule de Neige'; 6-foot white 'Catawbiense Album'; 6- to 8-foot rose-lilac 'Roseum Elegans', which does well in the sun; 6- to 8-foot rosy pink 'English Roseum'; and 5-foot red 'Nova Zembla'. André likes the Dexter hybrids of 5-foot pink 'Scintillation' and 'Wyandanch Pink', and the small-leaved lavender-pink PJM hybrids for fall color.

Rose-of-Sharon

Hibiscus syriacus

Botanical Pronunciation
hye-BISS-kiss seer-ee-AY-kus

Other Name
Shrub althea

Bloom Period and Seasonal Color
July to September; luminous white, pink, lavender blue, lilac, deep red

Mature Height × Spread
8 to 12 feet × 6 to 10 feet

This is an old-fashioned, tall, spreading shrub, or small upright tree, that bears a profusion of flowers in July and goes on blooming until the end of September. The blossoms are trumpet shaped, like its relative the exotic tropical hibiscus, and about 2 to 3 inches across with ruffled petals crinkled on the margins. The usual colors are white, pink, crimson, and purple, most with an eye in a vivid contrasting color. Look for one of the newer cultivars introduced through the U.S. National Arboretum by the late, great Dr. Donald Egolf. They are sterile triploids that have a longer blooming season and set less fruit, which can be a nuisance.

When, Where, and How to Plant
Choose a young—under 6 foot—container-grown shrub, and plant it in fall before Indian summer, or in early spring. Rose-of-Sharon flowers best growing in full sun. It thrives in a wide variety of soils, and in a pH ranging between 5.5 to 7.0. Provide a site that is well-drained and has about 50 percent leaf mold, peat moss, or acid humus. See "Soil Preparation and Improvement" in the introduction, and the planting instructions at the beginning of this chapter. Provide a planting hole three times the width of the rootball and twice as deep. Set the shrub so the crown will be an inch or two above ground level. Shape the soil around the crown into a wide saucer. Water slowly and deeply. Apply mulch 3 inches deep starting 3 inches from the crown.

Growing Tips
The first year, unless there's a soaking rain, in spring and fall slowly and gently pour two to three buckets of water around the roots every two weeks; in summer every week or ten days. Water at the same time you water flower borders during prolonged droughts. Maintain the mulch. Using a slow-release organic fertilizer for acid-loving plants, fertilize lightly in fall and again in late winter or early spring. Replenish the mulch.

Regional Advice and Care
In early spring before the buds break, prune the branches back heavily to a pair of outward-facing buds. If you want larger flowers, prune the branches all the way back to three or four outward-facing buds.

Companion Planting and Design
Rose-of-Sharon looks great anchoring a corner of a mixed border fronting a building. It can be used for screening and to create a tall hedge.

Try These
'Diana' bears big, beautiful, pure white flowers that last more than a day. 'Blue Bird' produces beautiful lavender blue flowers. Blue Satin® and Blue Chiffon™ are lovely.

Spirea

Spiraea japonica

Botanical Pronuciation
spy-REE-uh juh-PON-ih-kuh

Other Name
Japanese spirea

Bloom Period and Seasonal Color
July and August; rose-pink flowers; pink-tinted foliage in spring turning wine-red

Mature Height × Spread
4 to 6 feet × 5 to 7 feet

Japanese spirea is a low, very wide, twiggy shrub with dainty leaves and arching branches that literally cover themselves with rounded clusters of exquisite flowers in the summer. Undemanding, and one of the most successful of the spireas, it has been much hybridized. A long-time favorite variety is 3- to 4-foot 'Anthony Waterer', whose 4- to 6-inch-wide rose-pink flower heads open in July and remain in bloom into August. The new foliage has a pink tinge, and in fall, the leaves turn to wine-red. Several pink-flowered varieties with colorful foliage have been introduced. 'Goldflame' is our favorite. It's a smaller plant, 3 to 4 feet high, with compact pink flowers, whose foliage is a fiery gold in spring and in fall turns to red, copper, and orange. Bumald, *Spiraea* x *bumalda*, is dwarf, with dark pink flowers.

When, Where, and How to Plant

Plant a balled-and-burlapped spirea in fall or in early spring; a container-grown plant can be set out spring, summer, or fall. Spirea flowers best in full sun and an airy site but it tolerates shade a portion of the day. It handles all but very wet soil; ideal pH is 6.0 to 7.0. See "Soil Preparation and Improvement" in the introduction, and the planting instructions at the beginning of this chapter. Provide a planting hole three times the width of the rootball and twice as deep. Set the shrub so the crown will be an inch or two above ground level. Shape the soil around the crown into a wide saucer. Water slowly and deeply. Apply mulch 3 inches deep starting 3 inches from the crown.

Growing Tips

The first year, unless there's a soaking rain, in spring and fall slowly and gently pour two to three buckets of water around the roots every two weeks; in summer, water every week or ten days. Maintain the mulch. Using a slow-release organic fertilizer, fertilize lightly in late fall and again in late winter or early spring. Replenish the mulch.

Regional Advice and Care

To maintain the shape and to increase flowering of low, shrubby spireas, snip off stem tips before growth begins. Bridal wreath spireas need little attention, except to remove dead interior wood after the shrub has bloomed.

Companion Planting and Design

Shrubby spireas are used to cover sloping beds and planted banks. Their twiggy mass adds texture as well as flower power to perennial beds.

Try These

Other compact spireas we recommend are *Spiraea japonica* 'Alpina', 'Goldmound', and 'Little Princess', plants between 15 to 36 inches tall. We still love the old-fashioned, 4- to 8-foot bridal wreath spirea, *S. prunifolia*, whose graceful branches arch to the ground, and are covered with showy, small white flowers in mid-spring. Not all gardens today are big enough to accommodate *S.* x *vanhouttei*, which grows up to 8 feet tall and 8 to 10 feet wide. *S. nipponica* 'Snowmound' is replacing the bridal wreath your grandmother planted.

Viburnum

Viburnum spp. and hybrids

Botanical Pronunciation
vye-BUR-num

Bloom Period and Seasonal Color
Spring; pure white, pink, scarlet; red or black summer and fall fruits

Mature Height × Spread
3 to 20 feet × 5 to 12 feet

Viburnums are magnificent spring-flowering shrubs. Two distinct forms are popular; the scented viburnums are planted for their fragrance, and the large, strikingly handsome doublefile viburnums are planted for their flower display. Both develop colorful berries and fall foliage. Our favorite fragrant viburnums are the cinnamon-scented Koreanspice viburnum, *Viburnum carlesii*, whose fall foliage is a cheerful red, and *V. × burkwoodii* 'Mohawk', a U.S. National Arboretum introduction whose fall foliage is red-plum. In early spring, both bear beautiful rounded clusters of deep pink buds that open to a cream-pink. The perfume is intoxicating. Doublefile viburnum, *V. plicatum*, is different altogether—a big, handsome bush with beautifully layered branches covered in mid-spring with a snowfall of white blossoms. Tree expert Michael Dirr has called it "possibly the most elegant of flowering shrubs."

When, Where, and How to Plant

Plant container-grown and balled-and-burlapped viburnums in fall before Indian summer, or in early spring. Viburnums thrive in full sun but also do well in bright, all-day filtered light. Most species prefer well-drained, humusy slightly acidic soils, pH 6.0 to 7.0. See "Soil Preparation and Improvement" in the introduction, and the planting instructions at the beginning of this chapter. Provide a planting hole three times the width of the rootball and twice as deep. Set the shrub so the crown will be an inch or two above ground. Shape the soil around the crown into a wide saucer. Water slowly and deeply. Apply mulch 3 inches deep starting 3 inches from the crown.

Growing Tips

The first year, unless there's a soaking rain, in spring and fall slowly and gently pour two to three buckets of water around the roots every two weeks; in summer, water every week or ten days. Maintain the mulch. Fertilize lightly in fall and again in late winter or early spring. Maintain the mulch.

Regional Advice and Care

With viburnums, be sure to use low-analysis, natural organic fertilizers that don't force or stimulate excessive growth. To keep the shape of this spring-flowering shrub, shortly after it finishes blooming, prune protruding branches back to outward-facing buds, and cut old branches to the ground.

Companion Planting and Design

Plant fragrant viburnums by a porch, patio, and near house windows, or along a well-traveled path near the house. Doublefile viburnum needs plenty of space all around; it's a choice plant for the entrance to a property, by a stone wall, or cloaking a garage corner.

Try These

Our favorite variety of Koreanspice viburnum, *V. carlesii*, is 'Aurora'. In a flowering border we like another hybrid, *V. × carlcephalum*, a tall, open shrub whose flowers change from pink bud to white when open. For hot areas of the Mid-Atlantic a very similar hybrid is the best choice, *V. × juddii*. Our doublefile viburnum favorites are 'Shasta', a spectacular U.S. National Arboretum introduction by Donald Egolf, and 'Mariesii', which is lovely in bloom and spectacular in fruit.

Weigela

Weigela florida hybrids

Botanical Pronunciation
wye-JEE-luh FLORE-ih-duh

Other Name
Old-fashioned weigela

Bloom Period and Seasonal Color
Mid-May and June; rosy shades of pink, crimson, white

Mature Height × Spread
3 to 10 feet × 3 to 12 feet

The weigelas are foolproof members of the honeysuckle family, dense-flowering shrubs with spreading branches that arch to the ground in maturity. Their gift to the gardener is late color and a disposition to thrive no matter what the conditions. The flowers are showy clusters of 1-inch long tubular blooms that cover the plant in late spring and early summer. Some have a slight fragrance, and some repeat a few blooms later in the season. The most ornamental form is old-fashioned *Weigela florida* 'Variegata', whose leaves are edged with a creamy white margin. It's a tidy 4- to 6-foot shrub whose flowers are a deep rose. For smaller gardens, the 3-foot dwarf 'Variegata Nana' is a good choice.

When, Where, and How to Plant
A container-grown weigela transplants easily in spring, summer, or fall. Growing in full sun it will flower most satisfactorily, but it also will bloom in partial shade. The ideal soil is well drained and has a nearly neutral pH between 6.0 to 7.5. But almost any soil will do as long as it is fertile and contains enough humus to maintain moisture around the roots. See "Soil Preparation and Improvement" in the introduction, and the planting instructions at the beginning of this chapter. Provide a planting hole three times the width of the rootball and twice as deep. Set the shrub so the crown will be an inch above ground level. Shape the soil around the crown into a wide saucer. Water slowly and deeply. Apply mulch 3 inches deep starting 3 inches from the crown.

Growing Tips
The first year, unless there's a soaking rain, in spring and fall slowly and gently pour two to three buckets of water around the roots every two weeks; in summer, water every week or ten days. Maintain the mulch. Using a slow-release organic fertilizer, fertilize lightly in fall and again in late winter or early spring. Replenish the mulch periodically.

Regional Advice and Care
A weigela flowers mostly on old wood. Wait until the branches leaf out to cut back tips that have died during the winter. 'Variegata' is somewhat compact and should be allowed to develop freely. Branches that fail to show the variegation should be cut back to older wood.

Companion Planting and Design
We like weigela 'Variegata' planted in an evergreen shrub border where the flowers and foliage will really stand out. It's a good choice when you are looking for a shrub that will do well almost anywhere without much help.

Try These
My Monet® has beautiful cream-and-green leaves touched with pink and rose-pink flowers. 'Bristol Ruby' bears ruby-red flowers; big 'Mont-Blanc' has somewhat fragrant white flowers (may be hard to find); and Wine & Roses® has three-season appeal—the new foliage that is a fresh green, pink-rose flowers, and in fall, glossy burgundy-purple foliage.

Witch-Hazel

Hamamelis × intermedia

Botanical Pronunciation
ham-uh-MEE-liss in-tur-MEE-dee-uh

Bloom Period and Seasonal Color
Late January to Mid-March; yellow or bronzed red; rich yellow with red tints fall foliage

Mature Height × Spread
15 to 20 feet × 15 to 20 feet

The witch-hazels are tall shrubs and small picturesque trees that flower in the winter or very early spring, and turn lovely shades of yellow, orange, and carmine red in the fall. The blossoms, which consist of four twisted ribbon-like petals dangling on bare branches, survive temperature drops by curling up. The leaves appear later. The best known witch-hazels are varieties of *Hamamelis × intermedia*, a classification that includes a number of hybrids resulting from crossing *H. japonica* and *H. mollis*. They bear wonderfully fragrant flowers that are a soft yellow or a bronzed red, and the fall foliage is rich yellow with red tints. Each has its special appeal. 'Arnold Promise', one of the last to bloom, has large flowers that are a clear yellow and have a rich fragrance. It is considered one of the best.

When, Where, and How to Plant
Plant a balled-and-burlapped witch-hazel in early spring or early fall. Plant a container-grown specimen in spring, summer, or fall. It may be a few years before it blooms. Witch-hazel does well in full sun or partial shade. It prefers moist loam that is well drained and somewhat acidic, in the pH range between 6.0 to 7.0. See "Soil Preparation and Improvement" in the introduction, and the planting instructions at the beginning of this chapter. Provide a planting hole three times the width of the rootball and twice as deep. Set the shrub so the crown will be an inch or so above ground level. Shape the earth around the crown into a wide saucer. Water slowly and deeply. Apply a 3-inch mulch starting 3 inches from the stem.

Growing Tips
The first year, unless there's a soaking rain, in spring and fall slowly and gently pour two to three buckets of water around the roots every two weeks; in summer, water every week or ten days. Maintain the mulch. Apply a slow-release organic fertilizer for acid-loving plants in late winter or early spring. Water it in. Replenish the mulch.

Regional Advice and Care
After a witch-hazel has bloomed, cut away sprigs that will grow into the center of the shrub or that will rub against other branches.

Companion Planting and Design
Witch-hazels are successful in the light shade of deciduous woods. Their picturesque form is well suited to naturalized settings. They do very well in city conditions and are attractive as container plants, and as specimens in small gardens.

Try These
We like 8- to 12-foot *H. × intermedia* 'Diane', which has copper-red blossoms and rich orange-red fall color. The Chinese witch-hazel, *H. mollis*, blooms later, in March usually, and it is the most fragrant; however, the blooms can be lost when temperatures go below -10 degrees Fahrenheit. Japanese witch-hazel, *H. japonica*, is a 10- to 15-foot tree, with somewhat fragrant yellow flowers, and foliage that turns yellow, red, and purple. The winter hazels, *Corylopsis* species, are beautiful shrubby relatives that bear fragrant flowers in April.

TREES
FOR THE MID-ATLANTIC

A tree is such a large presence in a landscape; its every aspect—habit, color, and texture—can contribute to your pleasure in fall and winter as well as in spring and summer. In this chapter we have included deciduous and broadleaved evergreen trees, and trees we plant for their flowers. Needled evergreen trees and shrubs can be found in the Conifers chapter.

In choosing a tree, beauty is the first thing we look for, and we think of foliage. A maple's flaming fall color can be breathtaking. But when the leaves go, it's the bark, bole, and branch structure that lend beauty to your garden view. Imagine white birches against a stand of evergreens. A tree's silhouette, whether columnar, pyramidal, oval, vase-shaped, round, clumping, or weeping, also makes a deep impression. By repeating the same silhouette, color, and texture—the symmetry of paired blue spruces flanking an entrance, or an allée of columnar flowering apple trees—you create an air of gracious formality. By combining a variety of forms, such as a symmetrical incense cedar and a stylized Serbian spruce with a wide-branching maple and a clump of birches, you create a natural, informal effect, add a hint of mystery, a little excitement.

When it's shade we need, we look to wide-branched trees whose silhouettes are oval, pyramidal, vase-shaped, or round. Maples and oaks are excellent shade trees, and some evergreens make good shade trees too—hollies and magnolias for example. Limbed up, small flowering trees can provide all the shade a small urban garden needs—the dogwoods and some flowering fruit trees, for example.

For style and for the fun of something different, we look to columnar trees. Many species now are offered in this form—red maple, European hornbeam, beech, and apple. 'Princeton Sentry'® is a beautiful columnar ginkgo. Small columnar forms even grow well in big tubs, adding style to patios, roof gardens, and decks.

For romance, grace, and movement, weeping trees are tops. They're especially effective planted where their drooping branches will be reflected in water. The graceful weeping willow loves wet places but the roots invade underground water pipes too regularly for us to recommend it. A weeping birch or a weeping beech, or the gorgeous weeping crabapple 'Red Jade' can be very beautiful. And weeping varieties of the flowering and the kousa dogwoods are lovely.

To create a seasonal parade that is a true delight, we plant small flowering trees. The shrubby witch-hazels open the season at the U.S. National Arboretum with fragrant ribbon-like blossoms, followed by the flowering fruit trees—almond, plum, cherry, pear, crabapple, apple. Some flowering trees bear colorful fruits—the fruits of the dogwoods and flowering crabapples are among many that attract birds. Most small flowering trees developed in the bright shade of taller trees, so, while they can

What a wonderful spring scene of *Betula, Tulipa* 'Maywonder', *Tulipa* 'Ile de France', and *Muscari*.

stand full sun, they also do well in a partly shaded city garden. A few big trees rival the show staged by the small flowering trees. In early spring, the maples are outlined in tiny garnet-red buds. In summer a mature Japanese pagoda tree bears showy panicles of creamy white, fragrant, pea-like flowers followed in September by beautiful showers of winged, yellow-green seedpods.

Size can be an asset or a debit. A tree that will grow out of scale with a dwelling is a debit. The heights we give in this chapter are for trees in cultivation—in the wild and in arboreta they can often be twice as big.

When, Where, and How to Plant

Young trees knit into their new environments quickly: trees 7 to 8 feet tall can overtake the growth of 15-foot trees set out at the same time. Early fall and early spring are the best planting seasons for trees. Choose early spring for trees difficult to transplant. Most large trees need full sun; many small flowering trees are understory plants that developed in the partial shade of a forest and do well in partial shade.

Make the planting hole for a tree three times as wide as the rootball and twice as deep. Mix into the soil from the hole the amendments described in "Soil Preparation and Improvement" in the introduction. Fill half of the bottom of the hole with loosened soil, and tamp it down to make a firm base for the tree to rest on.

Trees are sold balled-and-burlapped, or growing in containers. To free a containerized tree, tip the container on its side and roll it around until the rootball

White oak, Quercua alba is a large, majestic tree that grows slowly—but is spectacular upon maturity. Many consider it our finest native tree.

loosens, or slit the pot open. If roots wrap the rootball, before planting make four deep vertical cuts in the sides and slice the matted roots off the bottom 2 inches. A balled-and-burlapped tree goes into the hole in its wrapping, then you cut the rope or wires and remove as much of the burlap as you can. Set the tree in the hole so the crown will be 1 to 2 inches above ground level (the weight on unsettled soil will cause it to sink some after planting). Half-fill the hole again with loosened soil and tamp it down. Fill the hole to the top with improved soil and tamp it down firmly. Shape the soil around the trunk into a wide saucer. Water slowly and gently with a sprinkler, a soaker hose, a bubbler, or by hand. Put down ½ inch of water measured in a regular-sized coffee can, or pour 10 to 15 gallons of water slowly from a bucket.

Apply 3 inches of mulch starting 3 inches from the trunk and extending to the edge of the saucer. Stake a young tree so the trunk will grow up straight, and wrap the lower trunk to protect the bark from sunscald and deer rubbing. Remove the stake and wrapping as the trunk fills out. Or, paint the trunk with whitewash, which is calcium carbonate with resins in it.

Care

The first year, unless there's a soaking rain, in spring and fall slowly and gently pour two to three buckets of water around the roots every two weeks; in summer every week or ten days. Maintain the mulch. The slow-release organic additives mixed into the soil at planting time are sufficient fertilizer for that year (see page 222 in the appendix for more information on fertilizers). For flowering trees, use a slow-release organic fertilizer for acid-loving plants. For trees whose flowers are not the show, use a complete, slow-release, long-lasting, organic lawn fertilizer. In the following years, in late winter or early spring apply one of these fertilizers from the drip line outward to a distance that equals the height of the tree, plus half again its height. And compost the leaves you rake up in the fall. The nutrients they contain should go to enriching your soil, not clogging a landfill!

Pruning Trees

Most new trees require periodic light pruning. The first few years are the most important times to prune and shape a new tree. When needed, remove branches growing into the center of the tree or crossing other branches. Never remove more than 25 percent; such "dehorning" causes "water sprout" growth. Before cutting a branch, find the collar or ring at the base where it springs from the trunk. Taking care not to damage the ring, make the cut just to the outside of it. From the collar an attractive, healthy covering for the wounded area can develop. Current wisdom says "no" to painting or tarring these cuts. That said, André prefers to paint with orange shellac any wounds caused by removing big branches; it disinfects and seals the cuts.

The best time to prune is when the tree is dormant in late winter, just after the coldest part of the season. If sap starts to flow, never mind. It will stop when the tree leafs out. Light pruning in summer is not harmful, and you can see what you're doing. Pruning stimulates growth and you can use that to encourage bushier growth and more flowering stems. Prune a spring-flowering tree that blooms on last year's wood after the flowers fade. Prune a summer-flowering tree that blooms on current growth shortly before growth begins.

Nurturing a beautiful tree for years and then losing it leaves a gap in the heart as big as the gap in the garden. For an extra fee, some nurseries will plant your purchase and guarantee replacement if it fails. Still, the best protection against loss or disappointment is to choose disease-resistant trees and to plant, water, and feed them wisely.

Other Choices

While the trees in this chapter are the very best for Mid-Atlantic gardens, here are a few others we like:

Small Flowering Trees

Carolina silverbell, *Halesia tetraptera, H. monticola*

Chaste tree, *Vitex negundo* (Zones 7 to 10), *V. agnus-castus* (Zones 6 to 9)

English hawthorn, *Crataegus laevigata*

Washington hawthorn, *C. phaenopyrum*

Winter King hawthorn, *C. viridis* 'Winter King'

Large Deciduous Trees

American hornbeam, Blue beech, Ironwood, *Carpinus caroliniana*

European hornbeam, *C. betulus* 'Fastigiata'

Kentucky Coffeetree, *Gymnocladus dioicus*

Thornless honeylocust, *Gleditsia triacanthos* var. *inermis*; cultivars 'Moraine', 'Rubylace', 'Shade Master', 'Sunburst'

Yellowwood, American yellowwood, *Cladrastis kentukea (C. lutea)*

American Beech

Fagus grandifolia and spp.

Botanical Pronunciation
FAY-gus gran-dih-FOH-lee-uh

Bloom Period and Seasonal Color
Fall; russet-gold-brown foliage

Mature Height × Spread
50 to 80 feet × 40 to 80 feet

The American beech is a grand tree, a magnificent pyramidal native species that needs plenty of space all around and belongs in a park-like setting. It has silky silver-gray bark and beautifully symmetrical branches that reach to the ground, shading out weeds and creating a hiding place for nut-loving squirrels, and children. The shimmery green leaves appear late in spring, turn russet-gold-brown in fall and cling to lower branches well into winter. The big oily seeds appeal to many species of birds and animals. This species is slow growing and rather difficult to transplant. The European beech, *Fagus sylvatica*, and its cultivars transplant more readily and are successful in all but the warmest parts of the Mid-Atlantic.

When, Where, and How to Plant

Transplant a young container-grown or balled-and-burlapped tree with great care in early spring. Take care not to break the rootball—American beech does not transplant easily. It needs space all around and full sun, though it can handle dappled shade when young. The brow of a low hill, and toward the top of a slope is a likely site. It does best in soil in the somewhat acid range, pH 5.0 to 6.5, well drained, loose, and humusy enough to hold moisture. See "Soil Preparation and Improvement" in the introduction, and the planting instructions at the beginning of this chapter. Provide a planting hole three times the width of the rootball and twice as deep. Set the tree so the crown will be an inch or so above ground level. Staking might help the tree grow straighter, but remove it once the tree is established. Shape the earth around the crown

into a wide saucer. Water slowly and deeply. Apply mulch 3 inches deep starting 3 inches from the stem.

Growing Tips

The first year, unless there's a soaking rain, in spring and fall slowly and gently pour two to three buckets of water around the roots every two weeks; in summer, water every week or ten days. Maintain the mulch. Apply a complete, slow-release, long-lasting, organic lawn fertilizer in late winter or early spring from the drip line out to a distance equal to 1½ times the tree's height. Water it in. Replenish the mulch.

Regional Advice and Care

Beech trees can sucker; prune out any that come up. It's relatively pest-free and it's deer-resistant. Sometimes tree litter is an issue.

Companion Planting and Design

The American beech has high surface roots that are hard to cover, but are attractive when interplanted with small flowering bulbs.

Try These

The European beech is smaller and easier to transplant than the American species, and many fine cultivars are available. 'Pendula' is a striking weeping form. The young leaves of the purple beech, 'Atropunicea' ('Purpurea'), are an extraordinary black-red that change to purple-green. The purple leaves of the tricolor beech, 'Purpurea Tricolor' ('Roseo-marginata'), have an irregular edge of rose and pinkish white. (It's shown in the photo.)

Birch

Betula spp. and cultivars

Botanical Pronunciation
BET-you-luh

Bloom Period and Seasonal Color
April; 2- to 3-inch catkins; chalk-white bark
patterned with black triangles

Mature Height × Spread
30 to 80 feet × 10 to 60 feet

As a group, the birches are fast-growing, tall, slender trees known for beautiful bark. They have graceful crowns of dainty pointed leaves that move in every breeze and turn to yellow and yellow-green in fall. In our mild climate, birches are especially susceptible to birch leaf miner and bronze birch borer, so choosing a resistant cultivar is a wise move, such as Himalayan birch, *Betula utilis* var. *jacquemontii*, which has beautiful, strikingly white bark. One of the most beautiful resistant birches is a single-trunk cultivar, the Asian white birch, *B. populifolia* 'Whitespire'. Introduced by John L. Creech, late director of the U.S. National Arboretum, it has chalk-white bark enhanced by contrasting triangles of black at the base of the branches. The bark doesn't peel off, like that of the canoe birch, and the structure of the tree is very appealing.

When, Where, and How to Plant
The birches transplant easily in early spring or fall. They thrive in full sun, but accept bright shade. Most cultivated varieties grow well in somewhat wet or dry soils and are not particular as to pH. Provide soil that is well drained, fertile, and humusy. See "Soil Preparation and Improvement" in the introduction. Follow the planting instructions at the beginning of this chapter. Staking might help the tree grow straighter, but remove it once the tree is established. Water well. Mulch 3 inches deep starting 3 inches from the main stem.

Growing Tips
The first year, unless there's a soaking rain, in spring and fall slowly and gently pour two to three buckets of water around the roots every two weeks; in summer, water every week or ten days. Maintain the mulch. Apply a complete, slow-release, long-lasting lawn fertilizer in late winter or early spring from the drip line out to a distance equal to 1½ times the tree's height. Water it in. Replenish the mulch.

Regional Advice and Care
In summer or fall, prune out limbs that threaten to cross others or grow in the wrong direction.

Companion Planting and Design
Beautiful, resistant birches are at their best standing alone as specimens with a background of evergreens.

Try These
'Whitespire' may be the most resistant of the white barked birches but there are others. Chinese paper birch, *B. albo-sinensis*, is one of the whitest of all the birches—but not easy to find; the handsome bark of *B. nigra* 'Heritage', river birch, peels to expose inner bark that may be salmon-pink to grayish, cinnamon, or reddish brown. The older bark of monarch birch, *B. maximowicziana*, is white, and it is represented as exceptionally resistant. Weeping birch, *B. pendula* 'Youngii', has a graceful habit, but may be vulnerable to the bronze birch borer.

Callery Pear

Pyrus calleryana and cultivars

Botanical Pronunciation
PYE-rus kal-ler-ee-AY-nuh

Other Name
Flowering pear

Bloom Period and Seasonal Color
Early spring, white; wine-red foliage in fall

Mature Height × Spread
30 to 50 feet × 20 to 30 feet

Flowering pear is a beautiful, pyramidal tree bigger than most flowering fruit trees, and one of few guaranteed to bloom annually. In very early spring, before the leaves appear, it covers itself with clusters of small, white blooms. In fall, glossy green leaves turn an attractive wine-red and stay into late October and November. The fruits are small and russet-colored and attract birds. Flowering pear has been widely planted as a street tree. The first was 'Bradford', a beautiful tree that unfortunately tends to split as it matures. It is being replaced with stronger varieties such as 'Aristocrat', which we planted years ago when it was first introduced. It's now a very large, magnificent tree that never has broken a branch. Flowering pear is a little too big for a small city garden, but handsome in a larger suburban landscape.

When, Where, and How to Plant
Plant balled-and-burlapped trees in late winter or early spring before the plant leafs out. Callery pear flowers most fully and produces the brightest fruits when growing in full sun. However, like most small flowering trees, with four to six hours of sun or daylong bright, filtered light, it will perform well. The callery pears succeed in soils with a broad pH range, 5.5 to 7.5. See "Soil Preparation and Improvement" in the introduction, and the planting instructions at the beginning of this chapter. Provide a planting hole three times the width of the rootball and twice as deep. Set the tree so the crown will be an inch or so above ground level. The tree might grow straighter if it's staked, but remove the stake once

the tree is established. Shape earth around the crown into a wide saucer. Water slowly and deeply. Mulch 3 inches deep starting 3 inches from the trunk.

Growing Tips
The first year, spring and fall gently pour two to three buckets of water around the roots every two weeks; in summer every week or ten days. Maintain the mulch. Apply a slow-release organic fertilizer for acid-loving plants in late winter or early spring to just beyond the drip line, at half the recommended rate, and water in. Replenish the mulch.

Regional Advice and Care
Thin, prune, and tip the tree to reduce damage by wind, ice, and snow. In late winter or early spring, cut away branches that will grow into the center of the tree or rub against other branches—keep it open and airy.

Companion Planting and Design
Callery pear tolerates urban conditions, and it's a superb street tree and park specimen.

Try These
'Chanticleer' (which may be the same as 'Select' and 'Cleveland Select') has a distinctive conical form ideal for street planting. André recommends 'White House', a larger U.S. National Arboretum introduction, for boulevards and parks; it has a strongly developed central stem, produces masses of pure white flowers, and colors red-purple early in fall.

Crape Myrtle

Lagerstroemia indica and hybrids

Botanical Pronunciation
lag-ur-STREE-mee-uh IN-dih-kuh

Other Name Southern summer lilac

Bloom Period and Seasonal Color
July and August; warm raspberry, melting
shades of rose, pink, melon, mauve, red, purple,
white; colorful foliage; colorful bark

Mature Height × Spread
24 inches to 40 feet × 24 inches to 25 feet

The crape myrtles are flowering trees and shrubs that light up July and August with sprays of blooms that look like lilacs and last for months. The crape myrtles you see in gardens and parks all over the Mid-Atlantic are likely to be disease- and mildew-resistant hybrids developed by the late, great hybridizer Don Egolf, and introduced by the U.S. National Arboretum. Named for Native American tribes, these new varieties have cinnamon-colored, exfoliating bark, and the foliage of pink varieties turns showy colors in fall. There are dwarfs, low shrubs, shrubs, and small and large tree forms. Most grow relatively quickly, but they can be kept to shrub-size by cutting the plants back to the ground before they leaf out.

When, Where, and How to Plant
Plant a balled-and-burlapped crape myrtle in early spring or early fall. Plant a container-grown specimen in spring, summer, or fall. Crape myrtles leaf out late, especially when young. Full sun is best but four to six hours of sun or all-day dappled light will do. Moist, fertile, heavy loam and clay soils in the acid range, pH 5.0 to 6.5, are best. See "Soil Preparation and Improvement" in the introduction, and the planting instructions at the beginning of this chapter. Provide a planting hole three times the width of the rootball and twice as deep. Set the tree so the crown will be an inch or so above ground level. To encourage a single trunk, prune out all but the main stem; cut back a shrubby crape myrtle to the desired height. Shape the soil around the crown into a wide saucer. Water slowly

and deeply. Apply mulch 3 inches deep starting 3 inches from the crown.

Growing Tips
The first year, unless there's a soaking rain, in spring and fall slowly and gently pour two to three buckets of water around the roots every two weeks; in summer, water every week or ten days. Maintain the mulch. Water during dry spells. Apply a slow-release, organic, acid fertilizer lightly in fall and again in late winter or early spring. Replenish the mulch.

Regional Advice and Care
In colder areas of Zone 6, a crape myrtle may die back and re-grow from the base. If that happens, thin the suckers to three, five, or seven stems and they will grow and bloom. To maintain the height you wish, and to have lots of flowers, prune the plant back every year in early spring.

Companion Planting and Design
Underplant with small spring bulbs, wood hyacinths, and mixed flowering groundcovers such as ajuga and periwinkle.

Try These
Choose the color and height that will do the most for your landscape. A miniature crape myrtle with mildew resistance has been introduced by the National Arboretum. Named 'Chickasaw', it is pink-lavender, and will remain between 24 to 36 inches tall.

Common Smoke Tree

Cotinus coggygria

Botanical Pronunciation
KOTT-ih-nus kog-GIG-ree-uh

Other Name Smokebush

Bloom Period and Seasonal Color
Smoky effect July and August; yellow, red, purple fall foliage

Mature Height × Spread
10 to 20 feet × 10 to 20 feet

A favorite of the Victorians, beautiful in every season, the smoke tree can be counted on for beautiful foliage, romantic effect, and intense fall color. In June and early July, tiny, inconspicuous, yellowish flowers appear; then, in midsummer clouds of long, pink-gray fruiting panicles envelop the branches in misty halos that create a smoky effect. The source is thousands of tiny hairs attached to the developing fruit that dangles in clusters at the ends of the branches. Rounded, bluish purple or wine-colored to dark green in summer, the leaves change in fall to yellow, red, and purple. The fall color is most pronounced in the hybrids. Medium to slow growing, as the tree matures the bark becomes corky and quite beautiful.

When, Where, and How to Plant

The smoke tree transplants readily in spring while the plant is still dormant, and in fall before Indian summer. It achieves the best color growing in full sun but grows well in part shade. Almost any soil will do; it can handle dry rocky soils, but in well-drained loam it thrives. See "Soil Preparation and Improvement" in the introduction, and the planting instructions at the beginning of this chapter. Provide a planting hole three times the width of the rootball and twice as deep. Set the tree so the crown will be an inch or so above ground level. Shape the earth around the crown into a wide saucer. Water slowly and deeply. Apply mulch 3 inches deep starting 3 inches from the trunk.

Growing Tips

The first year, unless there's a soaking rain, in spring and fall slowly and gently pour two to three buckets of water around the roots every two weeks; in summer, water every week or ten days. Maintain the mulch. Apply a slow-release organic fertilizer for acid-loving plants in late winter or early spring, at half the recommended rate, from the drip line out to a distance equal to 1½ times the tree's height. Water it in. Replenish the mulch.

Regional Advice and Care

The flowers appear on new growth, so you can cut the plant back in late winter or early spring to keep it small, and to encourage greater flowering.

Companion Planting and Design

Smoke tree is a lovely addition to any shrub grouping, and makes a beautiful hedge.

Try These

We like several of the colorful named varieties. 'Royal Purple' unfolds from a rich maroon-red to a rich purple that doesn't fade; 'Velvet Cloak' is a luminous dark purple; 'Black Velvet' has dark purple foliage. 'Notcutts' Variety' is a strikingly rich dark maroon-purple. Where a larger plant can be used, the 20- to 30-foot native American smoke tree, *Cotinus obovatus*, would be our choice because the color is more spectacular. Michael Dirr says, "It may be the best of all American shrub trees for intensity of color."

Dogwood

Cornus spp. and cultivars

Botanical Pronuciation
KORE-nus

Bloom Period and Seasonal Color
Spring, white, pink, and pink-red; red-plum fall foliage; red fruits

Mature Height × Spread
20 to 30 feet × 20 to 25 feet

The dogwood is a graceful tree whose layered branches are covered in mid-spring with sparkling white, star-shaped flowers (actually bracts), followed in fall by bright red fruits that attract birds. Cold turns the foliage red-plum. The flowering dogwood that blooms with the redbuds at the edges of our woodlands is the 15- to 30-foot *Cornus florida*, Virginia's state tree. Dr. Elwin Orton of Rutgers University crossed *C. florida* with the Kousa dogwood, *C. kousa*, and produced *C. × rutgeriensis*, and a group of hybrids resistant to anthracnose and borers. This patented series is marketed as the Stellar® series. The other dogwood we recommend is the late-blooming, disease-resistant Chinese dogwood, *C. kousa* var. *chinensis*, whose flowers perch on branches that droop a little. The bark exfoliates attractively as the plant matures.

When, Where, and How to Plant
Plant a young, container-grown or balled-and-burlapped dogwood in early spring while it's dormant; handle rootball with care. Dogwoods do best in dappled light though they handle full sun if soil is humusy and moist. Ideal is a well-drained site with acid pH, 5.5 to 6.5, and about 40 percent humus. See "Soil Preparation and Improvement" in introduction, and planting instructions at the beginning of this chapter. Provide a planting hole three times the width of the rootball and twice as deep. Set the tree so the crown is an inch or so above ground level. Staking might help the tree grow straighter but remove once the tree is established. Shape the earth around the crown into a wide saucer. Water slowly and deeply. Mulch 3 inches deep starting 3 inches from the trunk.

Growing Tips
The first year, unless there's a soaking rain, in spring and fall slowly and gently pour two to three buckets of water around the roots every two weeks; in summer, water every week or ten days. Apply slow-release, organic, acid fertilizer in late winter or early spring from the drip line to a distance equal to 1½ times the tree's height. Water it in. Replenish the mulch.

Regional Advice and Care
Prune dead or diseased branches anytime. Dogwood anthracnose is a serious threat; plant resistant cultivars.

Companion Planting and Design
Dogwoods are beautiful at the edge of a woodland, centering a lawn, or by a stone wall.

Try These
'Cloud 9' is one of the best large-flowering white cultivars of *C. florida*; 'Multibracteata' and 'Pluribracteata' have double white flowers; 'Rubra' has pinkish red flowers and the foliage colors well in the fall. The Kousa dogwood 'Milky Way', a broad bushy tree, produces quantities of white blooms; the bracts of the hybrid 'Summer Stars' stay beautiful for up to six weeks. Other species with great appeal are 20- to 25-foot *C. mas*, cornelian cherry, a yellow-flowered tree with showy, edible, scarlet fruits that attract birds; and 30- to 40-foot giant dogwood *C. controversa* 'Variegata', whose foliage has an irregular yellowish white border.

Eastern Redbud

Cercis canadensis

Botanical Pronunciation
SUR-siss kan-uh-DEN-siss

Bloom Period and Seasonal Color
Early spring; red-purple, lavender-pink, rosy pink white; fall, yellow foliage

Mature Height × Spread
20 to 30 feet × 25 to 35

When the flowering dogwoods are just ready to bloom at the edge of the woodlands here, the slim branches of little redbuds growing nearby are covered with showy, red-purple or magenta buds opening into rosy pink flowers. Usually after it blooms, but sometimes before, this multistemmed or low-branching native tree puts forth reddish purple leaves that change to dark, lustrous green, which often turn to gold in fall. A mature redbud reaches 20 to 30 feet in the wild but is likely to be half that size in cultivation. The fruit is a brown beanlike pod. Some lovely cultivated varieties are available but the excitement these days is generated by a beautiful white form, *Cercis canadensis* forma *alba*—not to be confused with a white subspecies of *C. texensis*.

When, Where, and How to Plant

Plant balled-and-burlapped redbuds in early spring or early fall. Plant container-grown trees in spring, summer, or fall. Redbuds flower best in full sun but do well in open woodlands as long as they receive four to six hours of sun or all day dappled light. Redbud succeeds in well-drained sites in alkaline or acidic soil, not in a permanently wet location. See "Soil Preparation and Improvement" in the introduction and planting instructions at the beginning of this chapter. Provide a planting hole three times the width of the rootball and twice as deep. Set the tree so the crown is an inch or so above ground level. Staked trees might grow straighter, but remove stakes once a tree is established. Shape the earth around the crown into a wide saucer. Water slowly and deeply. Mulch 3 inches deep starting 3 inches from the trunk.

Growing Tips

The first year, unless there's a soaking rain, in spring and fall slowly and gently pour two to three buckets of water around the roots every two weeks; in summer, water weekly or ten days. Feed slow-release organic fertilizer for acid-loving plants in late winter or early spring from the drip line out to a distance equal to 1½ times the tree's height. Water in. Replenish the mulch.

Regional Advice and Care

Prune anytime as required. The most serious disease is a fungus, dieback/canker. A tree's leaves will wilt and turn brown; sometimes twigs and bark are affected with visible cankers. There's no control; prune out and destroy all affected parts.

Companion Planting and Design

Redbuds are small enough to use at the back of a shrub or a flower border; they will be large enough at maturity to be a specimen tree for a small yard. They're charming naturalized at the edge of a woodland.

Try These

'Royal White' is a beautiful white-flowered cultivar. 'Wither's Pink Charm' has clear pink flowers. 'Forest Pansy' is a favorite—strikingly colorful, purple leaves. 'Flame' is an attractive, double-flowered form. The showy, shrubby, multistemmed Chinese redbud, *C. chinensis*, is smaller and is an option for gardeners in warmer regions.

Flowering Cherry

Prunus spp. and hybrids

Botanical Pronunciation
PROO-nus

Bloom Period and Seasonal Color
April to May, pink flowers; leaves turn bronze-red in fall.

Mature Height × Spread
8 to 50 feet × 6 to 40 feet

After witch-hazel's early show the flowering fruit trees bloom—most are species and hybrids of *Prunus*. The most celebrated are flowering cherries, but there are plums, apricots, peaches, almonds, and nectarines. Bred for their blooms, they produce rudimentary fruit appealing to birds. Higan cherry, *P. subhirtella*, is a beautiful species that has given rise to numerous cultivars and forms. The four-season appeal of Sargent cherry, *P. sargentii*, makes it the most useful of the cherries; it bears showy clusters of single, deep pink flowers, is big enough to provide shade for a small garden, has bronzy leaves that turn a nice red in fall, and its polished mahogany bark is handsome in winter. It blooms later than the Yoshino cherries, *P. × yedoensis*, that flower at the Tidal Basin in Washington, D.C., often just in time to catch the last winter snow storm. Lovely hybrids have been developed by crossing these and other cherry species.

When, Where, and How to Plant
Transplant a balled-and-burlapped tree in early spring; a container-grown flowering fruit tree can be planted spring, summer, or fall. Flowering fruit trees bloom best in full sun. The ideal soil is well-drained, sandy loam, pH 6.0 to 7.5. See "Soil Preparation and Improvement" in the introduction, and the planting instructions at the beginning of this chapter. Provide a planting hole three times the width of the rootball and twice as deep. Set the tree so the crown will be an inch or so above ground level. The tree might grow straighter if it's staked, but remove the stake once the tree is established. Shape the soil around the crown into a wide saucer. Water slowly and deeply. Apply mulch 3 inches deep starting 3 inches from the trunk.

Growing Tips
The first year, unless there's a soaking rain, in spring and fall slowly and gently pour two to three buckets of water around the roots every two weeks; in summer every week or ten days. Apply a slow-release organic fertilizer for acid-loving plants in late winter or early spring from the drip line out to a distance equal to 1½ times the tree's height. Water it in. Replenish the mulch.

Regional Advice and Care
After a tree has bloomed, remove any sprigs that will become branches headed for the center of the tree or that will ultimately cross other branches.

Companion Planting and Design
Cultivars of the Sargent cherry are excellent street trees, and beautiful set out as specimens in lawns, large or small.

Try These
P. subhirtella 'Autumnalis' is a double-flowered pink cherry that blooms fully in early spring and repeats some in fall. The weeping cherry, *P. subhirtella* 'Pendula', blooms early. *P. pendula* 'Plena Rosea', a double-flowered form, blooms later and holds its flowers even in bad weather.

Flowering Crabapple

Malus spp. and cultivars

Botanical Pronunciation MAY-lus

Other Name Flowering crab

Bloom Period and Seasonal Color
Mid-spring; pink or carmine buds opening to
white; late summer, colorful fruits

Mature Height × Spread
6 to 30 feet × 5 to 30 feet

Apple orchards thrive in the Shenandoah Valley near the West Virginia border, where summers aren't quite so hot and fall is crisp and lingers—but the apple tree found in most gardens is the flowering crabapple. These small, spreading trees are covered in spring with exquisite apple blossoms, fragrant in some varieties, and the brilliant fall fruits attract birds. Older varieties have problems, but there are new and beautiful disease-resistant hybrids. One of the best is 'Donald Wyman', a showy crab with soft pink buds opening to white. The magnificent 15- to 20-foot Japanese crab, *Malus floribunda*, which does well in warm regions, has much to recommend it: a branch spread of 20 to 25 feet, a lovely silhouette in winter, buds that are deep pink opening to white, fragrant flowers, and yellow-red fruits.

When, Where, and How to Plant
A young container-grown or balled-and-burlapped crabapple transplants in early spring or fall. The best light is full sun. Eastern red cedar, *Juniperus virginiana*, is the alternate host of the cedar apple rust, so be sure to plant a rust-resistant crabapple. Crabs flourish in well-drained, heavy, loamy soil on the acidic side, pH 5.0 to 6.5. See "Soil Preparation and Improvement" in the introduction, and the planting instructions at the beginning of this chapter. Provide a planting hole three times the width of the rootball and twice as deep. Set the tree so the crown will be an inch or so above ground level. Staking may help the tree grow straighter, but remove it once the tree is established. Shape the earth around the crown into a wide saucer. Water slowly and

deeply. Apply mulch 3 inches deep starting 3 inches from the stem.

Growing Tips
The first year, unless there's a soaking rain, in spring and fall slowly and gently pour two to three buckets of water around the roots every two weeks; in summer, water every week or ten days. Apply a slow-release, organic, acid fertilizer in late winter or early spring from the drip line out to a distance equal to 1½ times the tree's height. Water it in. Replenish the mulch.

Regional Advice and Care
Remove branches heading to the center of the tree, or crossing others. Prune after the tree has bloomed, or in summer; orchardists are now pruning dwarf fruit trees in summer.

Companion Planting and Design
A flowering crabapple should be set out as a featured specimen. 'Narragansett', an introduction of the U.S. National Arboretum, is recommended for small gardens. Striking weeping forms included red-berried 'Red Jade' and white-flowered 'Sugar Tyme' and White Cascade®.

Try These
Disease-resistant crabs that André's father Martin grew include: *M. hupehensis*, the picturesque tea crab with wandlike branches; 'Katherine', a double-flowered hybrid; 'Sargentii', the Sargent crab, which is just 6 to 8 feet high and 9 to 15 wide; and the Asiatic apple, *M. spectabilis*, a 30-foot tree with double flowers.

Ginkgo

Ginkgo biloba

Botanical Pronunciation
GINK-oh by-LOE-buh

Other Name Maidenhair tree

Bloom Period and Seasonal Color
March and April; gold fall foliage

Mature Height × Spread
50 to 80 feet × 30 to 40 feet and more with age

A tall, stately tree ideal for city parks, the ginkgo has easily recognized, fan-shaped leaves and turns a truly luminous butter-yellow-gold in fall, and the color lasts. It forms a rounded crown near the top of the tall, straight trunk. Because it tolerates pollution and salt, it has been used as a street tree, but that isn't its best use. Though it bears these broad, triangular leaves, it is more closely related to conifers (cone-bearing trees and shrubs). This ancient species is estimated to have been growing on the planet for 150 million years; a Korean ginkgo has been documented as 1,100 years old. The strain we have now comes from China, but at one time it grew wild on this continent. Several beautiful specimens are growing on the grounds of the Capitol in Washington, D.C.

When, Where, and How to Plant
Gingkos transplant readily in spring while the plant is still dormant, and in fall before Indian summer. The ginkgo requires full sun, at least six hours a day. It does well in almost any soil, but thrives in sandy, deeply dug, well-drained, moist soil with a pH of 5.5 to 7.5. See "Soil Preparation and Improvement" in the introduction, and the planting instructions at the beginning of this chapter. Provide a planting hole three times the width of the rootball and twice as deep. Set the tree so the crown will be an inch or so above ground level. Staking might help the tree grow straighter, but remove it once the tree is established. Shape the earth around the crown into a wide saucer. Water slowly and deeply. Apply mulch 3 inches deep starting 3 inches from the stem.

Growing Tips
The first year, unless there's a soaking rain, in spring and fall slowly and gently pour two to three buckets of water around the roots every two weeks; in summer every week or ten days. Apply a complete, slow-release, long-lasting lawn fertilizer in late winter or early spring from the drip line out to a distance equal to 1½ times the tree's height. Water it in. Replenish the mulch.

Regional Advice and Care
Cut away any young branches that will grow into the center of the tree or rub against other branches.

Companion Planting and Design
A mature ginkgo is a tall, stately, handsome tree at its best growing in a large landscape or park setting. Its open form is not that attractive as a young tree, and it's too tall to look well in a small garden when it begins to mature.

Try These
Ask for and make sure you get a male ginkgo. The female tree produces a messy, plum-like fruit/seed that, in André's words, "is vile, stinky, not just bad." One of the best-looking cultivars is a broad-headed male called 'Autumn Gold'. The male clone 'Princeton Sentry' has a narrow, upright form.

Golden Rain Tree

Koelreuteria paniculata

Botanical Pronunciation
kole-roo-TEER-ee-uh puh-nick-you-LAY-tuh

Other Name
Varnish tree

Bloom Period and Seasonal Color
July; yellow flowers followed decorative seed capsules; yellow fall foliage

Mature Height × Spread
30 to 40 feet × 30 to 40 feet

This tree deserves its romantic name. Small to medium in height, open-branched and flat-topped, it's a shade tree that from early to midsummer bears showy 12- to 15-inch panicles of yellow flowers a ½-inch long. But this is only the opening show! The flowers are followed in late summer by cascades of segmented papery capsules that look like tiny Chinese lanterns. As autumn advances, they change from green to gold-buff to a vivid cinnamon-brown while the feathery and very graceful foliage turns a lovely yellow. The tree is fast growing, pest- and disease-resistant, and is a lovely specimen for the middle of a large lawn. The common name sometimes is confused with the laburnums, whose common name is golden-chain tree.

When, Where, and How to Plant

The golden rain tree transplants well when it is purchased as a young container-grown plant. Plant it in early spring while still it's dormant. The best location is a well-drained site with space all around and in full sun. However, it adapts to less light and a wide range of soils. It is tolerant of wind, pollution, drought, heat, and alkalinity. See "Soil Preparation and Improvement" in the introduction, and the planting instructions at the beginning of this chapter. Provide a planting hole three times the width of the rootball and twice as deep. Set the tree so the crown will be an inch or so above ground level. Staking might help the tree grow straighter, but remove it

once the tree is established. Shape the earth around the crown into a wide saucer. Water slowly and deeply. Apply mulch 3 inches deep starting 3 inches from the trunk.

Growing Tips

The first year, unless there's a soaking rain, in spring and fall slowly and gently pour two to three buckets of water around the roots every two weeks; in summer, water every week or ten days. Apply a complete, slow-release, long-lasting, organic fertilizer in late winter from the drip line out to a distance equal to 1½ times the tree's height and water it in. Replenish the mulch.

Regional Advice and Care

In winter while the plant is still dormant, prune out young branches that will grow into the center of the tree or rub against other branches.

Companion Planting and Design

The golden rain tree is used as a street tree, along interstate highways, and is featured in parks in our region.

Try These

André recommends 'September', a late-blooming cultivar. Another exceptionally lovely species, the Chinese flametree, *Koelreuteria bipinnata*, bears pink to rose-pink flowers, but it is reliably hardy only in the Zones 7b and 8 of the Mid-Atlantic.

Holly

Ilex spp. and hybrids

Botanical Pronunciation
EYE-lecks

Bloom Period and Seasonal Color
Insignificant flowers in spring; red, white, yellow, inky blue berries in fall and winter

Mature Height × Spread
½ to 60 feet × 1 to 35 feet

Hollies thrive in our gardens. There are three types: evergreen trees and evergreen shrubs, both planted for their foliage, form, and berries; and the shrubby, deciduous hollies, whose berry display in fall is the main show. Evergreen *Ilex opaca*, American holly, which is native to the eastern United States, grows into a handsome pyramidal tree 15 to 30 feet tall, and ripens single red berries in October that persist through winter—unless the birds get them. It is practically indestructible here. Female plants bear lots of berries if there's a male pollinator in the neighborhood; if there isn't one, plant a male American holly. There are shrubby hollies for almost every landscape purpose and climate.

When, Where, and How to Plant

Plant a container-grown shrub or a balled-and-burlapped tree holly in early spring. Hollies do well in full or part sun. It needs protection from strong winds and well-drained, humusy, acidic soil, pH 5.0 to 6.0. See "Soil Preparation and Improvement" in the introduction, and planting instructions at the beginning of this chapter. Provide a planting hole three times the width of the rootball and twice as deep. Set the plant so the crown will be an inch or so above ground level. Shape the soil around the crown into a wide saucer. Water slowly and deeply. Apply mulch 3 inches deep starting 3 inches from the crown.

Growing Tips

The first year, unless there's a soaking rain, in spring and fall pour a bucket of water around the roots every two weeks; in summer, water every week or ten days. Apply a slow-release, organic, acid fertilizer lightly in fall and again in late winter or early spring. Replenish the mulch.

Regional Advice and Care

To keep the plants trim, you can shear them when their spring growth is complete.

Companion Planting and Design

For hedges, varieties of the boxwood-like, shearable Japanese holly, *I. crenata*, are excellent, especially 'Convexa', 'Microphylla', and 'Stokes' holly. 'Helleri' matures at 2 to 4 feet and makes a hedge tough enough to walk on. The 8- to 10-foot Meserve holly, *I. × meserveae* 'Blue Girl' and its pollinator 'Blue Boy', are also excellent hedge and specimen plants. Burford holly, *I. cornuta* 'Burfordii', is a 8- to 12-foot cultivar that bears some berries even without a pollinator. For the wild garden and mixed shrub borders, use deciduous hollies such as compact inkberry *I. glabra* 'Compacta', white-berried 'Leucocarpa', and 'Ivory Queen'. *I. verticillata* 'Sparkleberry', a female, and its pollinator, 'Apollo', make beautiful berries together.

Try These

André's favorite varieties of American holly trees are 'Merry Christmas', 'George E. Hart', 'Xanthocarpa', and 'Old Heavy Berry'. Other good tree hollies are longstalk holly, *I. pedunculosa*; English holly, *I. aquifolium*; and slender 25-foot *I. × attenuata* 'Foster's Holly #2'.

Japanese Maple

Acer palmatum

Botanical Pronunciation
AY-sur pal-MAY-tum

Bloom Period and Seasonal Color
Red spring foliage; fiery foliage shades in fall

Mature Height × Spread
10 to 25 feet × 10 to 25 feet

The most elegant foliage tree used in landscaping is the Japanese maple, *Acer palmatum*. It comes in various sizes, shapes, and colors—weeping, upright, tall shrub, or small tree, and the foliage may be green, pink, red, or black-red. The best upright, deep red variety is probably *A. palmatum* 'Bloodgood', which is about 15 to 20 feet tall. The leaves hold their brilliant spring red and in fall become a rich scarlet. The most beautiful of the smaller forms is the threadleaf Japanese maple, *A. palmatum* 'Dissectum Atropurpureum', which is 6- to 8-foot tall, and has exquisite, deeply cut leaves and a picturesque weeping form. The ferny foliage is a rich purple-red in spring, fades toward green-plum in summer, then turns a spectacular orange in the fall.

When, Where, and How to Plant

Japanese maples benefit from special care in transplanting. In early spring, set out a container-grown plant, or a young balled-and-burlapped specimen. The Japanese maple needs four to seven hours of sun to color well, but it may burn if it is without some protection from the hot noon to afternoon sun in summer. It does best in a well-drained site and humusy, slightly acidic soil but it is fairly adaptable, so almost any well-drained, rich, moist soil will do. See "Soil Preparation and Improvement" in the introduction, and the planting instructions at the beginning of this chapter. Provide a planting hole three times the width of the rootball and twice as deep. Set the shrub so the crown will be an inch or two above ground level. The taller

Japanese maples may grow straighter if staked for the first year—don't leave a stake on after the tree is growing strongly. Shape the soil around the crown into a wide saucer. Water slowly and deeply. Apply mulch 3 inches deep starting 3 inches from the crown.

Growing Tips

The first year, unless there's a soaking rain, in spring and fall slowly and gently pour two to three buckets of water around the roots every two weeks; in summer every week or ten days. Maintain the mulch. In droughts, water a Japanese maple slowly and deeply every two weeks.

Regional Advice and Care

Japanese maples rarely require pruning to develop a beautiful form.

Companion Planting and Design

André has used vinca and ajuga as groundcovers under a Japanese maple; if the shade cast is dense, you can thin a few branches.

Try These

'Bloodgood', whose vivid color André remembers from his childhood at the Martin Viette Nursery, and the threadleaf Japanese maple are our recommendations. Another of André's favorites is the full moon Japanese maple, *A. japonicum*, a 10- to 20-foot tree whose foliage in spring is a soft glowing green and in fall turns to luminous yellow and crimson.

Japanese Pagoda Tree

Styphnolobium japonicum

Botanical Pronunciation
so-FOR-uh juh-PAW-nick-uh

Other Name Chinese scholar-tree

Bloom Period and Seasonal Color
July through mid-August; creamy white flowers
followed by pale green winged pods

Mature Height × Spread
50 to 75 feet × 30 to 40 feet

An airy, exceptionally beautiful tree for parks, the Japanese pagoda tree, formerly *Sophora japonica*, bears showy panicles of creamy white, somewhat fragrant, pea-like flowers for several weeks in summer. The flowers are followed by drooping clusters of fruits—showers of pale green, winged pods that look like beads and are persistent and just as beautiful as the flowers. Gardeners who have planted the species often are disappointed to discover that the flowers don't begin to appear until the tree is ten to fourteen years old—but the display is worth waiting for. The bark is pale gray and the foliage handsome. A rapid grower, the Japanese pagoda tree thrives under heat and tolerates drought and difficult city conditions; it's a good specimen plant for large lawns, parks, and golf courses.

When, Where, and How to Plant
Plant a young balled-and-burlapped or container-grown tree in spring while it is still dormant. The Japanese pagoda tree is somewhat tender to cold when it's young, but when it matures it will withstand more cold than it's likely to encounter in our region. The Japanese pagoda tree flowers most fully when growing in full sun. Provide a well-drained site with space all around. It adapts to a wide range of soils, tolerates poor soil, pollution, and, once mature, drought. See "Soil Preparation and Improvement" in the introduction, and the planting instructions at the beginning of this chapter. Provide a planting hole three times the width of the rootball and twice as deep. Set the tree so the crown will be an inch or so above ground level. Staking might help the tree grow straighter, but remove it once the tree is established. Shape the earth around the crown into a wide saucer. Water slowly and deeply. Apply mulch 3 inches deep starting 3 inches from the stem.

Growing Tips
The first year, unless there's a soaking rain, in spring and fall slowly and gently pour two to three buckets of water around the roots every two weeks; in summer every week or ten days. Maintain the mulch. Apply a complete, slow-release, long-lasting, organic fertilizer in late winter before growth begins to just beyond the drip line at half the recommended rate, and water it in. Replenish the mulch. Repeat in November.

Regional Advice and Care
In the fall after the leaves go, prune to create a strong central leader.

Companion Planting and Design
The tree is lovely underplanted with a living mulch of any one of the drought-tolerant groundcovers, such as periwinkle or ajuga. Hostas, liriope, mondo grass, and small spring-flowering bulbs such as wood hyacinths are also acceptable groundcovers.

Try These
Princeton Nurseries has introduced a cultivar, 'Regent', that has a large oval crown of glossy, dark green leaves; it comes into bloom at six to eight years of age.

Katsura Tree

Cercidiphyllum japonicum

Botanical Pronunciation
sur-sid-ih-FILL-um juh-PON-ih-kum

Bloom Period and Seasonal Color
Spring foliage changes from bronze or reddish purple, summer blue-green, fall apricot-orange and gold

Mature Height × Spread
40 to 60 feet × 25 to 60 feet

"If I could use only one tree, this would be my first tree." We are quoting noted plantsman and author Michael Dirr. This is a fast- to medium-fast-growing, very beautiful, refined shade tree planted for its foliage. The new leaves are reddish purple, changing to blue-green in summer, then in fall transformed into a spectacular, glowing, apricot-orange and golden yellow—a show described as very well worth traveling to see. The aging leaves give off a faint spicy scent. The tree has a dense rounded form and shaggy brown bark that add interest to the winter landscape. The katsura is an excellent tree for medium-sized landscapes and parks, and it also is useful for street planting.

When, Where, and How to Plant

The katsura tree is not easy to transplant. Set out a young, dormant, container-grown or balled-and-burlapped tree from a reliable nursery in early spring. The color is remarkable when the tree is growing in full sun and in soil in the acidic range, pH 5.0 to 6.5. Provide a well-drained site and soil that is rich, loose, and humusy enough to hold moisture. The brow of a low hill, and toward the top of a slope is a likely situation. See "Soil Preparation and Improvement" in the introduction, and the planting instructions at the beginning of this chapter. Provide a planting hole three times the width of the rootball and twice as deep. Set the tree so the crown will be an inch or so above ground level. Staking might help the tree grow straighter, but remove it once the tree is

established. Shape the earth around the crown into a wide saucer. Water slowly and deeply. Apply mulch 3 inches deep starting 3 inches from the trunk.

Growing Tips

The first year, unless there's a soaking rain, in spring and fall slowly and gently pour two to three buckets of water around the roots every two weeks; in summer, water every week or ten days. Apply a complete, slow-release, long-lasting, organic fertilizer in late winter from the drip line out to a distance equal to 1½ times the tree's height, and water it in. Replenish the mulch. The first two or three seasons, water the tree deeply as often as the flower beds need watering.

Regional Advice and Care

Prune in late winter to feature the main stem and create a broad-spreading crown.

Companion Planting and Design

The best use of this tree is as a specimen, set out where it can be seen throughout the seasons. Make a point of buying a single-stemmed plant.

Try These

For its beauty, we recommend planting the species. But, if you would like to add a weeping tree to your landscape, consider the weeping form of the katsura tree, 'Pendulum', a lovely small tree 15 to 25 feet tall in cultivation.

Maple

Acer spp. and cultivars

Botanical Pronunciation
AY-sur

Bloom Period and Seasonal Color
March to April; greenish yellow to red;
yellow, orange, and bright red fall foliage

Mature Height × Spread
15 to 80 feet × 15 to 70 feet

For the home garden perhaps the most valuable shade tree is the majestic maple. In spring, it covers itself with colorful buds, and in fall, the leaves turn to yellow, orange, and bright red. The species renowned for fall color is the big, beautiful, slow-growing sugar maple, *Acer saccharum*, the source of maple sap that is boiled into syrup. A mature sugar maple has a pyramidal shape, great strength and character, and wide branches that provide dappled shade. In the wild, it reaches 100 feet and more. Though smaller in cultivation it's a magnificent tree for parks and large landscapes. For home gardens and in our climate, plant the faster-growing, smaller swamp or red maple, *A. rubrum*; its fall color is often a more intense red. But it has more root problems than sugar maple. Maples withstand some pollution.

When, Where, and How to Plant
Plant a container-grown or balled-and-burlapped tree in fall before Indian summer, or in early spring while the tree is dormant. Most maples do best in slightly acidic soil and full sun, but almost any well-drained, rich, moist soil will do. Very young swamp maple saplings transplant readily bareroot; this species does best in slightly acidic soil and moist conditions. See "Soil Preparation and Improvement" in the introduction, and the planting instructions at the beginning of this chapter. Provide a planting hole three times the width of the rootball and twice as deep. Set trees so the crown is an inch or so above ground level. Staking may help trees grow straighter; remove stakes once a tree is established. Shape the earth around the crown into a wide saucer. Water slowly and deeply. Mulch 3 inches deep starting 3 inches from the trunk.

Growing Tips
The first year, unless there's a soaking rain, in spring and fall slowly pour two to three buckets of water around the roots every two weeks; in summer, water every week or ten days. Do not ever let the soil around young maples go dry; in dry spells, water even mature maples deeply, since they have a very shallow root system. In late winter feed a complete, slow-release, long-lasting, organic lawn fertilizer from the drip line to a distance equal to 1½ times the tree's height and water in. Replenish the mulch.

Regional Advice and Care
Maples need little care or pruning once established.

Companion Planting and Design
Most large maples are better in large landscapes, and as park trees rather than street trees unless watered in droughts. The roots of a vigorous maple will buckle cement sidewalks and patios.

Try These
'Green Mountain' (sugar maple) is heat tolerant and can handle more drought than some others. 'Bonfire' may grow faster than the species and has more reliable fall color. Outstanding red maples are Red Sunset®, which has orange-red fall color; Autumn Flame®, which colors earlier than the species; and October Glory®, which holds its leaves later.

Oak

Quercus spp.

Botanical Pronunciation
KWURK-us

Bloom Period and Seasonal Color
Fall foliage in yellow, nut brown, shades of red and russet

Mature Height × Spread
40 to 80 feet × 25 to 75 feet

The oaks are magnificent spreading shade trees suited to parks, large landscapes, and city streets—long-lived, symmetrical, and handsome. In Washington, D.C., there are well-grown examples of some that excel as street trees. The finest of the oaks for fall color is *Quercus coccinea*, the scarlet oak; *Q. rubra*, the Northern red oak, is not quite as showy but grows more quickly; *Q. shumardii*, the shumard or Southern scarlet oak, is the largest of the native red oaks and has deeply cut, lustrous leaves that turn scarlet in the fall. Many midtown Washington, D.C., areas are lined with willow oak, *Q. phellos*, an elegant smaller native oak with willow-like leaves that turn yellow, yellow-brown, and russet-red in the fall.

When, Where, and How to Plant
Plant an oak while it is still dormant in early spring. Buy a young container-grown or balled-and-burlapped tree and handle it with TLC: most oak species have taproots that can be damaged. The pin oak, *Q. palustrus,* has a shallow, fibrous root system that transplants more easily. Most species do best growing in full sun and in slightly acidic soil, but they are tolerant of other soils. The willow oak succeeds even in poorly drained clay soil; the shumard oak withstands moist soil. See "Soil Preparation and Improvement" in the introduction, and the planting instructions at the beginning of this chapter. Provide a planting hole three times the width of the rootball and twice as deep. Set the tree

so the crown will be an inch or so above ground level. Staking can help the tree grow straighter, but remove it once the tree is established. Shape the earth around the crown into a wide saucer. Water slowly and deeply. Apply mulch 3 inches deep starting 3 inches from the trunk.

Growing Tips
The first year, unless there's a soaking rain, in spring and fall slowly and gently pour two to three buckets of water around the roots every two weeks; in summer, water every week or ten days. Apply a complete, slow-release, long-lasting, organic lawn fertilizer in late winter from the drip line out to a distance equal to 1½ times the tree's height. Water it in. Replenish the mulch. Water deeply during droughts until the plant is growing well.

Regional Advice and Care
In late winter, prune to develop a strong central leader.

Companion Planting and Design
The oaks mentioned all do well in urban situations.

Try These
For a large landscape, we also recommend the majestic white oak, *Q. alba*, which has an arresting silhouette and is considered by many the finest of all our native oaks; it develops slowly and attains heights of 50 to 80 feet.

Sour Gum

Nyssa sylvatica

Botanical Pronunciation
NISS-uh sill-VAT-ih-kuh

Other Name
Black gum

Bloom Period and Seasonal Color
Spring; small greenish white flowers; fall foliage is fluorescent yellow to orange, scarlet to purple

Mature Height × Spread
30 to 50 feet × 20 to 30 feet

In fall, this is one of the most beautiful of all our native trees—the leaves change to fluorescent yellow, orange, scarlet, and purple. The tree is pyramidal in form, with somewhat drooping branches. The usual height is 30 to 50 feet, but it grows taller in the wild, especially near water. Bees visit the small, nectar-rich, greenish white flowers that appear in spring, and an exceptionally flavorful honey is made from it. The flowers are followed by bluish fruits that are somewhat hidden by the leaves and are relished by bears and other wildlife. The bark is dark charcoal gray, broken into thick blocky ridges, giving the plant winter appeal. It tolerates pollution well enough to be used as a street tree in the suburbs.

When, Where, and How to Plant

The sour gum has a taproot, which makes it difficult to transplant. Choose a thriving, young, container-grown plant, and set it out with TLC. In cultivation it does best in full sun or bright, dappled shade. It requires moist, well-drained, acidic soil, pH 5.5 to 6.5, and needs some protection from wind. See "Soil Preparation and Improvement" in the introduction, and planting instructions at the beginning of this chapter. Provide a planting hole three times the width of the rootball and twice as deep. Set the tree so the crown will be an inch or so above ground level. Staking might help the tree grow straighter, but remove it once the tree is established. Shape the earth around the crown into a wide saucer. Water slowly and deeply. Apply mulch 3 inches deep starting 3 inches from the stem.

Growing Tips

The first year, unless there's a soaking rain, in spring and fall slowly and gently pour two to three buckets of water around the roots every two weeks; in summer, water every week or ten days. Apply a complete, slow-release, long-lasting, organic fertilizer for acid-loving plants in late winter before growth begins from the drip line out to a distance equal to 1½ times the tree's height. Water it in. Replenish the mulch.

Regional Advice and Care

In late fall, cut away any branches that might grow into the center of the tree or rub against other branches.

Companion Planting and Design

The black gum looks its best featured at the edge of a lawn or near a stream or a pond where its autumn foliage will be seen. It is also successful at the shore.

Try These

We recommend the species but for water sites there is a handsome swamp species of the sour gum, *Nyssa aquatic*, the water tupelo or tupelo gum. The national champion of the species is 100 feet tall and 55 feet wide, and is growing in Southhampton County, VA.

Sourwood

Oxydendrum arboretum

Botanical Pronunciation
ock-sih-DEN-drum are-BORE-ee-um

Other Name
Lily-of-the-valley tree

Bloom Period and Seasonal Color
Late June to early July, white flowers; yellow, orange, red, and purple fall foliage

Mature Height × Spread
20 to 50 feet × 10 to 25 feet

This lovely native tree of modest height veils itself in drooping racemes of fragrant white, urn-shaped flowers in early summer. Then in fall, large, dark green leaves turn yellow, orange, red, and purple. Attractive seedpods follow the flowers and persist through fall, and deeply furrowed bark makes an attractive winter feature. Sourwood is a slow-growing tree that takes a dozen years to reach 15 feet or so. It is attractive to bees and is a source of a superb honey. Sourwood grows wild along the banks and streams of coastal Virginia, a beautiful tree that naturalizes fairly easily and is well worth the effort needed to establish it in the home landscape. It does not transplant easily nor does it tolerate urban pollution.

When, Where, and How to Plant
In early spring, buy a still-dormant container-grown plant from a reliable source, and handle the transplanting with great care. Sourwood does well in full sun, but it tolerates bright filtered light all day or partial bright shade. It requires a well-drained site and acidic soil, pH 5.5 to 6.5. See "Soil Preparation and Improvement" in the introduction, and the planting instructions at the beginning of this chapter. Provide a planting hole three times the width of the rootball and twice as deep. Set the tree so the crown will be an inch or so above ground level. Staking may help the tree grow straighter, but remove it once the tree

is established. Shape the earth around the crown into a wide saucer. Water slowly and deeply. Apply mulch 3 inches deep starting 3 inches from the stem.

Growing Tips
The first year, unless there's a soaking rain, in spring and fall slowly and gently pour two to three buckets of water around the roots every two weeks; in summer, water every week or ten days. Spread a compete, slow-release, long-lasting, organic fertilizer for acid-loving plants in late winter before growth begins out to a distance equal to 1½ times the tree's height. Water it in. Replenish the mulch.

Regional Advice and Care
Prune in early spring before growth begins, if needed. Two possible pests are dogwood stem borers and twig girdlers; a healthy tree is the best defense.

Companion Planting and Design
It's also known as the lily-of-the-valley tree—and considered second only to one other native flowering tree, the dogwood. So make it a feature of your landscape in a spot where it will be seen year-round.

Try These
Plant the species. But it's so spectacular you won't miss other options.

Southern Magnolia

Magnolia grandiflora

Botanical Pronunciation
mag-NOLE-yuh gran-dih-FLORE-uh

Other Name
Bullbay magnolia

Bloom Period and Seasonal Color
Intermittent summer, creamy white; evergreen foliage has handsome cinnamon reverse

Mature Height × Spread
60 to 80 feet × 30 to 50 feet

The majestic 80-foot bullbay magnolia, a very ancient evergreen tree, is a symbol of the Southern plantation. The foot-long leaves are oblong, glossy, stiff, almost indestructible, and are enhanced by cinnamon-brown undersides. The flowers are fragrant, immense, shaped like a saucer or a water lily, and appear intermittently in summer. Dark red, cone-shaped fruits with bright red decorative seeds follow the flowers and are Christmas arrangement staples at Colonial Williamsburg. There are magnificent specimens on Capitol Hill in Washington, D.C. For small gardens and Zone 6, the Chinese, or saucer magnolia, *Magnolia × soulangiana*, is a wise choice. A 20- to 25-foot deciduous tree, the blooms are purplish pink on the outside and cream or white inside, and they appear before the leaves.

When, Where, and How to Plant
Transplant a young container-grown or balled-and-burlapped magnolia with care, before new growth begins in early spring. Full sun is best but four to six hours of sun, or all-day filtered light will do. The ideal soil is acidic, pH 5.0 to 6.5, fertile, humusy, and well drained, but not dry. See "Soil Preparation and Improvement" in the introduction, and follow the planting instructions at the beginning of this chapter. Make the hole three times as wide and twice as deep as the rootball. Set the tree so the crown will be about 1 or 2 inches above ground level. Staking may keep the tree growing straight, but remove it once the tree is established. Shape the soil around the crown into a wide saucer. Water slowly and deeply. Apply mulch 3 inches deep starting 3 inches from the trunk.

Growing Tips
The first year, unless there's a soaking rain, in spring and fall slowly pour two to three buckets of water around the roots every two weeks; in summer, water every week or ten days. Apply a slow-release, organic, acidic fertilizer in late winter or early spring from the drip line out to 1½ times the tree's height. Water it in. Replenish the mulch.

Regional Advice and Care
Magnolias are most beautiful when allowed to develop without pruning; any pruning should be done after the tree has bloomed.

Companion Planting and Design
This majestic tree belongs as a specimen in the middle of a large lawn, or flanking a formal entrance, or as foundation plant for grounds around large buildings.

Try These
André's favorite Southern magnolia is pyramidal Majestic Beauty™, with large, lustrous green leaves and cup-shaped, white, 12-inch flowers. Outstanding half-sized varieties are 'Little Gem', which bears 6-inch flowers in spring, and 'St. Mary', which produces full-sized flowers while still young. He also likes *M. × soulangiana* 'Lennei' whose blooms are rich deep purple outside, pure white inside. They appear late and so escape late frosts. The star magnolia, *M. stellata*, another beautiful, small, deciduous magnolia, blooms before the leaves appear; 'Waterlily' is a lovely variety.

Sweet Gum

Liquidambar styraciflua

Botanical Pronunciation
lick-wid-AM-bur stye-ruh-SIFF-loo-uh

Other Name
American sweet gum

Bloom Period and Seasonal Color
April to May; inconspicuous flowers; true yellow, orange, red, purple fall foliage

Mature Height × Spread
60 to 80 feet × 35 to 45 feet

The American sweet gum is a tall, handsome shade tree with large, five-pointed leaves that in fall turn to true yellow, red, and purple—a spectacular show most years. In summer, the leaves are a deep, attractive, glossy green. The bark is grayish brown and interestingly corky. A big tree, in moist soil it grows rather quickly, 2 to 3 feet a year. In dry soil, the growth is a little slower. The common name refers to the sap, which is rather sweet and gummy. Male and female flowers are produced in dense clusters and mature into prickly, woody seedpods that litter. It makes a superb lawn tree as long as the means exist to remove the prickly fruit before mowing.

When, Where, and How to Plant
Plant a young container-grown or balled-and-burlapped tree in early spring while the tree is still dormant. Handle the rootball with care; under the best of circumstances it takes a while to recover from a move. Sweet gum requires full sun and tolerates part shade, but not pollution. Set the tree where there will be lots of space all around for the development of its root system. It does best in well-drained, moist, acidic soil, pH 5.5 to 6.5. See "Soil Preparation and Improvement" in the introduction, and planting instructions at the beginning of this chapter. Provide a planting hole three times the width of the rootball and twice as deep. Set the tree so the crown will be an inch or so above ground

level. Staking may help the tree grow straighter, but remove it once the tree is established. Shape the earth around the crown into a wide saucer. Water slowly and deeply. Apply mulch 3 inches deep starting 3 inches from the stem.

Growing Tips
The first year, unless there's a soaking rain, in spring and fall slowly and gently pour two to three buckets of water around the roots every two weeks; in summer every week or ten days. Apply a complete, slow-release, long-lasting, organic lawn fertilizer in late winter before growth begins to a distance equal to 1½ times the tree's height. Water it in. Replenish the mulch. Repeat in November.

Regional Advice and Care
If any pruning is required, do it in late winter before the buds swell.

Companion Planting and Design
Sweet gum is an excellent choice for a large, open landscape that was previously forested wetland, for example. It's a superb lawn tree, but its prickly fruit must be removed before mowing.

Try These
'Rotundiloba' does not produce the prickly balls that are such a nuisance. 'Burgundy' has dark red to maroon fall color and holds its color late.

Tuliptree

Liriodendron tulipifera

Botanical Pronunciation
leer-ee-oh-DEN-drun too-lip-IFF-ur-uh

Other Name
Tulip poplar

Bloom Period and Seasonal Color
Late May or early June, chartreuse blossoms touched at the base with bright orange; canary-yellow fall leaves

Mature Height × Spread
60 to 90 feet × 30 to 50 feet

The tuliptree is a tall, majestic, native shade tree that probably is the tallest and straightest hardwood in America. There's a beautiful specimen on the grounds of the Capitol in Washington, D.C., and a wonderful tree at Mount Vernon, supposedly planted by George Washington. The tuliptree grows wild from Massachusetts to Florida, and westward to Wisconsin and Mississippi. It is named for the greenish yellow, tuliplike flowers that appear in late spring or early summer. Unfortunately, they're borne high in the branches, and aren't readily visible from below. The seeds in the conelike fruits, which resemble those of the large magnolias, to which it is related, attract finches and cardinals. The leaves are quite distinctive—blue-green and rather like a maple leaf with its end squared off. In fall, the leaves turn a rich, handsome, canary-yellow that makes a very nice show.

When, Where, and How to Plant
The tuliptree requires care in transplanting. Plant a young, container-grown or balled-and-burlapped tree in early spring while it is still dormant. The tuliptree requires full sun. It does well in almost any soil, but thrives in sandy, deeply dug, well-drained, moist soil that is slightly acidic, pH 5.5 to 6.5. See "Soil Preparation and Improvement" in the introduction, and planting instructions at the beginning of this chapter. Provide a planting hole three times the width of the rootball and twice as deep. Set the tree so the crown will be an inch or so above ground level. Staking may help the tree grow straighter, but remove it once the tree is established. Shape the earth around the crown into a wide

saucer. Water slowly and deeply. Apply mulch 3 inches deep starting 3 inches from the stem.

Growing Tips
The first year, unless there's a soaking rain, in spring and fall slowly and gently pour two to three buckets of water around the roots every two weeks; in summer, water every week or ten days. In periods of drought water even well established trees deeply every week. Spread a complete, slow-release, long-lasting, organic lawn fertilizer in late winter from the drip line to a distance equal to 1½ times the tree's height. Water it in. Replenish the mulch.

Regional Advice and Care
Any pruning should be done in winter; remove young branches that will grow into the center of the tree or rub against other branches.

Companion Planting and Design
This majestic, long-lived native tree is suited to large parks and landscapes and should be allowed enough space all around to be seen. If seeing the flowers is part of the purpose of planting the tree, you will have to place near an observation point that looks toward or down onto the top of the tree. The tuliptree can tolerate city conditions and is handsome in a park, but can be too big for street planting.

Try These
Plant the species. There is a variegated variety, 'Aureomarginatum', which has leaves edged with yellow.

White Fringe Tree

Chionanthus virginicus

Botanical Pronunciation
ky-uh-NAN-thuss vur-JIN-ih-kuss

Bloom Period and Seasonal Color
Mid-spring with white flowers; fall foliage is
pure yellow

Mature Height × Spread
12 to 20 feet × 12 to 20 feet

In mid-spring, just as the leaves are filling in, this lovely little tree is wrapped in a mist of delicate, 6- to 8-inch-long panicles of lightly scented, greenish white flowers that consist of drooping, fringelike petals. With the first real cold in autumn, the leaves turn luminous yellow-gold and hang on as long as the weather stays fairly moderate. The female plants bear bloomy, purple fruits the birds relish. The petals of the flowers on male trees are larger and showier. The fringe tree is slow growing and tolerates urban pollution. It's often found in the Blue Ridge Mountains growing wild. It is very pretty seen at a distance—across a lawn for example, or near a pond or a stream.

When, Where, and How to Plant

Set out a young container-grown or a balled-and-burlapped tree in early spring while the tree is still dormant. Handle the rootball with care. The fringe tree flowers best in full sun but makes do with four to six hours of sun or bright, filtered light all day. The ideal site is near water in slightly acidic soil, pH 5.5 to 6.5. See "Soil Preparation and Improvement" in the introduction, and the planting instructions at the beginning of this chapter. Provide a planting hole three times the width of the rootball and twice as deep. Set the tree so the crown will be an inch or so above ground level. Staking might help the tree grow straighter, but remove it once the tree is established. Shape the earth around the crown into a wide saucer. Water slowly and deeply. Apply mulch 3 inches deep starting 3 inches from the trunk.

Growing Tips

The first year, unless there's a soaking rain, in spring and fall slowly and gently pour two to three buckets of water around the roots every two weeks; in summer, water every week or ten days. Apply a slow-release organic fertilizer for acid-loving plants in late winter or early spring from the drip line out to a distance equal to 1½ times the tree's height. Water it in. Replenish the mulch.

Regional Advice and Care

The white fringe tree flowers on the previous season's growth; after flowering, cut out young branches that will grow into the center of the tree or rub against other branches.

Companion Planting and Design

White fringe tree is beautiful as a specimen in the center of a lawn. An underplanting of periwinkle, ajuga, and small, spring-flowering bulbs such as wood hyacinths set the tree off nicely.

Try These

André also likes the Chinese fringe tree, *Chionanthus retusus*; it's a smaller, multistemmed plant that blooms two or three weeks before the American species. It bears male and female flowers on the same plant and has a more formal appearance. The Chinese fringe tree flowers on the current season's new growth, so it should be pruned in late winter before growth begins.

Zelkova

Zelkova serrata

Botanical Pronunciation
zell-KOE-vuh sair-AY-tuh

Other Name
Japanese zelkova

Bloom Period and Seasonal Color
Fall foliage is yellow-orange-buff

Mature Height × Spread
50 to 80 feet × 50 to 80 feet

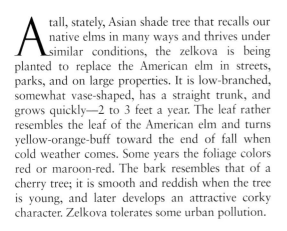

A tall, stately, Asian shade tree that recalls our native elms in many ways and thrives under similar conditions, the zelkova is being planted to replace the American elm in streets, parks, and on large properties. It is low-branched, somewhat vase-shaped, has a straight trunk, and grows quickly—2 to 3 feet a year. The leaf rather resembles the leaf of the American elm and turns yellow-orange-buff toward the end of fall when cold weather comes. Some years the foliage colors red or maroon-red. The bark resembles that of a cherry tree; it is smooth and reddish when the tree is young, and later develops an attractive corky character. Zelkova tolerates some urban pollution.

When, Where, and How to Plant
Plant a container-grown or balled-and-burlapped tree in early spring while the tree is still dormant. You can also set a zelkova out in fall, well before Indian summer, but in that case, protect it with burlap for winter, because young trees are susceptible to frost damage. The zelkova grows best in full sun but tolerates bright, filtered light when young. It adapts to a broad pH range and prefers soil that is deeply dug and moist. See "Soil Preparation and Improvement" in the introduction, and planting instructions at the beginning of this chapter. Provide a planting hole three times the width of the rootball and twice as deep. Set the tree so the crown will be an inch or so above ground level. Staking might help the tree grow straighter, but remove it once

the tree is established. Shape the earth around the crown into a wide saucer. Water slowly and deeply. Apply mulch 3 inches deep starting 3 inches from the trunk.

Growing Tips
The first year, unless there's a soaking rain, in spring and fall slowly and gently pour two to three buckets of water around the roots every two weeks; in summer, water every week or ten days. Broadcast a complete, slow-release, long-lasting, organic lawn fertilizer in late winter before growth begins from the drip line out to a distance equal to 1½ times the tree's height and water it in. Replenish the mulch.

Regional Advice and Care
In fall, prune out limbs that threaten to cross others or grow in the wrong direction. Zelkova is drought tolerant once it's established.

Companion Planting and Design
Zelkovas are excellent lawn and street trees, well suited to taking the place of our lost elms.

Try These
Two excellent varieties resistant to Dutch elm disease are 'Green Vase', a rapidly growing taller cultivar with bronze-red fall color, and Village Green®, a very resistant Princeton Nursery selection that grows more rapidly than the species, and has foliage that turns a warm rusty red in fall.

VINES
FOR THE MID-ATLANTIC

Vines create lush vertical accents, invaluable when you want a real visual impact taking up little space in the ground. The leafy greens soften, beautify, transform, and hide problems. You can create an (almost) instant shade garden by training a leafy vine—trumpet vine, for example—to cover a pergola or a trellis. A climbing rose romances a balcony. Ivy greens ugly stumps. Vines climbing wires between the railing and the roof of a porch make a privacy screen. A vine can frame an attractive view and draw your eye to it. You can clothe a barren slope with a waterfall of vines by planting several at the top of a slope and training the runners to grow down. Fragrant vines belong where you can enjoy the scent. Sweet autumn clematis is especially fragrant—it grows like a tidal wave all summer then covers itself with a foam of small, sweetly fragrant white flowers in fall.

Vines grow rapidly—up or down, or sideways, according to how you train the leading stems, and the supports you provide. When choosing a vine, consider how you are going to prune it when it gets to the top of its support. How a vine climbs dictates what it needs as support. Vines that climb by twining stems require a narrow support such as a wooden post, a pipe, wires, or strings. Vines that climb by twining tendrils

Clematis 'Madame Julia Correvon'

or leaf petioles—clematis, for example—require a structure of wires or wire mesh. Vines that climb by aerial rootlets that secrete an adhesive glue, like English ivy, need only a rugged surface, such as a brick or stucco wall, or a rough, unpainted fence. Vines that eventually will be very heavy—climbing hydrangea, and wisteria—need the support of heavy timbers, or a dead tree, to hold them up.

Vines hold moisture: Make sure the lumber that will support a vine is pressure-treated. Don't set a vine to grow up a wooden wall, because its moisture can cause rot. Allow 3 inches or more air space between foliage and a house wall—vines need air circulation all the way around. Avoid planting vines that climb by tendrils near trees, large shrubs, windows, or shutters.

Planting and Care

You plant a container-grown vine the same way you plant a shrub: see "Soil Preparation and Improvement" in the introduction, and planting instructions in the Shrubs chapter. The first year, slowly and gently pour two to three buckets of water around the roots every week or ten days unless there's a soaking rain. Maintain the mulch throughout the year. If the vine is sheltered from rain, hose it down now and then in summer—but don't hose it when it is coming into—or already in—bloom as that will spoil the blossoms. In late winter or early spring before growth begins, broadcast a slow-release organic fertilizer around the plant and scratch it in. Replenish the mulch if necessary. Repeat in the fall.

A beautiful container planted with million bells, sweet potato vine, and geraniums.

Pruning Vines

We can't give instructions for pruning vines that will apply to all. Wisteria requires special handling, as do some others. But to keep all vines healthy and good-looking, be sure to remove dead, extraneous, or weak wood. Monitor the growth of large, fast-growing vines and prune them severely every year. When your vine will need to be pruned depends on the plant itself. The rule of thumb is, prune flowering vines that bloom on wood that grows in the current year in late winter. A good time is anytime just after the coldest part of the winter season, and before growth begins. Prune spring flowering vines that bloom on wood produced the year before right after the flowers fade. That gives the plant time to mature the wood that will flower the following year. Prune in the summer those vines that do not flower. The best time is right after the major thrust of seasonal growth is over. Generally, it is best to avoid pruning in fall. The wounds heal more slowly during that season. And pruning stimulates growth, which may come too late to harden off before the first frosts. It isn't necessary to paint, tar, or otherwise cover a pruning cut.

Other Options

If you want to try the effect of a vine without making it a permanent fixture in your landscape, plant one of the fast-growing annual climbers. The three best are the lovely purple-podded, scented hyacinth bean, *Lablab purpureus* (also known as *Dolichos lablab*); white-flowered moonvine, *Ipomea alba* (formerly *Calonyction aculeatum*); or morning glory, *Ipomea tricolor* 'Heavenly Blue'.

Carolina Jessamine

Gelsemium sempervirens

Botanical Pronunciation
jell-SEEM-ee-um sem-PUR-vur-enz

Bloom Period and Seasonal Color
Late winter to early spring; golden yellow

Mature Length
12 to 20 feet

A fast-growing native woodland vine with dainty foliage, in late winter Carolina jessamine covers itself with masses of fragrant, funnel-shaped golden flowers, very welcome at that time of the year. The stems are reddish and wiry, and the plant climbs by twining around anything handy, including fencing, porches, or trellises. It is often used for screening mailboxes and downspouts. It makes a good groundcover for slopes if you pin the stems to the ground to prevent them from twining around one another. It's evergreen in the Deep South, but in our area severe cold damages the leaf tips. It is not reliably winter hardy in the uplands near West Virginia. And don't chew on it! It's considered toxic.

When, Where, and How to Plant

The best times for planting Carolina jessamine are in fall before Indian summer, and in late winter and very early spring before the vine blooms. It blooms lavishly planted in full sun, but it also produces flowers in partial shade. It tolerates slightly acidic and slightly alkaline soil. Provide a planting hole twice the size of the rootball with soil that is well drained, humusy, and moist. See "Soil Preparation and Improvement" in the introduction, and planting instructions in the Shrubs chapter. Provide a planting hole three times the width of the rootball and twice as deep. Set the vine so the crown will be an inch or two above ground level. With soft twine, tie the longer branches to whatever you want the vine to grow over. Shape the soil around the crown into a wide saucer. Water slowly and deeply. Apply mulch 3 inches deep starting 3 inches from the crown.

Growing Tips

The first year, unless there's a soaking rain, in spring and fall slowly and gently pour two to three buckets of water around the roots every two weeks; in summer, water every week or ten days. In late winter before growth begins, broadcast a slow-release organic fertilizer over the area and water it in. Replenish the mulch if necessary. Repeat in fall.

Regional Advice and Care

When flowering is over for the season, prune out all the stems twining around one another, and any that are heading in unwanted directions.

Companion Planting and Design

If the vine is to climb, it will in time become woody, like a small tree, and is attractive underplanted with a living mulch of periwinkle, ajuga, or a slow-growing, small-leaved variegated ivy. Don't let the periwinkle crowd, or the ivy climb, the jessamine.

Try These

The cultivar called 'Pride of Augusta' is a beautiful, double-flowered form.

Clematis

Clematis spp. and hybrids

Botanical Pronunciation
KLEM-uh-tiss

Bloom Period and Seasonal Color
Spring, summer, or fall; white, shades of blue, mauve, pink, red, lavender, purple, yellow, bicolors

Mature Length
8 to 20 feet

The clematis hybrids have made this the most popular—and most hybridized—of all the climbers. Deciduous vines with attractive dark green foliage, clematis climbs by attaching leaf petioles (stalks) to the support provided. In time, a clematis will sprawl over other vegetation, walls, trellises, posts, fences, and arbors. Most clematis hybrids bloom in spring or summer; some bloom twice and others bloom in fall. Clematis isn't a difficult plant, but pruning affects the way it blooms—timing is important. To help the plant do its best, before you buy a clematis, make sure you will be able to acquire the pruning information you need. The vines expand at a rate of 5 to 10 feet in a single season.

When, Where, and How to Plant
Set out healthy, vigorously growing container plants in spring after the soil has begun to dry and warm. Clematis vines need to be in the sun, but the roots need to be cool. If the roots aren't shaded, mulch heavily. A site with protection from strong winds is best; avoid hot, dry, airless sites. Soils with a pH between 6.0 and 7.5 are recommended, but clematis tolerates somewhat acidic soils. See "Soil Preparation and Improvement" in the introduction, and planting instructions in the Shrubs chapter. Provide a planting hole three times the width of the rootball and twice as deep. Set the vine so the crown is at ground level. Provide a structure of twine or wire for support, or to lead the vines to a fence, a tree, or other support. Make a saucer of earth around the plant. Apply and maintain a 3-inch mulch starting 3 inches from the stem.

Growing Tips
The first year, unless there's a soaking rain, in spring and fall pour a bucket of water around the roots every two weeks; in summer, water every week or ten days. Using a slow-release organic fertilizer, fertilize lightly in fall and again in spring.

Regional Advice and Care
Check the vines often and prune to train them in the desired direction. Prune clematis that bloom in spring on last year's wood lightly right after the vines finish blooming; prune clematis that bloom on new wood just as the leaf buds begin to swell by cutting the flowering stems back to buds within 4 to 6 inches of the main branches.

Companion Planting and Design
The big-flowered hybrids are lovely paired with open-branched shrubs or roses.

Try These
For spectacular flowers in summer, plant 'Duchess of Edinburgh', a double white; 'Henryi', a large single white; 'Jackmanii Superba', dark purple; or 'Nelly Moser', mauve pink. For masses of small fragrant flowers in spring, plant anemone clematis, rosy red *Clematis montana* var. *rubens*, and white 'Alba'. For fall fragrance, plant (and control) sweet autumn clematis, *C. terniflora* (formerly *C. maximowicziana* and *C. paniculata*), a rampant vine that produces a froth of tiny, fragrant, whitish flowers.

Climbing Hydrangea

Hydrangea petiolaris

Botanical Pronunciation
hye-DRAIN-juh pet-ee-oh-LAIR-iss

Bloom Period and Seasonal Color
Spring and early summer; white bracts

Mature Length
30 to 50 feet

This slow-growing, climbing vine with its lustrous, dark green leaves is probably the most beautiful, massive, and formal climber we have. A mature specimen is magnificent in late spring and early summer when it opens clusters of small, fragrant florets backed by showy white bracts. Clinging by means of rootlike attachments, the branches extend 2 to 3 feet outward, which gives the vine a full, rich silhouette. Though not evergreen, the leaves are a fine green, and they stay that color until late fall. In time, the central stem thickens and becomes woody, and the cinnamon-colored bark exfoliates in an attractive way. It will grow up brick, stucco and stone walls, chimneys, arbors, and trees. It becomes massive and must have strong support.

When, Where, and How to Plant
Set out a container-grown plant in early spring, disturbing the rootball as little as possible. It will be slow to re-establish and show new growth. The climbing hydrangea grows in part shade to full shade. It tolerates salt air. Provide deeply dug, rich, moist, loamy soil. See "Soil Preparation and Improvement" in the introduction, and planting instructions in the Shrubs chapter. Provide a planting hole three times the width of the rootball and twice as deep. Set the vine so the crown is at ground level. With soft twine, tie the vine to the structure that will support it. Shape the soil around the crown into a wide saucer. Water slowly and deeply. Apply mulch 3 inches deep starting 3 inches from the crown.

Growing Tips
The first year, unless there's a soaking rain, in spring and fall slowly and gently pour two to three buckets of water around the roots every two weeks; in summer, water every week or ten days. Using a slow-release organic fertilizer for acid-loving plants, fertilize in fall and again in spring. Replenish the mulch.

Regional Advice and Care
Prune after flowering; though it's slow growing, once a climbing hydrangea matures, it can become invasive and will need to be controlled.

Companion Planting and Design
Climbing hydrangea becomes a massive many-layered, strong, structural landscape element used to enhance a brick or stone wall, trees, arbors, and other freestanding structures.

Try These
Plant the species.

Goldflame Honeysuckle

Lonicera × heckrottii

Botanical Pronunciation
luh-NISS-ur-uh heck-ROT-ee-eye

Other Name
Coral honeysuckle

Bloom Period and Seasonal Color
Late spring to fall; carmine buds open to yellow
and change to pink

Mature Length 10 to 15 feet

Honeysuckles are fast-spreading, climbing, twining vines or tall shrubs that often bear sweetly scented flowers followed by bright, berrylike fruits attractive to many types of birds. Birds disperse seeds, so some types (such as Japanese honeysuckle and Japanese bush honeysuckle) turn up as weeds in your garden, making it a sweetly scented jungle—uncontrolled, they will take over. Goldflame, or coral, honeysuckle is a cross between two native species which do not possess the same aggressive habits of their Asian counterparts, and is considered the most beautiful of the twining, climbing types. It bears carmine buds opening to yellow and changing to pink; it blooms from late spring to fall. The fruit is red and not borne as profusely as other species, nor is the vine as vigorous, which keeps it well behaved. Although scented, it does not possess the same intensity of fragrance as the invasive Japanese species so familiar along the roadsides.

When, Where, and How to Plant

The best times for planting honeysuckle are in fall before Indian summer and in early spring while the plant is still dormant. Honeysuckle is most happy, and fragrant, growing in full sun, but with four to six hours of sun, or all-day filtered light, goldflame performs well. It does best when its roots are shaded and cool, and the vine is in the sun. Honeysuckles thrive in moist, loamy soils in the neutral range, pH 6.0 to 7.5, but tolerate other soils. See "Soil Preparation and Improvement" in the introduction, and planting instructions in the Shrubs chapter. Provide a planting hole three times the width of the rootball and twice as deep. Set the vine so the crown is at ground level. Prune back to the main two or three stems and tie these to the structure that will support the vine. Shape the soil around the crown into a wide saucer. Water slowly and deeply. Apply mulch 3 inches deep starting 2 to 3 inches from the crown.

Growing Tips

The first year, unless there's a soaking rain, in spring and fall slowly and gently pour two to three buckets of water around the roots every two weeks; in summer every week or ten days. Using a slow-release organic fertilizer, fertilize lightly in fall and again in spring.

Regional Advice and Care

Before growth begins in late winter, cut out weak, crowded, or dead growth, and trim long shoots back to a pair of buds near the main stem.

Companion Planting and Design

Goldflame is perfect in a cottage garden, and shows well climbing archways, fences, arbors, mailboxes, and lampposts. Combined with a climbing rose and clematis, it makes a beautiful flowering pillar.

Try These

Goldflame is our favorite, but we also like yellow trumpet honeysuckle, *Lonicera sempervirens* 'Sulphurea'; the flowers aren't fragrant but they and the foliage are beautiful. *L. × brownii* 'Dropmore Scarlet' is hardy in Zones 3 to 9.

Japanese Wisteria

Wisteria floribunda, and spp.

Botanical Pronunciation
wiss-TEER-ee-uh flore-ih-BUN-duh

Bloom Period and Seasonal Color
April, May, or June; pink, white, lilac

Mature Length
10 to 25 feet

Dreamy, romantic, seductive, irresistible, a wisteria in full bloom is everything a flowering vine can be! Picture long drooping clusters of lightly scented, pastel-colored single or double blooms dripping from gnarly vines and sprays of dainty new leaves. That said, wisteria should be approached with caution. You can plant it to climb pillars and arbors, as "green roofing" for porches, and to soften the harsh lines of stone walls. But do not plant where it can reach windows, doors, shutters, or gutters, or near a live tree. It can invade and damage attics, and it destroys trees. As it matures, the weight is considerable, so you must provide a strong support. The cultivars tend to be less invasive than the species. And there are native species with smaller flower clusters. But if you're a romantic at heart . . .

When, Where, and How to Plant
Set out a container-grown plant in spring, summer, or fall. Plant it in full sun. Wisteria is said to do better in soil with a high pH, but it is adaptable to soil that is somewhat acidic too. Provide soil that is deeply dug and well drained. See "Soil Preparation and Improvement" in the introduction, and planting instructions in the Shrubs chapter. Provide a planting hole three times the width of the rootball and twice as deep. Set the vine so the crown is at ground level. Prune the vine to one main stem, or more according to your plan for it. With soft twine, tie the stem, or stems, to a support. Shape the soil around the crown into a wide saucer. Water slowly and deeply. Apply mulch 2 inches deep starting at the crown.

Growing Tips
The first year, unless there's a soaking rain, in spring and fall slowly and gently pour two to three buckets of water around the roots every two weeks; in summer, water every week or ten days. Using a low-nitrogen slow-release fertilizer, fertilize in early spring.

Regional Advice and Care
Prune the vine ruthlessly to restrict it to the branching structure you want. When it reaches the desired height, prune the main stem, or the several stems, back so the laterals will develop, and tie the laterals to supports leading them in the direction you want them to grow. Japanese wisteria blooms on old wood and last season's growth; to keep it blooming, cut back all big, old shoots, leaving only three to four buds on each shoot. This is called spur pruning.

Companion Planting and Design
Plant the area around the vine with a living mulch of drought-tolerant groundcovers, like periwinkle, ajuga, or a slow-growing, small-leaved ivy. Hostas, liriope, mondo grass, and small, spring-flowering bulbs are also good.

Try These
We plant 'Longissima Alba', which bears fragrant white flowers in clusters 15 to 18 inches long; 'Issai Perfect', a blue-violet with 14- to 24-inch racemes; 'Macrobotrys', with violet to red-violet flowers in 18- to 36-inch racemes; and 'Rosea', a lovely pale rose with 12- to 18-inch racemes.

Mandevilla

Mandevilla spp. and cultivars

Botanical Pronunciation
man-dah-VILL-ah

Bloom Period and Seasonal Color
May to October; pink, rose, red, white flowers

Mature Length
1 to 2 feet

That gloriously pink-flowered (or rose, red, or white) vine climbing porch pillars and trellises is mandevilla, a Brazilian perennial grown here as an annual. The showy flowers bloom as temperatures warm and appear nonstop till night temperatures head below 50 degrees Fahrenheit. Most grow 6 to 8 feet in a season, but if summer lingers they can get to be 8 to 10 feet tall. They will overwinter in a warm Florida room or a greenhouse and will grow and make a bigger and better show once you move them out to the sun the following summer. The foot-high 'Garden Crimson' has been bred to stay small, as has the Rio series, which stays under 2 feet. Check the height on the plant tag before you buy.

When, Where, and How to Plant
Buy vigorous young container plants already heavily budded and ready to bloom, but don't set them out until nighttime temperatures are staying above 50 degrees Fahrenheit or they will do very little and be off to a poor start. Transplant to a larger container and set the crown level with the top of the soil. They need loose, well-drained soil containing a slow-release fertilizer for flowering plants and enough compost to so they stay evenly damp. If you are planting several next to a wall or fence, space them 12 to 18 inches apart and cover the surrounding soil with an inch or so of mulch to help maintain spoil moisture during the hot dry months.

Growing Tips
Since they grow rapidly once they start moving, for the first few weeks check the soil moisture several times a week and add just enough water each time to keep the soil evenly damp. After they start growing, they will need rain or watering weekly throughout the season to keep the vines growing rapidly. To encourage lots of flowers, fertilize the plants every two weeks with a liquid fertilizer formulated for flowers.

Regional Advice and Care
Potted mandevillas winter well in a warm Florida room or heated greenhouse. Move them as temperatures head for 50 degrees Fahrenheit. Cut the plants back to about a foot, hose them well, and apply an insecticidal soap. Set the pots near a sunny window. Keep the soil evenly damp but do not fertilize until they show signs of growth in early spring. They can go back outdoors after temperatures reach 50 degrees Fahrenheit.

Companion Planting and Design
Mandevillas grace anything vertical—mailboxes, porch columns, and light posts. It's lovely underplanted with blue and purple annuals, such as verbena, angelonia, or salvia.

Try These
The Sun Parasol® series has many shades, flower forms, and plant heights. 'Cream Pink' is especially appealing. 'Red Riding Hood' has red blossoms with yellow throats, and stays between 6 to 8 feet high. 'Alice du Pont' is a beautiful pale pink with a red throat, reaching 15 to 20 feet.

Sweet Potato Vine

Ipomea batatas

Botanical Pronunciation
ih-poe-MEE-ah ba-TAH-tahz

Bloom Period and Seasonal Color
Summer, occasional lavender flowers; foliage is chartreuse, bronzed, purple, near black, variegated

Mature Length
4 to 10 feet

Deer, wild turkeys, and people love the handsome foliage of the sweet potato. It's a vine that, when tubers are the goal, will wander 3 to 4 feet across the ground at about a foot high. Developed now as an ornamental in an array of shades and variegations, the sweet potato vine has large heart-shaped leaves that are lacy in some varieties. It is most often seen dripping from window boxes, barrels, and other large containers but it can be trained to climb vertically. Its development as an ornamental began in the 1990s. At the end of the season, the tubers, which are starchy but edible, are there in the ground if you choose to dig a few and try them out.

When, Where, and How to Plant

This vine comes from south of the border and sulks if planted before the temperature is reliably above 50 degrees Fahrenheit. It looks great dripping from window boxes, tubs, half-barrels and does best in a sunny spot. Buy container plants and set them in well-drained containers in damp soil that includes lots of compost and slow-release fertilizer for foliage plants.

Growing Tips

To get the vines off to a good start for the first month or so water weekly often enough to keep the soil evenly damp—but not soggy wet. After that, water weekly unless you have a good soaking rain: the soil mustn't dry out. If the vines are growing well, fertilize at half-strength every three or four weeks.

Regional Advice and Care

As summer winds down, try growing tip cuttings 6 to 8 inches long in water indoors in a sunny window. If they root, as they almost surely will, plant them in humusy potting soil. If they do well, you can transplant them to outdoor containers next summer. Another way to grow your own is to dig the tubers at the end of the summer and overwinter them indoors in a cool closet in peat moss or vermiculite. The eyes will sprout in spring, as they do in white potatoes, and these you can cut out and replant.

Companion Planting and Design

We love to see these beautiful leaves—especially the chartreuse and variegated varieties—draping half-barrels, edging window boxes, rambling across garden patches left bare after the spring bulbs have gone to sleep. It makes a charming background for colorful annuals such as zinnias.

Try These

We like the Sweet Caroline series, which is compact and comes in many colors. The Illusion® series has lacy foliage and offers a variety of shades. A favorite is 'Tricolor' whose cream, green, and pink leaves may be the showiest. For good chartreuse color, try 'Margarita'. 'Blackie' and 'Black Heart' are two nearly black varieties.

Trumpet Vine

Campsis radicans

Botanical Pronunciation
KAMP-siss RAD-ih-kanz

Other Name
Trumpet creeper

Bloom Period and Seasonal Color
Spring through early fall; orange, yellow, red

Mature Length
20 to 40 feet

The trumpet vines are woody, vigorous (read: rampant), indomitable, and fast-growing deciduous climbing vines that will quickly provide you with a dense, leafy "green roof" for arbors and pergolas. The delightful bonus is a long-season crop of fresh, showy, trumpet-shaped flowers that appeal mightily to hummingbirds. You can also use a trumpet vine to cover fence posts and to soften bleak corners and bare stone and masonry walls. The vines climb by means of aerial rootlets, and grow at a run to 20 to 40 feet. As trumpet vine matures, it becomes woody and very heavy, so provide a strong support. You must be prepared to prune this vine often: although it is native to the United States, do not plant it where it can escape and invade wild areas.

When, Where, and How to Plant

Set out container-grown plants in early spring, or in early fall. Trumpet vine grows almost anywhere in almost any soil and almost any light, but it flowers best growing against a warm wall and in full sun. See "Soil Preparation and Improvement" in the introduction, and planting instructions in the Shrubs chapter. Provide a planting hole three times the width of the rootball and twice as deep. Set the vine so the crown is at ground level. With soft twine, tie or lead the vine to the structure that will support it. Shape the soil around the crown into a wide saucer. Water slowly and deeply. Apply mulch 3 inches deep starting 1 to 2 inches from the crown.

Growing Tips

The first year, unless there's a soaking rain, in spring and fall slowly and gently pour two to three buckets of water around the roots every two weeks; in summer every week or ten days.

Regional Advice and Care

Do not allow the roots to dry out in summer. In late winter, replenish the mulch. The colorful trumpets are produced on new growth, so early every spring prune the secondary stems back to a few buds—really, do it!—to encourage new flowering spurs. After the first year or two, when the vine is filling its space, in late fall or in early spring, prune leafy young shoots to within a few buds of old wood. Remove any out-of-control stems at any time during the growing season.

Companion Planting and Design

Trumpet vine really doesn't need companion plants. It grows into a floriferous, beautiful (heavy!) green roof for a pergola or a terrace; give it solid supports and you can also use it to soften corners, hide drain pipes, and to screen ugly structures.

Try These

We love *Campsis radicans* 'Flava', which has been popular for more than a century, for its rich yellow or yellow-orange blossoms and 'Crimson Trumpet', whose blossoms are a velvety red. 'Madame Galen', a form of *C. × tagliabuana*, is a superior plant that thrives in our region and bears larger orange flowers.

MORE ABOUT
FERTILIZERS & PLANT NUTRITION

Our all-purpose recipe for fertilizing, followed by an explanation of why and when we use which product:

Flower and Shrub Garden

For each 100 square feet of new garden space add:

	Sun Garden	Shade Garden
Plant-Tone®	5–10 lbs.	0
Holly-Tone®	0	4–7 lbs.
Rock Phosphate	5–10 lbs.	0
Super Phosphate	0	3–5 lbs.
Greensand	5–10 lbs.	5–10 lbs.
Gypsum (clay soils)	5–10 lbs.	5–10 lbs.

Till all these amendments plus organic matter into the soil, rake smooth, and your bed is ready to be planted.

Know What's in Your Fertilizer

In our experience, plant health depends on more than just the three essential nutrients, nitrogen, phosphorus, and potash provided in an all-purpose chemical fertilizer. The Viette family has been growing plants for more than eighty years using natural, organic, blended fertilizers made up of at least eight to fourteen ingredients. These are earth-friendly products that include the three essential nutrients, and in addition, have beneficial effects on the environment and the soil.

Adding natural organics to the soil has a positive effect on soil microorganisms, the micro-fauna and micro-flora of the soil, and beneficial earthworms. The soil structure and aeration is improved. Natural organics don't dissolve quickly and do not easily run off into rivers and lakes. Their breakdown is dependent on three factors—soil moisture, temperature, and microbial activity. The nutrient microbial release is a slow, gradual process that makes nutrients available exactly when the plants need them and over an extended period of time. The result is overall plant health, and plants with luxuriant and robust foliage and superb flowers.

In the past, we mixed our own blends of organic fertilizers in the nursery garage. Today the marketplace offers packaged fertilizers that are blends of natural organics. Bulb-Tone®, Holly-Tone®, Plant-Tone®, Rose-Tone® and other "Tones" are 100 percent natural and organic and contain beneficial microbes.

APPLICATION AMOUNTS		
	New Bed	**Established Bed**
Bulb-Tone® 3-5-3	10 pounds per 100 square feet	5 pounds per 100 square feet
Holly-Tone® 4-3-4	10 pounds per 100 square feet	5 pounds per 100 square feet
Plant-Tone® 5-3-3	10 pounds per 100 square feet	5 pounds per 100 square feet
Rose-Tone® 4-3-2	4 cups per plant	2 cups per plant

Greensand

Greensand is a mined mineral-rich marine deposit, also known as glauconite. These ancient sea deposits are an all-natural source of potash. It is an iron potassium silicate in which the potassium is the important element in the potash. Thirty-two or more micro ingredients are contained in greensand. Greensand is non-burning and helps to loosen heavy clay soil. It also binds sandy soil for a better structure. It increases the water holding capacity of soils and it considered an excellent soil conditioner. Greensand promotes plant vigor, disease resistance, and good color in fruit. Greensand also contains silica, iron oxides, magnesia, and lime. Dr. J.C.F. Tedrew, Rutgers University Soil Specialist, mentions that glauconite may have a considerable capacity for gradual release of certain plant food elements, particularly the so-called trace elements (micronutrients).

Gypsum

Gypsum is a hydrated calcium sulfate. The actual amounts of calcium and sulfur can vary, but 22 percent calcium and 17 percent sulfur occur in some formulations. Gypsum improves the drainage and aeration. Gypsum is applied at the rate of 10 pounds per 100 square feet in heavy clay soil and 5 pounds per 100 square feet in moderately clay soil. Gypsum improves the structure of the heavier clay soils.

A wonderful organic starter fertilizer is Espoma's Bio-Tone R Starter Plus 4-3-3. This all-natural plant food contains hundreds of thousands of living microbes. These beneficial soil microbes have been shown to increase root growth, bloom count, and yields in fruits and vegetables. In addition, a blend of mycorrhizae has been added. These are naturally occurring fungi that have been shown to enhance plant growth and reduce the amount of watering required.

Use Bio-Tone R Starter Plus at time of planting, 4 pounds (12 cups) per 100 square feet.

Potting mixes: 1 cup per cubic foot.

1 to 4 cups per plant depending on size.

For more information, go to www.espoma.com.

MORE ABOUT
PRUNING TREES & SHRUBS

Pruning is part of regular garden maintenance, not just a solution to things gone wrong. The thing to keep in mind when you prune is that it stimulates growth, which dictates what you should prune, and when.

What to Prune

To keep trees and shrubs looking their best and growing well, regularly remove weak, crowded stems; branches that will eventually cross each other; suckers, which are shoots growing at the base of a tree or shrub; and water sprouts, which are vigorous upright shoots that develop along a branch, usually where it has been pruned. Pruning is sometimes needed to open up the canopy of a tree or a shrub to let in air and sun. Pruning also causes denser growth, and can be used to encourage height and to control size. For the most appealing results, when you prune, follow the lines of the plant's natural growth habit.

When to Prune

Our plant pages suggest a best time for pruning each plant. The rule is that trees and shrubs that bloom on this year's growth—hydrangeas for example, rose-of-Sharon, chaste tree, butterfly bush—are pruned early in the year, before growth begins. The growth that pruning encourages provides more places for flowers. Plants that bloom on wood from the previous year—ornamental fruit trees and most spring flowering trees and shrubs such as azaleas—are pruned as soon as possible after they bloom. Shade and evergreen trees are typically pruned every three or four years.

Flowering and evergreen shrubs may need maintenance pruning every season. Young vigorous plants will need more pruning than mature plants. Winter and early spring pruning stimulates plants to produce more unwanted suckers than late spring or summer pruning. So if it's a plant's nature to sucker heavily, as with lilacs and crabapples, summer is a better time to prune. On the other hand, pruning in late summer or early fall can cause growth that won't have time to harden off before winter.

Pruning Large Trees

When a large limb is involved, pruning is best undertaken in spring just before growth begins, or after maximum leaf expansion in June. Pruned then, the tree will likely roll calluses over the external wound, and, internally, it will protect itself by walling off the damaged tissue. Painting a wound has fallen out of favor but the Cornell Cooperative Extension *Illustrated Guide to Pruning* says "certain materials such as orange shellac may provide a temporary barrier to certain pathogens until a tree's natural barrier zones form." The alcohol in shellac is a disinfectant.

Evergreen trees are usually allowed to develop naturally, but deciduous trees may need pruning to grow up to be all they can be. After planting a balled-and-burlapped, or a container-grown, deciduous tree, remove any weak and injured branches, and those that will eventually rub across each other. For bare-root trees, some experts recommend thinning out one-quarter of the branches so the canopy will be in better balance with the reduced root system. The year after planting, pruning to shape a deciduous tree begins, and that continues over the next three to five years. The first step is to identify the strongest terminal leader, unless the tree is naturally multi-stemmed, the leader will become the trunk. Then prune all but the main limbs—the "scaffold branches"—that will define the structure of the tree. Choose as scaffolding those branches whose crotch is at a wide angle to the trunk. The height of the lowest scaffold branches depends on the activities planned under the tree. You can leave them in place for the first few years to protect the bark from sunscald and to provide more leaves to nourish the root system. The scaffold branches at each level should be a fairly equal distance from each other: spaced evenly all around the trunk, they make for better balance. For each next level of scaffold branches, choose limbs developing between or offset from, not directly over, the branches of the level below. In the following years, watch the growth of the tree and trim back any side branches growing taller than the leader.

Pruning and Rejuvenating Shrubs

At planting time, prune out weak and injured branches, and any crossing each other. To keep the shrub airy, then and later, you may need to remove a few branches from the base and to head back others. "Heading back" means cutting an unwanted branchlet back to where there is an outward facing branchlet or bud on the main stem. Shearing shrubs, unless they are growing as a hedge, is discouraged because it stimulates dense growth at the tips of the branches and distorts the natural shape of the plant.

You can use pruning to rejuvenate older shrubs grown leggy or out of scale with their place in the garden. There are three ways to rejuvenate deciduous shrubs, all initiated before growth begins in early spring. The most drastic way is to cut the whole plant back to within 6 to 10 inches of the ground, by July it will be a mass of upright canes. Remove half or more of these, and head the others back to outward facing buds at half or less of the height you want the shrub to be. A slightly less drastic way is to cut half, or more, of the older branches, including any that cross, and all suckers, back to the ground: at midsummer, remove all new canes and head back branching that develops on the canes you kept. The least drastic method is to remove one-third to one-quarter of the older branches over three, or even four years, each year removing unwanted suckers and heading back crowded branching. You can rejuvenate broadleaved evergreen shrubs that have grown out of scale—rhododendrons, mountain laurels, boxwoods for example—by cutting them back to within 2 to 4 feet of the ground in late winter or early spring before growth begins. Leave branch ends at various heights so re-growth will appear natural. Re-growth will take two to four years.

GARDENING WITH WILDLIFE
WELCOME AND OTHERWISE

Birds

To *attract* birds—Birds adopt gardens that provide food, water, and shelter. To attract birds, plant trees and shrubs that have berries and small fruits. Let stand the seedheads of ornamental grasses and various flowers for fall and early winter. Provide a water basin/bird bath near a shrub, preferably a dense evergreen, where birds can check for predators before flying in. Plant, or keep, tall trees for perching and nesting; pines and hemlocks provide nesting materials as well. Finally, if you have space, allow milkweed and other wild plants useful to birds to develop in a bramble away from house traffic.

To *deter* birds—Our feathered friends are beautiful, lovable, inspiring, and useful in that they eat insects, some good and some bad. They also eat your berries and your flower and grass seeds. A mesh cover is almost the only way to protect berries. Remember when planting for birds that they drop seeds everywhere. Bears are eager for birdseed: if there are bears in your area, stocking a bird feeder may not be a good idea.

Hummingbirds

Hummingbirds rely on sight, not scent, to locate their food. They are attracted by tubular, brightly colored flowers, and prefer single-petaled varieties to doubles. Like butterflies, hummingbirds require a continuous supply of nectar.

Bears, bees, and wasps love nectar, too; think twice before putting out sugared water.

Butterflies

Ideal for a butterfly garden is the sun-warmed side of a south-facing fence, a wall, or a windbreak. Because this lovely thing is cold-blooded, it can fly only when warmed by the sun and in air that is 55 to 60 degrees Fahrenheit. On sunless days and at night butterflies roost in deeply fissured bark, or a butterfly hotel: a wooden box with perches and an entrance big enough for a butterfly with folded wings to slide through, a slot about ¼ inch wide by about 3½ inches high. For basking, butterflies also need tall verticals that hold warmth—statuary, stones, standing logs. And a puddling place—a patch of damp sand or drying mud where male butterflies can gather and take up moisture and dissolved salts, which we believe are helpful for mating. The food for adult butterflies is the nectar in flowers. They are drawn to brightly colored flowers—purple, yellow, orange, and red. The caterpillars of most species need a specific host plant; field guides can tell you which. Learn to recognize the caterpillars of butterflies, and even many moths, so that you won't be tempted to eliminate them from the garden when you see them eating your plants.

Deer

To *attract* Bambi and company—plant fruit trees. They relish apples and pears. They also adore hostas, daylilies, rhododendrons, and other large, succulent leaves, and roses, raspberries, impatiens—anything that doesn't have itsy bitsy leaves or flowers. Provide a salt lick and water in a secluded spot, and for winter put out bales of hay.

To *deter* these oversize white-tailed rats—Alternate your deer repellents. Wrapping evergreens with burlap in late fall and winter works: for summer, use chicken wire—at a distance you won't see it. Or plant in small, fully enclosed spaces. To protect a large property, try high tensile fencing 9 to 10 feet high, or double fences 4 to 5 feet apart. If you can't fence, you may be able to discourage them this way: at places where they enter your garden, hang tubes of crushed garlic, or predator urine, chunks of Irish Spring soap, or human hair damp with strongly scented lotions such as Avon's Skin So Soft. Hang them at the height of the deer's nose, a different scent at each entry point. Replace these scents with new different ones every four to six weeks of the gardening season.

Rabbits, Woodchucks, and Other Rodents

To *attract* these sweet critters—Develop a wilderness bramble with fallen logs far enough from the beaten path to let them feel safe. Provide a source of water. Time and nature will do the rest.

To *deter* these not-so-sweet critters—Use chicken wire fencing that starts 24 inches underground keeps out most rodents: for woodchucks, make it 4 to 6 feet tall as well and leave it loose and floppy, not stiff enough to climb. Keeping raccoons out too requires enclosing your garden overhead as well.

Good Plants for Songbirds

Annuals, Perennials, and Grasses
Ammophila breviligulata,
   American beachgrass
Echinacea purpurea 'Magnus',
   Purple coneflower
Echinops ritro, Globe thistle
Helianthus annuus, Sunflower
Panicum virgatum, Switchgrass
Rudbeckia fulgida var. *sullivantii*
   'Goldsturm', Black-eyed Susan

Trees, Shrubs, and Vines
Abies concolor, White fir

Acer saccharum, Sugar maple
Amelanchier arborea,
   Downy serviceberry
Arctostaphylos uva-ursi, Bearberry
Buxus spp., Boxwood
Cedrus atlantica 'Glauca',
   Blue Atlas cedar
Cercis canadensis, Eastern redbud
Chamaecyparis obtusa 'Nana Gracilis',
   Dwarf hinoki falsecypress
Chionanthus virginicus,
   White fringe tree
Cornus florida, Flowering dogwood

Cotinus spp., Smoke tree
Cotoneaster spp., Cotoneaster
Crataegus viridus, Hawthorn
× *Cupressocyparis leylandii*,
    Leyland Cypress
Euonymus alatus 'Compactus',
    Dwarf burning bush
Fagus grandifolia, American beech
Juniperus spp., Juniper
Liquidambar styraciflua, Sweet gum
Liriodendron tulipifera, Tuliptree
Lonicera × *heckrottii*,
    Goldflame honeysuckle
Malus spp. and cultivars,
    Flowering crabapple
Nyssa sylvatica, Sour gum
Oxydendrum arboreum, Sourwood
Parthenocissus quinquefolia,
    Virginia creeper
Picea pungens 'Glauca',
    Colorado blue spruce
Pinus strobus, Eastern white pine
Prunus spp., Flowering cherry
Pseudotsuga menziesii, Douglas fir
Pyracantha coccinea, Firethorn
Pyrus calleryana, Callery pear
Quercus spp., Oak
Rosa spp. and hybrids, Rose
Sciadopitys verticillata, Umbrella pine
Spiraea spp., Spirea
Stewartia pseudocamellia,
    Japanese stewartia
Taxus × *media*, Yew
Thuja occidentalis, Arborvitae
Tsuga canadensis, Canadian hemlock

Good Plants for Hummingbirds
Annuals, Perennials, and Bulbs
Ageratum houstonianum, Ageratum
Ajuga spp., Bugleweed
Alcea spp., Hollyhock
Allium spp., Flowering onion
Antirrhinum majus, Snapdragon

Aquilegia spp., Columbine
Asclepias tuberosa, Butterfly weed
Begonia grandis, Hardy begonia
Chelone spp., Turtlehead
Crocosmia spp., Crocosmia
Dahlia spp. and cultivars, Dahlia
Delphinium spp., Larkspur
Dianthus spp., Pinks
Digitalis spp., Foxglove
Heuchera spp. and cultivars, Coral bells
Hibiscus moscheutos,
    Marsh rose mallow
Hosta spp. and cultivars, Hosta
Impatiens walleriana, Impatiens
Kniphofia spp., Red hot poker
Lavandula spp., Lavender
Lilium spp., Lily
Lobelia cardinalis, Cardinal flower
Lobularia maritima, Sweet alyssum
Mentha spicata, Mint
Monarda didyma, Bee balm
Nepeta faassennii, Catmint
Pelargonium spp. and hybrids,
    Geranium, Cranesbill
Penstemon spp., Beardtongue
Petunia × *hybrida*, Petunia
Phlox paniculata, Phlox
Rosmarinus officinalis, Rosemary
Rudbeckia spp., Black-eyed Susan
Salvia spp., Salvia and sage
Scabiosa spp., Pincushion flower
Tropaeolum majus, Nasturtium
Verbena spp., Verbena
Zinnia elegans, Zinnia

Trees, Shrubs, and Vines
Buddleja davidii, Butterfly bush
Campsis radicans, Trumpet vine
Caryopteris × *clandonensis*, Blue spirea
Chaenomeles speciosa,
    Flowering quince
Daphne × *burkwoodii* 'Carol Mackie',
    Carol Mackie Daphne

Hibiscus syriacus, Rose-of-Sharon
Lonicera × heckrottii,
    Goldflame honeysuckle
Sophora japonica, Japanese pagoda tree
Stewartia pseudocamellia,
    Japanese stewartia
Syringa vulgaris, Lilac
Wisteria floribunda, Japanese wisteria

Good Plants for Butterflies
(Including plants for butterfly larvae or caterpillars)
Achillea millefolium, Yarrow
Agastache spp., Anise hyssop
Alcea spp., Hollyhock
Allium spp., Ornamental onion
Aquilegia spp., Columbine
Aristolochia spp., Dutchman's pipe
Arabis spp., Rockcress
Armeria maritima, Sea thrift
Asclepias tuberosa, Butterfly weed
Asimina triloba, Paw paw
Aster spp., Aster
Astilbe spp., Astilbe
Boltonia asteroides, Boltonia
Buddleja davidii, Butterfly bush
Caryopteris × clandonensis, Blue spirea
Centaurea spp., Bachelor's buttons
Centranthus ruber, Jupiter's beard
Ceratostigma plumbaginoides,
    Leadwort, Plumbago
Chelone spp., Turtlehead
Coreopsis spp., Tickseed
Crocosmia spp., Crocosmia
Delphinium spp., Larkspur
Dendranthema spp., Chrysanthemum
Dianthus spp., Pinks
Echinacea purpurea, Purple coneflower
Echinops ritro, Globe thistle
Eryngium spp., Sea Holly
Eutrochium spp., Perennial ageratum,
    Joe-pye weed, White snake root
Filipendula rubra, Meadowsweet

Foeniculum vulgare, Fennel
Gaillardia spp., Indian blanket
Helenium autumnale, Sneezeweed
Helianthus spp., Sunflower
Heliopsis helianthoides, Heliopsis
Hemerocallis spp., Daylily
Iberis spp., Candytuft
Iris pseudacorus, Yellow flag
Kniphofia uvaria, Red hot poker
Lavandula spp., Lavender
Liatris spicata, Gay feather
Lilium spp., Lily
Lindera benzoin, Spicebush
Lobelia spp., Cardinal flower,
    Blue lobelia
Monarda didyma, Bee balm
Nepeta faassenii, Catmint
Origanum spp., Oregano
Passiflora spp., Passion vine
Petroselinum crispum, Parsley
Petunia × hybrida, Petunia
Phlox spp., Phlox
Physostegia virginiana, Obedient Plant
Primula spp., Primrose
Rosmarinus officinalis, Rosemary
Rudbeckia spp., Black-eyed Susan
Ruta graveolens, Rue
Salvia spp., Salvia, sage
Scabiosa spp., Pincushion flower
Sedum spp., Stonecrop
Skimmia japonica, Japanese skimmia
Solidago spp., Goldenrod
Spiraea japonica, Spirea
Stokesia laevis, Stokes' aster
Vernonia noveboracensis, Ironweed
Verbena, spp., Verbena
Veronica spp., Speedwell
Zinnia elegans, Zinnia

INDEX

PHOTO CREDITS

André Viette: pp. 129, 130, 160, 215, 218

Bill Adams: pp. 81, 96, 108, 133

Bill Kersey: p. 17

Candace Edwards: pp. 9 (both), 10, 14,

Cathy Wilkinson Barash: p. 78

Charles Mann: pp. 83, 177

Conard-Pyle: p. 148

Cool Springs Press: pp. 13 (all)

George Weigel: p. 188

Getty Images: pp. 54, 167, 173, 171

Jerry Pavia: pp. 25, 27, 39, 50, 62, 69, 71, 74, 107, 109, 111, 113, 115, 117, 119, 124, 131, 137, 140, 142, 143, 145, 152, 155, 176, 178, 183, 185, 189, 193, 195, 200, 206, 210, 217

Katie Elzer-Peters: pp. 23, 43, 169,

Liz Ball: pp. 80, 203

Neil Soderstrom: pp. 11, 61, 64, 126,

Netherlands Flower Bulb Association: p. 49

Proven Winners® Sonic Bloom™ Pink Weigela: p. 182

Richard Shiell, courtesy Monrovia Nursery: p. 162

Shawna Coronado: pp. 87, 132, 179, 180, 197, 220

Shutterstock: pp. 6, 24, 26, 29, 31, 32, 33, 34, 36, 37, 40, 41, 44, 47, 48, 51, 52, 53, 55, 57, 84, 85, 88, 92, 94, 97, 101, 105, 114, 122, 127, 128, 134, 135, 136, 139, 141, 151, 157, 161, 164, 165, 170, 174, 175, 190, 194, 196, 207, 213, 216, 221

Tom Eltzroth: pp. 18, 19, 22, 28, 30, 35, 38, 46, 56, 58, 59, 60, 63, 65, 66, 67, 68, 72, 75, 76, 77, 82, 86, 89, 90, 91, 93, 95, 98, 99, 102, 103, 104, 106, 116, 118, 120, 123, 125, 138, 144, 146, 147, 149, 154, 158, 159, 163, 166, 168, 172, 186, 191, 192, 198, 199, 201, 202, 204, 209, 212, 219

Troy Marden: pp. 79, 121, 156, 208, 211, 214

MEET THE AUTHORS

André Viette

A distinguished horticulturist, author, and lecturer, André owns the Viette Farm and Nursery in Fishersville, Virginia. He is also radio host of the weekly three-hour, live, nationwide call-in radio program "In the Garden with André Viette." Viette is a graduate of the Floriculture School of Cornell University, New York, was instructor in horticulture at the Blue Ridge Community College for twenty-nine years, and past president of the Perennial Plant Association of America. André was honored in 2001 with the PPA Award of Merit. He holds the Garden Club of America 1999 Medal of Honor for

his outstanding contributions to horticulture. He has served on the Advisory Council of the National Arboretum. André is the recipient of the 2004 Liberty Hyde Bailey Award, the highest honor given by the American Horticultural Society.

Mark Viette

Mark Viette is a nurseryman, lecturer, hybridizer, and contributor to horticultural journals. A horticultural instructor at Blue Ridge Community College, Mark Viette is president of Viette Communications, which produces and distributes the national weekly radio call-in show "In the Garden with André Viette" (www.inthegardenradio.com). Mark has produced over 650 video gardening segments for TV stations and are available to view on YouTube. He holds a Bachelor of Science degree in Horticulture from Virginia Tech and after focused on plant propagation through tissue culture. He has been on numerous plant-finding trips to Europe and South America in search of new perennials to introduce to American home gardens. Mark's latest project is creating HD movies of flowers using time lapse photography with the hope that the movies will educate and inspire a younger audience.

Jacqueline Hériteau

Jacqueline (Jacqui) Hériteau is known for her many books featuring environmentally sound plants and garden solutions. She is the author of the *National Arboretum Book of Outstanding Garden Plants, The American Horticultural Society Flower Finder*, and *New England Gardener's Guide*. A Fellow of the Garden Writers Association, she holds the 1990 Garden Writer of the Year Award given by the American Nursery and Landscape Association. Her first book was *How to Grow and Cook It*. In 2007 Jacqui and her three children opened Your Country Bistro in Salisbury, Connecticut, a small, full-service restaurant dedicated to fine food.